PENNANTS & PINSTRIPES

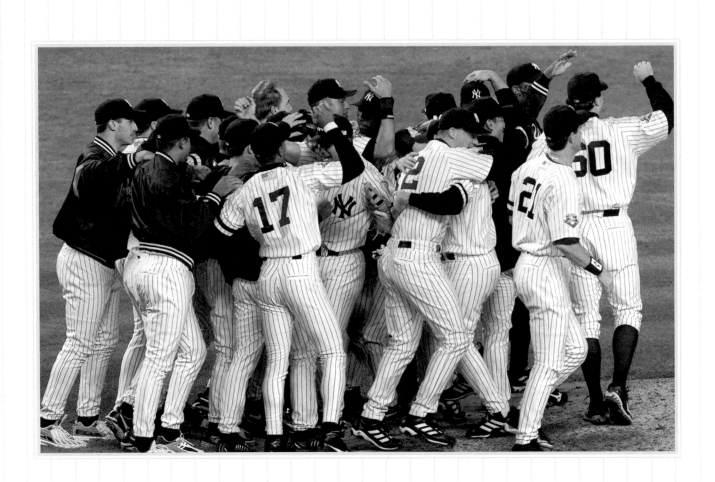

PENNANTS & PINSTRIPES
The New York Yankees 1903–2002

Ray Robinson & Christopher Jennison

Viking Studio

VIKING STUDIO

Published by the Penguin Group
Penguin Putnam Inc., 375 Hudson Street, New York, New York 10014, U.S.A.
Penguin Books Ltd, 80 Strand, London WC2R ORL, England
Penguin Books Australia Ltd, Ringwood, Victoria, Australia
Penguin Books Canada Ltd, 10 Alcorn Avenue, Toronto, Ontario, Canada M4V 3B2
Penguin Books (N.Z.) Ltd, 182–190 Wairau Road, Auckland 10, New Zealand

Penguin Books Ltd, Registered Offices: Harmondsworth, Middlesex, England

First published in 2002 by Viking Studio, a member of Penguin Putnam Inc.

10 9 8 7 6 5 4 3 2 1

CIP data available
ISBN 0-670-89214-9
This book is printed on acid-free paper. ∞

Printed in England

Editor: Christopher Sweet
Assistant Editor: Michelle Li
Managing Editor: Tory Klose
Production Manager: Ellen Schiller
Designer: Jaye Zimet

FRONTIS: **New York Yankees players celebrated after they defeated Seattle in game 5 of the American League Championship Series in New York, October 22, 2001. The Yankees defeated the Mariners 4 games to 1 to advance to the World Series.**

To Phyllis, who became a Yankee fan late in the game
—but with a fervor befitting a lifetime supporter
R.R.

To Nancy, a Bostonian with Fenway memories
and pinstripe affections.
C.J.

Acknowledgments

The authors would like to express their profound gratitude to all of those who provided their invaluable assistance in the preparation of this book:

Rick Cerrone, New York Yankees publicity director; Chris Sweet, editor in chief at Viking Studio and the talented catalyst for this book, and assistant editor Michelle Li; Jaye Zimet, for a marvelous book design, and production manager Ellen Schiller; Barry Popik, for his research on the Highlanders, who became the Yankees; and to baseball buddies Butch Geiger, Tony Gamboli, Andy Jurinko, Tony Morante, John Brooks, Lee Woodcock, Les Lowenfish, Marty Appel, Lane Akers, Mike Pressley, John Clarke, Bob Harrison, Bob Gruber, Steve Milman, Jim Kaat, Bill Purdom, Vince Russo, Linda Schacht, Tim Wiles, Bob Gormley, and Nick Jennison.

And an extra thanks to the "picture people":

Lou Requena; Mark Rucker at Transcendental Graphics; Elvis Brathwaite at AP/Wide World Photos; Rona Tuccillo at TimePix; Carol Butler at Brown Brothers; Susan and Dennis Brearley of the Brearley Collection; Pete Schroeder; Stephen Urgola at the Columbia University Archives; Francia Martinez at E/Z Photo on Spring Street.

Contents

PENNANTS & PINSTRIPES

1903–1912

AT THE OUTSET OF THE TWENTIETH CENTURY, NEW YORK, WITH ITS MORE THAN THREE MILLION PEOPLE, WAS ON ITS WAY TO BECOMING THE UNOFFICIAL CULTURAL CAPITAL OF THE WORLD. IT WAS ESTIMATED THAT THE CITY HAD MORE IRISH THAN DUBLIN, MORE ITALIANS THAN NAPLES, AND MORE GREEKS THAN ATHENS. BY 1897, THE FIVE BOROUGHS—MANHATTAN, THE BRONX, BROOKLYN, QUEENS, AND STATEN ISLAND—HAD BEEN CONSOLIDATED, THOUGH THERE WERE THOSE WHO SLYLY SUGGESTED

that this was done because Chicago was on the verge of surpassing Manhattan in population and prestige.

Flooded by immigrants in pursuit of opportunity, jobs, and money (and, incidentally, freedom), New York had become a magnet for thousands. The tired, huddled masses from Europe provided the brawn that built the city's roads, buildings, and subways, while their brains wrote the country's songs. There was more wealth circulating among the few—and more things to buy than anybody dreamed of. But uninhibited consumers conveniently forgot that New York, at the same time, had more misery and dense poverty than almost any other community in the world.

By now the theater district had moved up to Times Square from Union Square, giving the upward-striving locals and curious tourists a chance to visit the nickelodeons, cabarets, and flea circuses. The pulsating area remained impervious to reformers. At city hall, presided over by Mayor George McClellan (no relation to the Civil War general), the bureaucrats spent more time working on ticker-tape parades than looking for greedy Tammany rascals, while on stylish Fifth Avenue the rich and famous promenaded in all of their hauteur.

America had recently been engaged, for several months, in Rough Rider Teddy Roosevelt's excursion into Cuba (an event nudged along by the outrageous jingoism of newspaper baron William Randolph Hearst). Meanwhile, in organized baseball, Byron Bancroft Johnson, a burly, overbearing former newspaperman from Norwalk, Ohio, sought his own imperialism over a new American League.

OVERLEAF: Hilltop Park, where the Highlanders/Yankees played from 1903 through the 1912 season, was located in the Washington Heights section of Manhattan, several blocks north of the Polo Grounds. As this picture indicates, overflow crowds were permitted to sit and stand perilously close to the action.

Johnson had pounded heads together to create a rival baseball circuit to the venerable National League, which had been inaugurated in 1876. Teams from Boston, Washington, Philadelphia, and Baltimore quickly embraced Johnson's plan and joined the American League. Now Johnson wanted to place a franchise in New York, which made a good deal of sense. So when the Baltimore club self-destructed, thanks to the shenanigans of John J. McGraw, Johnson seized the moment to put New York into his master plan.

In truth, of course, Ban Johnson had hardly invented baseball for New Yorkers. The game already had made itself felt there following the Civil War. After the great unpleasantness, over a hundred ball clubs were formed in Manhattan and Brooklyn; by the end of the 1860s thousands of young men were playing professionally. Most of these participants were skilled workers—skilled also at heavy drinking and unruly behavior. They played before large crowds, predominantly men, for an admission price of twenty-five to fifty cents. The pastoral nature of the game was especially appealing to urban folks, as were the sharply defined rules and intriguing statistics.

By 1900, ballplayers were often regarded lower than itinerant actors, Bowery bums, or stagecoach robbers in the order of their social acceptance. "They were mostly young and uneducated," biologist Stephen Jay Gould has written. "Hardly any of these men went to college and few finished high school. Baseball, with all of its mythological hyping, really took root as a people's sport in America. Rube, the nickname of so many early players, reflected a common background."

Curiously, while many people of all ages were collecting baseball cards (first issued in the 1860s) and enjoyed arguing about the relative talents of their favorite ballplayers, *many of these same collectors also held them in contempt for their disruptive manners and unwholesome habits. Bryan DiSalvatore, the biographer of John Montgomery Ward (one ballplayer who did have a college education), wrote that in those early days, "the sport had a gawky, vituperative adolescence."*

The new team in New York town was called the Highlanders, who played at the high altitude venue called Hilltop Park, in the Washington Heights section of Manhattan. Hilltop, close to McGraw's Polo Grounds, was located on upper Broadway between 165th and 168th streets (today the Columbia Presbyterian Medical Center stands on the site); it was said to be the most elevated point in the borough. The ballpark, accommodating some 15,000 people, was also known as the New York American League Ball Park, but most people knew it as Hilltop. It opened on April 30, 1903, and was abandoned in 1912, when the field was adjudged to be too small and too out of date for further use as a big league playground. It was about an hour from downtown by the elevated train and just two blocks east of the Hudson River. The plot of land had originally been owned by the New York Institute for the Blind. Home plate at Hilltop faced Broadway, so the fans in the open wooden stands sat with their backs to the majestic river.

The *Evening World* often chose to call the Highlanders by another name—the Invaders—because the club had the effrontery to challenge McGraw and his uppity Giants. In those beginning years, the Highlander nickname didn't sit very well with New York's newspapers for the simple reason that it couldn't be squeezed too comfortably into box scores or headlines. The jazzy name "The Yankees" stuck like adhesive and for one hundred years it has had universal appeal, even where Confederates roam.

The two owners of the Highlanders were Frank Farrell and Big Bill Devery, who had bought the Baltimore franchise for $18,000 and turned it into the New York Highlanders, much to the satisfaction of the scheming Johnson. In later years, these two characters might have had a difficult time winning approval from a board of ethics or a baseball commissioner. But they did invest some $300,000 turning their rocky property

into a suitable playing field. An ex-bartender and saloon operator, Farrell also ran a stable of horses and liked, on occasion, to place a bet on them. It wouldn't have surprised anyone if he had also, on occasion, placed a bet *against* his own animals. (When Kenesaw Mountain Landis came on the scene in the 1920s as commissioner, Farrell would have been slapped down. After all, Landis had thrown the book at .400-hitter Rogers Hornsby for losing money at the race track.)

Devery was more of a polymath than Farrell. He had been a policeman, a trial-horse prizefighter, and a bartender. After he became chief of police, with important political connections, it was rumored that the crime rate rose dramatically. The two men agreed on the choice of Joseph Gordon as the team's president (another Joe Gordon played second base in the late thirties and early forties for the Yankees) and signed the White Sox's Clark Griffith as the club's first manager. Later, as owner of the Washington Senators, Griffith won the nickname of the "Old Fox." In his five-year tenure with the Highlanders, Griffith also was called on to pitch. He won 14 games in 1903, the year Boston defeated Pittsburgh in the first modern World Series, but after that it was all downhill for him. Instead, Griffith had to rely on Happy Jack Chesbro, a right-hander seemingly as durable as one of Mr. Henry Ford's newfangled inventions. Throwing a tantalizing spitball in the deadball era, Chesbro won 41 games in 1904, pitching 48 complete games in 51 starts. This remarkable performance, still a twentieth-century mark, was overshadowed that same season by Denton Tecumseh "Cy" Young's perfect game against Philadelphia, the first such game in the new century.

Sadly, Happy Jack also suffered the ignominy of tossing an errant pitch against Boston on the last day of the 1904 season that lost the American League flag to the Red Sox (then called the Pilgrims). Thus, if Chesbro is remembered at all, it is for being in the

The first Yankee star was "Wee Willie" Keeler, a small, crafty graduate of the old Baltimore Orioles school of baseball. With the Orioles in 1897, he set a consecutive game hit streak that stood until Joe DiMaggio broke it in 1941. He said the secret to his success was "Keep your eye clear and hit 'em where they ain't." He hit .343 for the Highlanders in 1904.

same company as Fred Merkle, who blundered at a critical moment in baseball history. "In the history of America, we reserve a niche," William B. Mead chortled, "for the moment back in nineteen-four: Chesbro's great wild pitch." The month after Chesbro's egregious misplay, Teddy Roosevelt, the passionate patriot, was elected president of the United States.

Chesbro's 455 innings of hurling in 1904 earned him the lordly sum of $1,500, though he may have picked up a few extra shillings when the fans passed the hat around, as was the custom at Hilltop.

In the years that followed, the Highlanders went from a second place finish in 1904 to Sisyphean depths. Accordingly, attendance plummeted from 211,000 the first season to half of that, even when such stellar attractions as the tempestuous Ty Cobb or the great Washington right-hander Walter Johnson came to town. Meanwhile, the Giants, with their gang of stalwarts including Christy Mathewson, Larry Doyle, Rube Marquard, and Fred Merkle, continued to attract standing room crowds at their swollen outdoor bathtub at Coogan's Bluff.

There were some epiphanic moments for the

Clark Griffith was the Highlanders' first manager, and also contributed 14 mound victories in the team's 1903 inaugural season. He continued as a player-manager for another five years, and over the course of a 20-year playing career won 236 games. He managed for a total of 20 years, mostly for underachieving teams. A longtime owner of the Washington Senators franchise, he gained notoriety by selling his son-in-law Joe Cronin to the Red Sox in 1934.

Highlanders in 1906, when the club surprised everybody by ending up in second place. But for the most part, they were out of contention, despite the presence of a few outstanding players such as Wee Willie Keeler, Branch Rickey (who caught in 1907 before moving on to greener pastures), and Prince Hal Chase. Keeler actually coined the immortal phrase, "Hit 'em where they ain't," which he invariably did.

Chase's colorful but questionable career is worth pondering here. He came from California to astound baseball people with his charm and acrobatic skills at first base. His hands were magic at the bag—he could charge in on bunts, throw runners out at second or third, swallow up grounders or pop flies with the grace of a cat. But in other respects he was a deeply flawed athlete. A compulsive gambler, Chase would bet on games, more often than not wagering against his own team.

A lifetime .291 hitter, Chase had become baseball's foremost recidivist, practicing his dishonesty even as many of his own teammates suspected him of consorting with gamblers. Despite such a reputation, he remained in New York until 1913, when Manager Frank Chance (part of the Tinker to Evers to Chance triad) disposed of his services. However, Prince Hal refused to mend his ways; it was strongly hinted that he had been one of those reptiles who had conspired to fix the outcome of the 1919 World Series between the Chicago White Sox (thereafter called the Black Sox) and the Cincinnati Reds.

Even in those "good old days," when things went wrong with a ball club the first person to suffer the consequences was always the manager. Thus, in 1908, when the Highlanders hit last place (and, obviously, hit little else), Griffith was dismissed. Arthur Norman Elberfeld, the team's shortstop, was handed the reins. "The Tabasco Kid," as he was called, led the team to a 27–71 mark, which could rival for ineptitude the Philadelphia Athletics of the 1930s, the Boston Braves of 1935, or the Mets of 1962.

Elberfeld's season climaxed, negatively, when the emerging pitching star of the Senators, Walter Johnson, hurled three shutouts in four days at Hilltop. If the Highlanders hadn't still been observing the Sunday blue law prohibiting baseball playing on that day, Johnson might well have pitched four shutouts in four days! Elberfeld was gone after the year was over, to be replaced by the former plantation owner, George Stallings.

Oddly, the Highlanders (by then generally called the Yankees) romped all the way to second place in 1910. Perhaps the most intriguing game they played all year took place in August when Tom Hughes pitched a no-hitter for nine innings against Cleveland only to lose in the eleventh inning.

However, the Yankees managed to achieve a certain status in the off-season when they engaged their

The graceful, gifted, and thoroughly corrupt Hal Chase. Babe Ruth said, "For my dough Chase was the greatest first baseman who ever lived." Cleveland's Bill Wambsganns said, "He was a cheater right from the beginning and everyone knew it." Chase reportedly won $40,000 betting on the Reds in the 1919 "Black Sox" World Series.

hated rivals, the Giants, in the first postseason city series in New York history. McGraw had everything to lose and little to gain by such a confrontation, while the opposite was true of the Yankees. When the Giants took the series four games to two—as the teams alternated games between Hilltop and the Polo Grounds—McGraw was spared apoplexy.

Despite this exposure to the Giants, attendance at Hilltop remained meager. During the American Revolution some skirmishes had been won on the Hilltop site—but the ball club failed to continue that winning tradition. Things got so bad that the corrupt Chase was named manager in 1911. But with all of Prince Hal's guile the club couldn't do better than sixth. Harry Wolverton, an infielder from Ohio, was a playing manager in 1912 but failed to rouse his tatterdemalion troops. Chance took over the job in 1913–1914, followed by the rangy shortstop Roger Peckinpaugh, who, as a Washington Senator in 1925, achieved reverse immortality by committing eight errors in the

World Series with Pittsburgh. After his sojourn with the Yankees, Peckinpaugh assessed the attitudes of his former players. "Their chief concern was not to get beaten too badly," he said. "Sometimes they started to sing songs in the infield right in the middle of the game. Nobody seemed to be bothered too much by the constant losing."

When a mysterious fire broke out in the Polo Grounds in April 1911, the most mordant suggestion was that McGraw might have burned down the place himself. Barring that, others said, it was a Bolshevik plot. More likely, a careless match had done the job. The wooden stands had been demolished by the blaze, making it impossible for the Giants to use the premises.

So who came to McGraw's rescue? None other than Messrs. Farrell and Devery, who were content for the moment to stop battling with each other. The two gentlemen magnanimously offered the Giants the use of Hilltop Park. Most agreed it was a gesture of unexpected civility and McGraw accepted the invitation immediately. By late June, when the damage to the Polo Grounds was finally repaired, the Giants returned to their home headquarters, still in a state of mild shock over the Yankees' hospitality.

By 1912, neither of the Yankees' owners were happy with the disintegrating state of Hilltop Park. It was almost in as bad shape as the ill-fated British ocean liner, *Titanic*, which sunk in the iceberg-cluttered North Atlantic on the night of April 14, causing the loss of 1500 lives. A week after the disaster, the Yankees and Giants played a special benefit game for the *Titanic*'s survivors. Once again, the Yankees lost.

Perhaps it was entirely fitting that the last thing most fans remembered about Hilltop Park was an incident involving Ty Cobb in mid-May 1912. In all the years that Cobb had restlessly dominated the American League with his hitting and base running, he had neglected to tame his volatile temper. Teammates and foes alike regarded him as being as angry as a warthog. More contemporary descriptions of him hint that he was a mental case. On this particular Saturday afternoon at Hilltop Park, with an unusually large crowd of 20,000 on hand, Cobb confirmed such negative impressions about himself when he climbed into the third-base stands and delivered a startling beating to a fan named Claude Leuker. After the assault was broken up, it became clear that Leuker was hardly a worthy adversary for Cobb: he had no hands. Cobb's excuse for his vicious behavior was that Leuker kept shouting that he was a "half nigger," words that couldn't possibly sit well with a man who had practiced relentless bigotry all his adult life. The brouhaha ultimately was resolved when Ban Johnson suspended Cobb for ten days and fined him a measly fifty dollars.

The 1912 season was the last hurrah for the Yankees at Hilltop Park. With their tenancy at Hilltop at an end, the Yankees chose to accept the Giants offer to play all their future home games at the Polo Grounds. In this instance, McGraw felt that one good turn deserved another. Also, he didn't believe that the team from Washington Heights would ever be able to find another home, a prospect that didn't upset him in the least.

Bad business for their club and bad feelings between the two of them then caused Farrell and Devery to seek a buyer for their team. McGraw had often rejected bids for the Giants, so when two distinguished gentlemen approached him about a possible deal for his team he referred them to the Yankees owners. The two interested buyers—Colonel Jacob Ruppert and Captain Tillinghast L'Hommedieu Huston—were vastly different in personality and character. But they had one thing in common: they wanted to buy a baseball team in a city they knew possessed unbounded kinetic energy. Negotiations for the purchase of the Yankees began in the waning days of 1914 and by January 1915 the deal was concluded. The estimated price paid by Ruppert and Huston was $460,000, about two weeks' pay for journeymen ballplayers in the twenty-first century.

Of the two new Yankees owners, Ruppert was the less baseball-oriented, though he'd known McGraw for years and was occasionally a guest of the Giants. He was a collector of things such as horses, yachts, dogs, monkeys, and first editions of books, so it wasn't surprising that he chose to add a ball club to his multifaceted possessions. A debonair man who spoke with a pronounced German accent, Ruppert had been elected four times to Congress and may have been the only member of that august body who had a valet to assemble his clothes. Ruppert enjoyed his honorary designation of colonel—but aside from an occasional visit to the Park Avenue Armory he had never served a day in the military. Ruppert was a confirmed bachelor and never

My All-Time Yankee Team

Selected by Bob Costas, announcer

1B	Gehrig
2B	Lazzeri
SS	Jeter
3B	Nettles
RF	Ruth
CF	DiMaggio
LF	Mantle
C	Berra
P (Lefty)	Ford
P (Righty)	Ruffing
Mgr	Stengel

seemed to be without a derby on his head, just as one of his Tammany friends, Al Smith, gloried in similar headgear. A man of considerable means, Ruppert liked to spend—always wisely—and he liked to win. As soon as the Yankees fell into his hands, Ruppert installed himself as president, while Huston had to settle for vice president.

Huston liked to talk and drink. Some laughed that his parents must have been drinking when they provided him with his two flatulent names. Unlike Ruppert, who inherited his father's east side Ruppert Brewery, Huston was a self-made man and never hesitated to remind people about it. Most of his money was made on construction projects in Cuba after the Spanish-American War. Prior to that good fortune he had been an engineering officer in the United States Army.

Irrepressible capitalists, Ruppert and Huston knew almost from the moment they bought the Yankees that some day they would have to build their own ballpark. That would come in time—and would change the face of baseball in New York.

Jack Chesbro

John Dwight "Happy Jack" Chesbro, never a household name, has become little more than a tough trivia question for latter-day baseball fans. But from 1903 to 1909 he was a remarkably effective right-handed pitcher for the Highlander/Yankees. In 1904, he won the preposterous total of 41 games, which included a winning streak of 14 games. The number of complete games he pitched in 1904—48—was more than most pitchers in the modern era complete in an entire career.

Unfortunately for Chesbro, he threw one pitch that year that brought the wrath of the New York press and fans down on his head, thus detracting from his sturdy accomplishments. This was the scenario: the Highlanders were a game and a half behind Boston (the Pilgrims) but could have won the American League pennant by sweeping both contests of a season-ending doubleheader at Hilltop Park. In the first game, with the score tied, 1–1, and two outs in the Boston half of the ninth, the Pilgrims' Lou Criger was perched on third base. With a two-nothing count on Fred Parent, Chesbro unleashed a wild pitch that sailed over the head of his catcher, John "Red" Kleinow, allowing Criger to scamper home with the winning run. That settled the pennant issue, even though the distraught Highlanders were able to win the second game of the doubleheader. That was as close as the Highlanders were ever to come to a flag during all the years at Hilltop Park. Chesbro went on to win 19 games in 1905 (with 24 complete games) and 23 in 1906 (with another 24 complete games). But New Yorkers could never forget that single pitch that had done them in in 1904. (Well, did Red Sox fans ever forgive Bill Buckner for his flub at first base against the Mets in 1986, or have Dodger fans ever forgotten that it was Ralph Branca who threw an equally infamous pitch to Bobby Thomson in 1951?)

Until the day he died in 1931, at the age of fifty-seven, Chesbro always maintained that Kleinow—a little fellow at 5'9"—should have reached up and caught that wayward pitch. Born in 1874 in North Adams, Massachusetts, Chesbro started out his base-ball life at a state mental hospital in Middletown, New York. As an employee there, not an inmate, he hurled for the hospital team. By 1899, Chesbro made it to Pittsburgh in the National League. Within two years he became a 21- and 28-game winner, with the help of his specialty—a baffling spitball. He had a total of 14 shutouts in the two seasons, as Pittsburgh finished in first place each time.

In a period when most men were paid salaries of less than $4,000, "everybody was jumping all over the lot," as outfielder Davy Jones told Lawrence Ritter in *The Glory of Their Times*. So Chesbro jumped to the Highlanders in 1903. Within a year, Happy Jack (so called because he was a man with a congenial disposition despite his meager pay) experienced the high of 41 victories and the low of an unforgettable pitch. He was elected to baseball's Hall of Fame in 1946.

1913–1922

I F EVER THERE WAS A TIME OF TURMOIL AND TRANSITION IN THE WORLD—
AND IN THE TIGHTLY KNIT UNIVERSE OF BASEBALL—IT WAS THAT
STRETCH OF YEARS FROM 1913 TO 1923. THE BLOODBATH IN THE
TRENCHES OF THE GREAT WAR, WHICH STARTED IN 1914, HAD EXHAUSTED
ENGLAND, FRANCE, AND GERMANY. MILLIONS OF YOUNG MEN IN THOSE COUN-
TRIES GAVE UP THEIR LIVES IN BATTLE OR FROM THE UNPRECEDENTED VIRU-
LENCE OF A PLAGUE THAT CAME TO BE KNOWN AS THE SPANISH FLU. IN SOME

city morgues around the United States bodies were stacked up like cordwood and on many ballfields players and spectators wore gauze masks.

When America entered World War I in April 1917, some celebrated players, including Ty Cobb, Christy Mathewson, Branch Rickey, Duster Mails, Grover Alexander, and Hank Gowdy answered the call of the colors, as President Woodrow Wilson exhorted his fellow citizens to "make the world safe for democracy." In all, over 250 players from both leagues went into the armed forces. The first casualty was the Giants' Eddie Grant, who was cut down by machine-gun fire in the Argonne Forest. The estimable heavyweight contender Jack Dempsey ducked out of military service, causing him to be regarded as a slacker. An enthusiastic backer of the war, Tillinghast Huston didn't insist that all of his players run off to enlist but he installed military drills for his Yankees charges following pregame practice. Military instructors were brought in to put the players through their paces. In this way, Charles Alexander wrote, "Ban Johnson's league could boast of giving an example of preparedness for the rest of the country."

Crowds continued to come to big league ballparks, even as American doughboys marched off to France in step to patriotic tunes or to the reproachful "I Didn't Raise My Boy To Be A Soldier." Many of them would face death and injury from the horrible new instruments of modern war—tanks, poison gas, machine guns, artillery. Then they came home to a country that, having eagerly supported the war, now sought a "return to normalcy." At least that was the presidential election slogan of Warren G. Harding, a lackluster Republican politician who preferred poker to politics.

Normalcy, unfortunately, included the gambler-driven, headline-grabbing Black Sox Scandal that involved eight players on the Chicago White Sox who were accused of dumping the World Series of 1919 to the underdog Cincinnati Reds. If baseball could now be seen as a corrupt pastime, the game would pay dearly at the gate and in diminished fan support. That the conspiring players were paid inadequately by the tight-fisted owner of the White Sox, Charles Comiskey, thus giving Shoeless Joe Jackson and his confederates a rationale for their sad behavior, was not considered a valid excuse by the press and the fans.

Something had to be done at once to restore baseball's integrity and loss of innocence. That "something" turned out to be George Herman "Babe" Ruth, an undisciplined kid whose thunderous home run bat literally revolutionized the game. Almost overnight, he made fans forget the shady dealings of the Black Sox as he turned a team sport into the cult of the individual. Joining the Yankees from Boston in 1920, Ruth became the most implausible sports figure of all time—a man who wildly overindulged and overdissipated, even as he smashed all records for long-distance clouting. Once a pitcher himself, the Babe reduced all other pitchers to their lowest estate in baseball history. He was "a hero in the image of Heracles and Beowulf," wrote Bill Curran.

But as Ruth went about the daily routine that hurtled the Yankees into contention, one of his team-

OVERLEAF: Lou Gehrig at Columbia. Lou Gehrig was a football as well as a baseball star during his stay at Columbia University. He set university records for batting average, slugging percentage, and home runs, and when he wasn't playing first base, he pitched. In the early 1920s the Columbia ballfield was right in the middle of the campus.

mates, the hard-edged pitcher Carl Mays, threw a ball one August afternoon in 1920 that ended a batter's life. The incident occurred at the Polo Grounds, where the Yankees were still playing their home games. As Cleveland's shortstop, Ray Chapman, stood at the right side of the plate, Mays shattered his skull with one of his typical "submarine" pitches. There were no batting helmets at the time and Chapman died the following morning.

To this day Chapman is the only ballplayer ever killed in a major league game. Mays always heatedly denied that he purposely threw at Chapman's head. Indeed, he was quickly absolved in the matter by Ban Johnson, despite demands for his banishment. Within a week the unpopular Mays was back on the mound. At season's end he had 26 victories, with a league-leading six shutouts.

The Black Sox culprits (no court ever convicted them of anything, but they were summarily thrown out of baseball by the newly installed commissioner Kenesaw Mountain Landis) plus Mays's deadly pitch could have added up to disaster for baseball. But the

rising popularity of the game didn't suffer. Babe Ruth and the Yankees saw to that in the incubating days of the Roaring Twenties.

The transfer of Ruth to the Yankees (a move since referred to as the Curse of the Bambino because of its devastating effect on the Red Sox) was the most ill-advised baseball deal ever concocted. It had its roots in the ludicrous business machinations of Harry Frazee, who owned the Red Sox but had his heart and pocketbook in the Broadway theater. Many of the shows he backed were outright turkeys. He had also wandered afield in 1915 when he helped to promote the Havana heavyweight fight between Jack Johnson and "White Hope" Jess Willard. To this day, many suspect that Johnson, a black man, took a Cuban dive so that the United States government and the bigots would stop pursuing him.

When Frazee bought the Red Sox in 1916, he was

Carl Mays, LEFT, who used a "submarine" pitch to intimidating effect, is very likely exaggerating his windup here for the benefit of the photographer. He was a talented and generally disliked performer. On August 16, 1920, he hit Cleveland's Ray Chapman, BELOW, in the temple with a fastball. Chapman died the next day.

The Pinstripes

The Yankees were not the first team to wear pin-stripes, but since putting them on for the first time in 1912 they have worn them with unmatched élan. The Boston Braves wore stripes on their road uniform in 1907, as did the Cleveland Indians a year later, and the Philadelphia Athletics in 1909. Pinstripes were seen on home uniforms for the first time in 1912, when several teams adopted the style. The Yanks dropped the look for two seasons, returned to it in 1915, and have displayed it ever since.

The signature pin-striped uniform has become a symbol of pride and accomplishment. It is even said to have restorative powers, capable of revitalizing veteran players that other teams have given up on. Opponents have also been affected, even one as determined to be unimpressed as Jackie Robinson. "They would come out and you could sense they thought they could beat you," Robinson said in 1955. Red Smith wrote that the uniform became "the surplice and stole of baseball."

No one wore the pinstripes with more pride than Tommy Henrich. He took it upon himself to remind rookies and new arrivals alike that the uniform conferred both a privilege and a challenge.

---

not yet debt ridden. He had made sound purchases of players like Joe Bush and Stuffy McInnis, thus helping the Red Sox to win a world championship in 1918 (a series in which Ruth was still a dominating pitcher.) But Frazee was not a winner in the highly speculative milieu of the Broadway musical. He turned to Colonel Ruppert and Captain Huston, who were eager to energize their New York entry, and asked them for a money transfusion. They were only too happy to oblige. In depositing the Babe into the Yankees' clutches Frazee had the chutzpah to insist that in the long run the Red Sox would benefit by such a move. "This was a level of hypocrisy that would have qualified him for political office," Donald Honig has written. It was also the kind of nonsense that won Frazee the reputation in Beantown of being "the original Boston Strangler."

However, even before Frazee had unloaded Ruth for some $125,000 in the pre-Christmas season of 1919, he had already negotiated other transactions with the Yankees that would set them on the road to baseball dominance in the 1920s. He sold pitchers Carl Mays and Ernie Shore to Ruppert and Company, as well as outfielder Duffy Lewis, once part of the great Red Sox outfield of Harry Hooper, Tris Speaker, and Lewis. Connie Mack, the ringmaster of the Philadelphia Athletics, provided additional sinew to the Yankees lineup by letting John Franklin "Home Run" Baker loose, after a salary dispute with the World Series hero of 1911 and 1913. Baker, a good third baseman and one fourth of the over-glorified A's "100,000 infield," (Jack Barry, Eddie Collins, Stuffy McInnis), would put together some good seasons for the Yankees, but hardly enough to support his nickname. He did hit ten home runs in two different seasons, but that was before the Babe changed the whole character of the game.

Another import from Mack was James Robert Shawkey, a former fireman on the Pennsylvania Railroad. Shawkey had won 16 games for the pennant-winning Athletics in 1914. But when Mack's team then proceeded to lose four straight games to the Miracle Braves in the World Series, Mack expressed his disgust by selling off many of his top players, including Bob Shawkey. In short order, Shawkey became the premier right-hander on the Yankees, winning 20 or more games in four seasons. He also went on to hold a record for 1–0 Yankees shutouts, pitching seven of them.

Frank Navin, Detroit's owner, joined the unofficial conspiracy to augment the talent on the Yankees roster. He let first baseman Wally Pipp go to the Yankees. Pipp not only distinguished himself for several years but he also became a historic footnote in the story of Lou Gehrig, in one of baseball's most dramatic tableaus.

However, the first important order of business for the Yankees was to get themselves another manager.

Bob Shawkey pitched in twelve seasons for the Yankees, and won 20 or more games in four of them. He managed the team in 1930, the year after Miller Huggins died and the year before Joe McCarthy was hired. He was the winning pitcher in the first game ever played at Yankee Stadium, a 4–1 victory over the Red Sox on April 18, 1923.

That turned out to be Wild Bill Donovan, a former pitcher for Detroit, who had gained experience as a pilot in the International League. Donovan took over the Yankees job in 1915 and stayed at the helm through 1917. A fourth-place finish in 1916 was the best Wild Bill could do. True, he had put the New Yorkers into the first division for the first time since 1910 but, sadly for Donovan, the fans continued to stay away. Home Run Baker was supposed to lure the patrons through the turnstiles but it didn't work out that way. In 1917, Donovan's men ended up in sixth place, miles away from the White Sox, who hadn't yet decided to prearrange the results of ball games. With attendance barely reaching 325,000, Donovan became the fall guy and was dropped as manager. Ruppert had always professed admiration for Wild Bill. "I like

you," the Colonel said, as he handed him the pink slip, "but we've got to get some other help."

At this moment, Huston, a patriot in the mold of Teddy Roosevelt, ran off to the widening war in Europe, leaving Ruppert to search for a manager. Communications with Huston were for the most part limited to Ruppert's transoceanic cables. Instead, Ruppert leaned heavily on the all-knowing, 300-pound Ban Johnson for advice. Huston, before he left for overseas, had favored Wilbert Robinson, the jovial tutor of the Brooklyn Dodgers. Uncle Robbie, as he was called, had learned to dislike John McGraw, his old Baltimore Orioles teammate, which would seem to have been a perfect credential for the open Yankees post. But somehow Ruppert didn't see it that way. He thought Uncle Robbie, at fifty-four, was too old for

the job and regarded him as not much more than a drinking and hunting companion for Huston.

Johnson strongly endorsed Miller Huggins, then the playing manager of the St. Louis Cardinals. "There is a place in our league for a man like him," Johnson told Ruppert. Though he knew hardly anything about Huggins, Ruppert asked Johnson to set up a meeting with him. When Ruppert took one look at Huggins he saw that the man was about half his size. At 5'3" and 130 pounds, Huggins might have been more equipped to be a jockey at Belmont Park but his curriculum vitae was more impressive than that.

Huggins possessed a law degree from the University of Cincinnati and had been a better-than-journeyman infielder for both the Reds and the Cardinals. He had a sharp sense of humor, was an amusing conversationalist and, at thirty-nine, was a bachelor who appeared to be married to the game. He was known as a strategist who utilized the bunt and believed that part of the manager's role was to discipline his players. Johnson emphasized to Ruppert that Huggins was a man of integrity who didn't need the Yankees job and could always go back to practicing law.

Baseball people had never gone out of their way to employ hyperintellects but Huggins may have rated that description. "The real ballplayer employs his brains as well as the shrewdest business man," Huggins once said, indicating that he prized cerebral athletes.

When J. G. Taylor Spink, the publisher of *The Sporting News*, baseball's bible, joined Johnson in heartily endorsing Huggins, Ruppert hired the little man. This unilateral decision was entirely too much for Huston to accept. Never having been too collegial with his partner, Huston bellyached to the press from his vantage point with the 16th Engineers and fired

LEFT: **Frank "Home Run" Baker. His nickname was bestowed on the strength of the two homers he hit in the 1911 World Series while playing for the Philadelphia Athletics. One was hit off the Giants' Christy Mathewson, which enlarged his fame. Baker joined the Yankees in 1916, after leading the league in home runs for four consecutive seasons, averaging a little more than nine homers per year.**

off blistering messages to Ruppert. The relationship between the two men was now doomed. As far as Ruppert was concerned, he was concentrating more on strengthening his team than on patching things up with Huston. When Huston returned to the United States, as a bona fide colonel as opposed to Ruppert's honorary title, he continued to raise hell with his partner, accusing him of everything except murder and treason.

Meanwhile, Huggins, who never actually wanted the Yankees job, found himself caught in the middle. His first challenge was the war-shortened season of 1918, when the schedule ended on Labor Day and all teams played 26 fewer games. The Yankees traded for a new second baseman, Del Pratt, who had covered the position well for the St. Louis Browns. Somehow the team looked better with Pratt in the infield, along with his mate at shortstop, Peckinpaugh. Nevertheless, the Yankees came home in fourth place, thus causing the usual verbal tremors from Huston.

As the 1919 season got under way, Huggins continued to have a tenuous hold on his job. Huston assailed Hug for his supposed inability to handle pitchers. At the same time, the troublesome Carl Mays was added to the staff from Boston. Mays was the storm center of a noisy dispute that he had helped to create. Charging that his Red Sox teammates were not putting forth their best efforts when he was on the mound, Mays pointed to his 5–10 mark to prove his point. It might have been more appropriate to blame himself, but that thought apparently never occurred to Mays. When Mays then abruptly walked out on his team (and manager Ed Barrow), Ban Johnson suspended the recalcitrant hurler and informed the Red Sox they couldn't trade him.

Frazee refused to obey such a Johnson ukase. In short order, he sent Mays to the Yankees for $40,000 and Bob McGraw and Allan Russell, two pitchers never heard from again. With Johnson's fangs removed, Mays proceeded to fit right into the Yankees rotation behind Shawkey. He became a winning pitcher, managing even to smile on occasion as he gazed at the men playing with him: Pipp at first, Pratt at second, Peckinpaugh at short, Baker at third, Ping

Bodie (real name: Francesco Stephano Pezzolo), Duffy Lewis, and Sammy Vick in the outfield and Herold "Muddy" Ruel catching. (Oddly, Ruel's appearance in a Yankee uniform enabled his team to boast of a quirky record: Huggins and Muddy were both lawyers.) This aggregation ended the year in third place, drew 620,000 fans into the seats of the Polo Grounds (only 95,000 less than the Giants), and hit 45 home runs collectively.

Turning a deaf ear to Huston's complaints, Ruppert rewarded Huggins with a one-year renewal in October 1919, only a few months before the earthshaking purchase of the Babe. The arrival of Ruth was truly a seminal moment for the game and, stretching a point, for an America that was about to embark on a postwar joyride. Even Ruppert couldn't have been prescient enough to comprehend fully what his money had wrought. Previously, the most money ever doled out for a ballplayer was the $50,000 paid for Philadelphia's Eddie Collins by Chicago in 1914 and an equal sum that Cleveland banked for Boston in 1916 in return for Boston's Grey Eagle, Tris Speaker.

In 1919, Ruth had hit 29 homers for the Red Sox, even as Ty Cobb won his twelfth and last American League batting title. Few may have suspected it at the time, but the torch had been passed from the singles-hitting, base-stealing Cobb to the cloud-scraping Babe. Everywhere in Gotham—except in John McGraw's tent—expectations were high for the new man in town. But could anyone have anticipated that with each blow-your-house-down swing Ruth would turn the grand old game upside down? He may have resembled Fatty Arbuckle, the reigning comic king of silent films (who, in a few months, was to be implicated in a devastating sex scandal that was to destroy his career), but the Babe was no overweight joke. Playing for his first Yankee salary of $20,000,

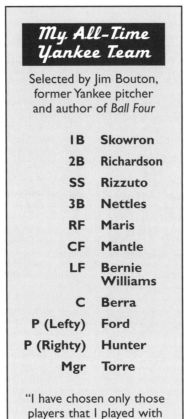

My All-Time Yankee Team

Selected by Jim Bouton, former Yankee pitcher and author of *Ball Four*

1B	Skowron
2B	Richardson
SS	Rizzuto
3B	Nettles
RF	Maris
CF	Mantle
LF	Bernie Williams
C	Berra
P (Lefty)	Ford
P (Righty)	Hunter
Mgr	Torre

"I have chosen only those players that I played with or against."

Ruth was well on his way to transforming the Yankees into the most explosive and remarkable team in baseball history.

The Babe finished the 1920 season at the Polo Grounds with numbers that caused statisticians to scratch their heads in disbelief. The reformed southpaw pitcher batted .376 with an unheard of 54 home runs (more than any of the 14 big league *teams* hit), 158 runs scored, and 137 runs batted in. Such productivity helped the New Yorkers to finish in third place. Just as impressive as the Babe's stats was the turnstile count for the Yankees: 1.3 million, double what the team had drawn in 1919. This, of course, represented a threat to McGraw's Giants, who, until now, had owned the hearts and minds of most New York baseball fans.

"I want these guys out of here," McGraw growled, as he pressured the Yankees to take their show out of the Polo Grounds. Ruppert took the unsubtle message seriously and began to search for a new home for his club. The proud man had long wanted his team released from tenancy at the Polo Grounds. McGraw wanted the Yankees as far away as possible, but Ruppert wasn't about to accommodate him by moving the club into the Sahara Desert.

Even before Ruppert could arrange another venue for the Yankees, his first priority was to acquire a knowledgeable general manager, one who would devote full time to the personnel needs of the Yankees. Naturally, Ruppert again looked to Boston, which had become the prep school for his emerging organization. In this instance, he lured Edward Grant Barrow to New York in October 1920. Barrow, now fifty-two years old, managed the Red Sox in 1918 and 1919. Although he had never played baseball, Barrow had been engaged in almost every aspect of the business. Born in Springfield, Illinois—and not in a covered wagon, as the game's mythmakers had asserted—Barrow had a middle name that was borrowed from the Civil War general. Ulysses Grant had been reputed to drink too much; Ed Barrow never had such a problem. He had become a hard-driving executive, after an apprenticeship as a mail clerk for the *Des Moines Register* and a job running concessions for Harry Stevens in Pittsburgh. In his years as a minor league executive at various ports of call Barrow exhibited flashes of innovativeness that would have brought an approving smile to Bill Veeck's face. Long before Babe Didrikson was born, Barrow employed a woman pitcher, and he once hired the boastful heavyweight champion John L. Sullivan to umpire a ball game. Gentleman Jim Corbett, another legendary heavyweight, played first base for the enterprising Barrow.

But Barrow's chief claim to fame was converting Babe Ruth into a full-time outfielder with the Red Sox, acting on the urgent advice of Harry Hooper, Boston's Hall of Fame outfielder. In 1918, Barrow managed the Red Sox to a pennant and World Series victory over the Chicago Cubs. But when he realized that Frazee was determined to tear the guts out of his team, he looked elsewhere for employment. Barrow was tough, explosive, shrewd, and careful with other people's money, attributes that endeared him to Ruppert.

When Barrow arrived in New York he promptly told Huggins that "your job is to win . . . I'll give you the players." Barrow was true to his word. It didn't take him long to dispossess the Red Sox of additional talent. In 1921, Barrow brought right-hander Waite Charles Hoyt to New York, a move that yielded great dividends on the mound. Hoyt was street smart, handsome, and Brooklyn born. He was more articulate and sophisticated than most players of his day and after his long career was over he became a popular broadcaster in Cincinnati. In 1923, Herb Pennock, a patrician southpaw who raised silver foxes in Kennett Square, Pennsylvania, and utilized splendid control to get batters out, joined Hoyt from the Red Sox. Both Hoyt and Pennock ultimately were voted into the Hall of Fame.

The plundering of Boston didn't stop with these two pitchers. The durable shortstop Everett Scott was obtained, as well as pitchers Sad Sam Jones and Bullet Joe Bush. Catcher Wally Schang, who hit .300 for the Sox, came to the Yankees in 1921, and Jumping Joe Dugan, a solid third baseman, arrived in 1922. He was a valuable addition to the club, not least because, like Hoyt and Pennock, he became an intimate buddy of the Babe. With Dugan's arrival, the aging Home Run Baker was moved out of the infield picture.

Frazee's moves literally destroyed Boston's franchise, while putting the Yankees on the road to glory. From 1922 on, the Red Sox practically had squatter rights to last place, while the Yankees galloped to six pennants in eight seasons. Commissioner Landis, so

Wally Pipp was the Yankees' regular first baseman for 10 years, beginning in 1915. Early in the 1925 season he was injured during batting practice and replaced in the lineup by Lou Gehrig, a twenty-one-year-old rookie. Gehrig remained on the job for the rest of the year, and for the next 13 seasons. Pipp was traded to Cincinnati in 1926.

unyielding in his dealings with the banned-for-life Black Soxers, failed to lift a finger to prevent Frazee from denuding his roster of its best players.

The Yankees broke quickly from the pack in 1921 and were challenged for a time by the Cleveland Indians, a club that included Tris Speaker, little Joe Sewell, Bill Wambganss, and pitchers George Uhle and Stan Coveleski. The Yankees wound up winning 98 games and achieved their first American League pennant. Chiefly responsible for the Yankees' climb to the top were, of course, the Babe, and pitchers Hoyt and Mays, who won 46 games between them.

Ruth was even better than he was in 1920. He hit 59 home runs, scored 177 runs, and drove in 170 runs. This output occurred even after he'd been declared "dead" in a newspaper headline, following a minor automobile accident outside Philadelphia. Another home run hitter emerged in the Yankee lineup in the dour person of Bob Meusel, who banged 24 after being purchased from the Pacific Coast League. As a team the Yankees amassed 134 home runs, a league-leading total that was to become an annual tradition with the team.

Heading into the World Series against the Giants, whose formidable roster included Irish Meusel, Bob's brother, "High Pockets" George Kelly at first base, and the Fordham Flash, Frankie Frisch, at second

base, the Yankees had good reason to be optimistic. But in the best-out-of-nine Series (the last ever played), with all games at the Polo Grounds, things didn't work out too well for the Yankees. After winning the first two games by shutouts—thanks to the pitching of Mays and Hoyt—the Yankees stopped hitting. The Giants rallied to win the Series, the first time a team had ever lost the first two games and had come back to win. Another first: Grantland Rice, the sportswriter who golfed with presidents, was at the KDKA radio microphone for the first game of the Series, although he always showed a strong preference for his typewriter. At the time there were about three million American homes with radios.

The Giants victory was in large part a result of the Babe's slump—he connected for only one home run in this first Series clash between the two bitter New York rivals. When Ruth attributed his failure at bat to a painful abscess on his elbow, several of his newspaper critics doubted him and said he "wasn't up to the competition." The Babe angrily exhibited his injury to these gentlemen and they promptly shut up.

Though the Yankees lost, each player picked up a losing share of $3,500, a pretty munificent sum in those years. The Giants each took home $5,265, which, in some cases, equaled a year's salary.

Following his explosive season, the Babe was de-

A panoramic view of Yankee Stadium under construction during the winter of 1922–1923. The extreme wide angle lens places the grandstand at a greater distance from the bleachers than was actually the case, but it was still an intimidating stretch for most hitters. The tracks of the Lexington Avenue el can be seen on the far right.

termined to further cash in on his celebrity. He joined Meusel and catcher Fred Hofmann on a barnstorming tour, thus flatly defying Judge Landis's ukase that forbade such activity. Never having cared much for rules, the Babe thumbed his nose at the commissioner and was forced to pay for his anarchy. The touring players were fined the amount of their Series shares and were suspended through the first six weeks of the 1922 season. The howls from the Babe and from not a few fans who sympathized with his position could be heard all the way to the equator. Out of the lineup, the Babe persisted in following his routine of lots of booze, food, and women. He embraced a three o'clock in the morning regimen befitting a deity.

Even in the absence of Babe and Bob, the Yankees proved at least one point—they were a powerful team. They clung to first place in a grueling race with the St. Louis Browns, managed by Lee Fohl and led by George Sisler, one of the great hitters in American League history—a .400 hitter disadvantaged by chronically poor eyesight. With the Babe back in the lineup, the race still remained close. At the end, however, the Yankees squeaked in over the Browns by a single game.

Though he missed forty games, Ruth hit 35 home runs, about double what most mortals could accumulate. Wally Schang hit .319 and Wally Pipp did better at .329. This time around what won for the Yankees was their superb five-man pitching rotation, led by Bullet Joe Bush with 26 victories.

It appeared that Huggins had his men primed for a good whack at the Giants that autumn, who, as usual, fielded a tough, disciplined club. But within a week's time, Yankee fans were growling in disappointment. Frisch teamed with third baseman Heinie Groh to bang out 17 hits in 36 times at bat, as the Giants had a picnic at bat and in the field. The Yankees wound up losing four straight games. Only a tie game, called on account of darkness (when there was still plenty of daylight left), gave the Yankees any surcease. In two of the games a bow-legged, thirty-three-year-old impish fellow named Casey Stengel covered center field for the Giants. He had only a minor impact on that Series. But in a later time Casey would play a significant role in Yankee affairs.

The disastrous Series against the Giants, with the Babe faltering badly (he had two hits in 17 at-bats, with nary a home run), produced the expected reaction from Huston. He called for Huggins's head on a platter, although nobody had seen the diminutive manager either bat or pitch during the Series.

"That guy Huggins has managed his last game for the Yankees," Huston informed his friend Fred Lieb, a trusted baseball writer. However, it was Huston himself, not Huggins, who shortly afterward left the Yankees. The following spring Ruppert bought out his partner for a sum approaching $1.5 million. To signal the end of a rancorous era, Ruppert went out and bought two sets of uniforms for each player.

Meanwhile, even in victory, McGraw remained

adamant about the Yankees. More than ever he wanted the them out of the Polo Grounds. It had become an embarrassment for him to watch his team trample the Yankees and still draw fewer fans to the old green bathtub than "the other team in town." Under the circumstances, Ruppert did not permit himself to fall asleep at the switch. He was determined to provide a new, spectacular park for his team and was confident that in short order the Babe and crew would catch up with the Giants. An increasing acceptance of Sunday baseball, he knew, was bound to assure large crowds at weekend games. He was also impressed with the bountiful postwar economy, as well as the almost reckless joie de vivre that pervaded the country.

After considering many sites around the city, as well as on Long Island, Ruppert finally located an appropriate venue. It turned out to be a characterless old lumberyard, full of rocks and garbage, in the western section of the Bronx, running from 158th Street to 161st Street on River Avenue. The parcel of land, some ten acres, was once owned by the estate of William Waldorf Astor, and was near the Grand Concourse, then a fashionable area. More important, it was within spying distance of the Polo Grounds. During the Revolutionary War the British had granted the land to one John Lion Gardiner. When the architects and engineers assured Ruppert that the site was ideal because of its soft granite bedding, the Yankees doled out $600,000 for the property. No less important was the fact that the new ballpark would be a neighbor of the subway that could transport Ruppert from his downtown office in less than twenty minutes.

Construction of the new stadium began in the first week of May 1922, under the direction of the

My All-Time Yankee Team

Selected by Tommy Henrich, the Yankees' Old Reliable

1B Gehrig
"He gave me tips on various pitchers; he didn't have to do it."

2B Gordon

SS Rizzuto
"Kubek was good, too."

3B McDougald
"I know what he's made of in tough situations. He gets tougher."

RF Ruth

CF DiMaggio

LF Mantle

C Dickey
"I was the only Yankee present at Dickey's funeral."

P (Lefty) Ford
"But Gomez was mighty good, too."

P (Righty) Reynolds

Mgr McCarthy
"Huggins could handle the Babe. McCarthy couldn't."

White Construction Company and the Osborn Engineering Company of Cleveland. (Osborn had previously helped to rebuild the Polo Grounds.) Within 284 working days the majestic edifice was completed. It was a steel and concrete structure, with massive triple-deck stands—the first in the game's history—and included 60,000 seats, which, some Euclideans pointed out, equaled the accommodations in the Roman Colosseum. In the years to come the crowds often numbered more than that, either because of flagrant violations of the fire laws or equally flagrant misreporting.

The component parts assembled for the park would have stunned a reader of "Ripley's Believe It Or Not." Almost a million feet of Pacific Coast fir were transported via the Panama Canal, to build the bleachers. More than 116,000 square feet of sod were used to convert an urban site into a pastoral mecca. Some 2300 tons of structural steel, one million brass screws, 135,000 steel castings, and 20,000 cubic yards of concrete helped to build the grandstand. One giveaway structural concession to the Babe's southpaw stroke was the 296-foot right field foul line, accompanied by a low fence. (When it came to "cheap" home runs, that couldn't compare to right field in the Polo Grounds, which measured only 257 feet.) In left field it was 281 feet down the foul line, while center field was a vast, unexplored territory of close to 500 feet, a veritable graveyard for sluggers.

However, of all the striking features of the park, it was the copper frieze, 16 feet deep and hanging from the roof of the upper grandstand, that at once became the most familiar signature to visitors from all over the country. True, there were some critics who complained that the stadium's sight lines were not adequate. They also insisted that many seats suffered from obstructed views and that there were mysterious angles of shadows and sunlight that often caused problems for players. But these were only isolated quibbles.

For the most part, the ballpark—built for $2.5 million—was the ultimate tribute to the rising popularity of the game. In short order, it was nicknamed "The House That Ruth Built," for obvious reasons, by Fred Lieb, the *New York Evening Telegram* baseball writer. This naturally pleased one particular round-faced gentleman.

But Ruppert refused to go along with such a name tag. He opted for Yankee Stadium, perhaps not as romantic a name, but one that has surely taken on universal resonance.

Babe Ruth

"The Babe isn't a man, he's an institution," Moe Berg, the cerebral catcher and contemporary of Ruth, once remarked.

Babe Ruth was called many things in his time and after his time. But Berg's description of the man who turned the game upside down and inside out is as appropriate as any.

To this day many think the Babe invented the home run. Not exactly. He just hit more of them, higher, farther, and more frequently than anybody who played in his era. By the force of his swing and the impact of his uninhibited personality he endeared himself to millions as he went about rescuing the game from the rottenness of the Black Sox scandal.

Everything about Ruth was different. He even had two reported birth dates. You can take your choice between February 7, 1894, or February 6, 1895. The myth about the Babe paints him as an orphan. He wasn't that, by his own admission. But he was left to fend for himself in a difficult childhood in Baltimore. His father was a horsedriver and bartender who paid little attention to him. His mother died when the Babe was thirteen.

"The Babe avoided school with a passion," Robert Creamer's biography notes. "Truckdrivers, cops and storekeepers were his enemies." The Babe didn't disagree with that summation. "I was a bum when I was a kid," the Babe said many times.

In 1902, when the Babe was seven, he was placed in St. Mary's Industrial School for Boys. St. Mary's was run by the Xaverian Brothers, a Catholic order, but non-Catholics were also welcome. (The other most famous alumnus of the school was the entertainer Al Jolson.) The Babe came out of St. Mary's in 1908, then went in again, and out again, in subsequent years. Harsh discipline was meted out at the school and the Babe had few visitors. He was assigned to study tailoring and shirtmaking but showed little aptitude for those trades. However, he did show extraordinary promise on the ball field as a left-handed catcher, and was forced to use a right-hander's mitt because the school's meager budget couldn't support the purchase of an additional glove.

By now Brother Matthias had taken an active interest in Ruth, primarily because he was a baseball fan. As long as he had a bat in his hand, Ruth never seemed to be a problem. Brother Matthias encouraged Jack Dunn, the owner of the Baltimore Orioles team of the International League, to take a look at Ruth. Dunn liked what he saw in this big, flat-nosed, homely kid and promptly offered him a contract for $600 to sign with the Orioles.

By virtue of this arrangement, Dunn became the guardian for the nineteen-year-old youngster. Soon Ruth, whom many of the tough, grizzled Orioles regarded as a child—a guileless one at that—was given the nickname of "Babe." Dunnie's "babe," his Oriole teammates called him. And it stuck. The only other baseball Babe at the time was Babe Adams, a pitcher for Pittsburgh.

Within two months, Babe was pitching so well with his left hand that Dunn doubled his salary to $200 a month, scarcely enough to keep the Babe in hot dogs. However, by midseason of 1914, when

Dunn was hard pressed for money, he sold the lad to the Boston Red Sox for $2,900, a transaction that has to rate right up there with the sale of Manhattan Island. The Red Sox farmed the Babe out briefly to Providence of the International League. But before the season was over he was back with the Red Sox, where he began a brilliant career as a southpaw pitcher. In May 1915, on a day when he was on the mound at the Polo Grounds against the Yankees, the Babe hit his first big league home run off Jack Warhop, a journeyman right-hander.

In two World Series, against Brooklyn and Chicago in 1916 and 1918, the Babe, working for managers Bill Carrigan and Ed Barrow, won three games. In the process he hung up 29 straight scoreless innings of pitching, a mark that stood until Yankee pitcher Whitey Ford broke it years later. It is hard to think of the Babe's pitching prowess (some even compared him to the great Walter Johnson, who was acknowledged as the best hurler of his day) when compared to his ultimate success as the premier home run hitter of the twenties. But in 1916, *Baseball Magazine* rated him as "one of the greatest natural pitchers ever to break into the game."

But in 1919 Ed Barrow made the move that literally revolutionized baseball: he switched Ruth to a full-time position in the outfield. "You'll help the team more if you play every day," Barrow said to the Babe. "Sure, put me in there," replied Ruth. Thus began the transformation of Ruth, as well as baseball. The rest is Yankee history, as the Babe, in 15 glorious years with New York, pioneered the age of long-distance slugging.

1923–1932

THE YANKEES DIDN'T CREATE THE ROARING TWENTIES ANY MORE THAN JOAN CRAWFORD'S FLICKS DID. BUT, WITH THE BABE AND LOU GEHRIG LEADING THE WAY, THEY WERE AN INTEGRAL PART OF A DIZZY DECADE IN WHICH MOVIES TALKED FOR THE FIRST TIME, WOMEN SMOKED IN PUBLIC SHAMELESSLY, AND SOME PEOPLE GOT THEIR SOULS SAVED BY EVANGEL- ICAL CON MEN LIKE THE EX-BALLPLAYER BILLY SUNDAY. ■ IT WAS A TIME OF FLAMING YOUTH, FLAPPERS, FATTY ARBUCKLE, BOOTLEG BOOZE, SEX SCAN-

dals, Red scares, lynch mobs, and lawless saloons. It was a time when mobsters like Scarface Al Capone oddly won more attention than Presidents Calvin Coolidge and Herbert Hoover, and Shipwreck Kelly had nothing better to do with his time than sit on the top of flagpoles.

In those years of excess and hyperbole, sports icons like the Babe, Lou, Jack Dempsey, Bobby Jones, Red Grange, Knute Rockne, Bill Tilden, Tommy Hitchcock, Helen Wills, and a handy guy called Earl Sande were mythologized by an adoring press. "They were all colorful extroverts of one kind or another," wrote Paul Gallico, a troubadour of the era.

Other lyricists of that time spoke gloomily about this postwar age of cynicism and disillusionment. "The hangover became part of the day, as well allowed for as the Spanish siesta," wrote F. Scott Fitzgerald, a celebrated victim of the period. Edna St. Vincent Mil- lay talked about her candle burning at both ends. "It will not last the night; But ah, my foes, and oh, my friends—it gives a lovely light."

But one optimist of the twenties, the Frenchman Emil Coué, offered his cure for whatever was ailing the body politic. "Every day, in every way, I'm getting better and better," he said. And Colonel Ruppert's Yankees fulfilled that dictum to perfection, beginning on the afternoon of April 18, 1923, when they chris- tened their cavernous new playground before a crowd of over 74,000 people. Everyone who was anyone

OVERLEAF: **The Yankees' first game in their new ballpark took place on April 18, 1923, a gray, chilly day. Undeterred, fans filled every seat and standing space. The Yanks beat the Red Sox 4–1, and Babe Ruth, with his instinctive flair for ceremony, hit a towering home run.**

seemed to be on hand for the event, including the grave Commissioner Landis and Governor Al Smith, wearing his signature brown derby. The *New York Times* claimed that 20,000 fans were turned away.

It was appropriate that Ruth, on a chilly day more suitable for football, delivered the coup de grace, a three-run home run in the bottom of the fourth in- ning off right-hander Howard Ehmke of the Red Sox. The ball landed in the right-field bleachers, which henceforth would be named Ruthville. The ball game went to the Yankees, 4–1.

Just as the Babe was doing what he was hired to do, a handsome, muscular Columbia University ballplayer named Lou Gehrig was pitching a few miles away against Williams College at South Field at 116th Street in Manhattan. Only a handful of people were there to watch Gehrig strike out 17 Williams bat- ters—at the time a Columbia record. One of those present was the perceptive Yankee scout Paul Krichell, who had been trailing Lou for some time like a base- ball Javert. Yes, he was impressed with Lou's pitching that day, but it was the young man's batting power that fascinated him. Some of the home runs that Gehrig had hit at South Field and other college parks had been gargantuan wallops, including one legendary poke that supposedly landed atop the Columbia dean's head 500 feet away from home plate. Within days, Gehrig, a poor youngster from the Yorkville section of Manhattan, accepted a $1500 offer to play for the Yankees. Krichell, a failed big league catcher with the St. Louis Browns, would uncover other nuggets for New York. (In the future he would sign stars such as Tony Lazzeri, Benny Bengough, Mark Koenig, Phil Rizzuto, Whitey Ford, Charlie Keller, and Leo Durocher.) Even before he ever planted his spikes at Yankee Stadium, Gehrig was being hailed as a second Ruth, an almost intolerable burden to place on the dimple-cheeked young lion. But in two years Gehrig would be batting fourth in the Yankee lineup behind the Babe, a symbiotic slugging tandem that has since defied all comparisons.

Ruth's home run in the opener, the first of 41 he would hit in 1923, was a resounding harbinger of things to come. Having added the slender southpaw Pennock to their staff, via the Red Sox, the Yankees now also featured the most competent array of pitchers in the American League. In 1923, Sad Sam Jones won 21 games, Pennock won 19, Bush won 19, and Hoyt took 17, as the team galloped off to its third straight American League pennant. In the process, Ty Cobb's Tigers were left in the dust, 16 games back.

The Yankees prepared to face the Giants again in an interborough rivalry that had become more heated than John McGraw's temper. The first game of the World Series was scheduled for Yankee Stadium. But McGraw insisted that his players suit up at the Polo Grounds locker room before each contest at the Stadium. He didn't mind paying the extra taxi fare for his men as they rode to what is now widely called the Subway Series.

On Wednesday, October 10, thousands of kids played hookey from school and many office workers reported in sick. The baseball obsession had swept the city. For those milling

around the midtown streets of Manhattan the *New York Times* had erected a huge magnetic play-by-play scoreboard so that Yankees and Giants fans could follow the progress of the games. For the first time, radio carried the World Series, with Graham MacNamee, a popular broadcaster, doing the play-by-play.

As over 55,000 fans watched at the Stadium, the game seesawed until the ninth inning. Then, with the score tied at 4–4, and two men out, outfielder Stengel, whose deeply wrinkled face made him look older than his years, pulled off the most unexpected of plays: an inside-the-park home run. Stengel hit one between Bob Meusel in left field and Whitey Witt in center, and before they could catch up with the ball, he had huffed and puffed his way around the bases and across home plate. The desperate scamper, memorialized in

Waite Hoyt pitched in the major leagues for 21 years, 10 for the Yankees, and led the club in wins and ERA in the team's dominant 1927 season. He was the opening day pitcher for the Yankees that year, and told a reporter, "It's great to be young and a Yankee." He later became the Cincinnati Reds' radio and television voice from 1942 through 1965. Hoyt was a first-rate raconteur, much in the style of today's broadcaster Ralph Kiner.

the next day's newspapers by that hard-crusted diarist of Broadway fables, Damon Runyon, won the game for the Giants. It also won a measure of overnight fame (thanks to Runyon) for Casey. "His flanks heaving, his mouth open, his breath whistling, his warped old legs twisted and bent . . . just barely held out, as he ran his home run home," wrote Runyon, in part.

In the third game it was Casey again, with another home run, this one over the right-field wall, who won the game, 1–0, for the Giants. As he rounded third base, Casey, always up to some mischief, thumbed his nose at the Yankee dugout. Fined $50 for the gesture, Casey laughingly explained that "a bee was bothering me." Years later, when Stengel became the surprise manager of the Yankees, the fans relished the opportunity to react more positively to his brand of humor.

Notwithstanding Casey's efforts, it was Ruth who seized the initiative and helped to win the Series for the Yankees, four games to two. He crushed three home runs, refused to swing at bad pitches, walking eight times, and batted .368. The Babe had arrived as a Series standout in a big way and Heywood Broun was moved to type that "The Ruth Is Mighty and Shall Prevail." Most of the 300,000 fans who sat in on the Series were inclined to believe Broun. By this time the Babe's porcine features were now as lovingly familiar as Charlie Chaplin's mustached face, Douglas Fairbanks's radiant smile, and Rudolph Valentino's darkly handsome looks.

Largely overlooked during the Yankees' first championship season was the twenty-year-old Gehrig. He came to bat 26 times, hit one homer and had 11 hits. But Wally Pipp still had squatter's rights at first base, causing Lou to be sent down to Hartford in the Eastern League for more seasoning.

Huggins was confident that his club would repeat in 1924. But he failed to account for the rapid rise of the Washington Senators, under their boy manager, twenty-seven-year-old Stanley "Bucky" Harris. The Yankees led for a good part of the campaign, at one stage even walloping the Senators five times in a row. But Walter Johnson, in his eighteenth season, finally got a chance to pitch in a World Series as the Senators finished two games ahead of the New Yorkers. The seven-game World Series that followed, with the Senators licking the Giants, was more thrilling than anything the Yankees and Giants had displayed from 1921 to 1923. There was little doubt that millions of fans were happy to see Johnson and his Senators win a title for the first time.

Expectations were high in the Yankees camp that the club would bounce back to head their league in 1925. But a funny thing happened on the way to the counting house. Naturally, it involved the Babe, who at thirty, should have been primed for a peak year. Instead, his outrageous lifestyle of gluttony, night-crawling and womanizing finally caught up with him. As the Yankees arrived in North Carolina on their preseason barnstorming tour, the Babe woke up with a high fever and excruciating stomach pains, which shouldn't have surprised anyone who ever caught a glimpse of his daily menus.

Early, ugly reports insisted that the Babe was near death's door. In fact, one newspaper headlined that he had died. Exactly what was afflicting him was hard to ascertain, although rumors circulated that he had everything from stomach poisoning to a venereal disease. New York journalists pronounced that Ruth's ailment was "The Bellyache Heard 'Round The World," which utterly failed to bring any laughter from Messrs. Ruppert and Huggins.

After a lengthy sojourn in a New York hospital, during which the Babe underwent a stomach operation, he finally returned to the Yankee lineup in June. By that time the team was sunk in despair and in the

My All-Time Yankee Team

Selected by Allen Barra, columnist, *Wall Street Journal*

1B	Gehrig
2B	Gordon
SS	Jeter
3B	Nettles
RF	Ruth
CF	DiMaggio
LF	Mantle
C	Berra
P (Lefty)	Ford
P (Righty)	Cone
Mgr	Stengel

His somewhat barrellike body notwithstanding, the Babe was a graceful athlete and displayed a supple batting stroke. He is seen here hitting against the Chicago White Sox at Comiskey Park. In 1933, he hit a home run there in baseball's first All-Star Game. A Chicago reporter described the scene: "The crowd gave the Babe a tremendous ovation as he doffed his cap and cantered around the bases with a wide grin on his face."

"Don't bother to suit up today," Huggins shouted at the Babe, who continued to break all records for tardy arrival at the ballpark.

"For two cents I'd smack you in your face, you flea son of a bitch," the Babe shouted back.

"If you didn't have seventy pounds on me, I'd lick you right now," replied Huggins, who, with all of his training in mathematics, didn't add very well.

The upshot of this noisy confrontation was that Ruth was fined $5,000 by the Yankees out of his fifty-grand salary. Ruppert and Ed Barrow were adamant in supporting Huggins, causing the Babe finally to issue an apology. When he returned to action in the first week in September, the contrite Babe appeared chastened. He picked up almost fifty points in his batting average, but by that time the Yankees were miles behind the pack. To be precise, they finished in seventh place, 28½ games behind Washington.

That winter the Babe, decked out in a tuxedo, appeared at a dinner in which the voluble playboy mayor of New York City, Jimmy Walker, sternly lectured him on the obligation he had toward all the "dirty-faced little urchins" who rooted for the Yankees. Almost as imprudent in his behavior as the Babe, Walker hadn't yet been caught at it.

Whatever mysterious chemistry had worked on the Babe, it was clear that he had turned over a new leaf in 1926. But in this instance the Babe wasn't totally responsible for the astonishing Yankee turnaround. There were others who also contributed to the cause. They now had the twenty-three-year-old Gehrig at first base, after he had taken over the post the previous June from Pipp. Wally made the mistake of reporting in one day with a headache (after being beaned in batting prac-

standings. In hardly any shape to slug the Yankees back into contention, the Babe was still "rooming with a suitcase," as his former teammate Ping Bodie once said of him. (He did manage to finish the year with 25 home runs and a subpar .290 batting average.) But late in August, Huggins, fed up and frustrated, confronted the Babe in St. Louis.

tice by Charlie Caldwell, who later would become Princeton's football coach). Huggins sent in Lou to replace the veteran. Thus began Lou's long and honorable progression of 2,130 consecutive ball games, the figure that stood up until 1995, when Cal Ripken, Jr., of Baltimore beat it.

The purchase of the Kentucky Colonel, Earle Combs, from the Louisville club, gave the Yankees a premier center-fielder until 1935. Combs, a wonderful leadoff man, established a tradition in center field that was carried on by Joe DiMaggio, then Mickey Mantle, then Bernie Williams. At shortstop, the durable Everett Scott had finally relinquished that position to Mark Koenig, another newcomer from San Francisco,

Herb Pennock was the winning pitcher the day Babe Ruth hit his 60th homer in 1927. He won 19 games for the Bombers that season, adding another victory in the World Series. Nicknamed "The Squire of Kennett Square" after his Pennsylvania birthplace, he attended prep school and conducted himself in a country gentleman fashion, persuading Babe Ruth to go fox hunting with him. He won 240 games over the course of his 22-year career and was serving as the general manager of the Phillies at the time of his death.

who was a switch-hitter. Pairing with Koenig at second base was the twenty-two-year-old Tony Lazzeri, a fellow San Franciscan who had amassed 60 home runs and 222 runs batted in with Salt Lake City in 1925. Ultimately, Poosh 'Em Up Tony, which is the way his delighted Italian fans referred to him, was rated by many as the top second baseman in Yankee history.

The Babe's numbers in 1926—47 homers, a .372 batting average, and 155 runs batted in—promised to make it tough on the St. Louis Cardinals in the World Series. Indeed, he was tough, but the underrated Cardinals were tougher. Appearing in the postseason for the first time, St. Louis battled down to the seventh game and won it. The Cards were led by player-manager Rogers Hornsby, who refused to read books or watch movies in order to preserve his eyes for better things—such as several over .400 batting averages in the twenties.

In the fourth game of the 1926 World Series, the Babe connected for three mammoth home runs, two off Flint Rhem, who enjoyed late nights as much as Ruth did. But the most dramatic moment of the Series occurred in the seventh inning of the seventh game, on a chilly, drizzly October Sunday at the Stadium. That episode has since become indelibly imprinted into the game's history.

With the Yankees trailing the Cards, 3–2, in that seventh inning, intentional walks to Ruth and Gehrig loaded the bases with two out. With Lazzeri coming to bat (he was behind only Ruth in the American League RBI standings that season), Hornsby decided to remove Jesse Haines, his veteran right-hander, who had opened a blister on his pitching hand. In from the bullpen strode the thirty-nine-year-old Grover Cleveland Alexander, who had already won two complete games from the Yankees in the Series, one the previous afternoon. The legend insists that Hornsby peered into old Alex's eyes before handing him the ball, for the former farm boy from Nebraska was known to enjoy a libation or two after his victories. Seemingly content with what he saw, Hornsby then put the fate of the Series into Alexander's hands. "Well, the bases are full," said the Cards manager, "Lazzeri's up and there ain't no place to put him."

Using the guile of a lifetime, Alex, a World War I veteran who had seen tougher times, threw four pitches to Lazzeri. Tony swung mightily at three. The first swing was a bad miss. The second swing produced one of the loudest fouls in history, as the ball went screeching for the left-field stands and then twisted foul at the last second. The fourth pitch broke on the outside corner of the plate as Lazzeri swung awkwardly and missed. After turning back Lazzeri, Alex stayed in the game through the eighth and ninth innings. With two out in the ninth, he walked the Babe, because, as he explained later, "I'd never give the big son of a bitch anything good to hit." The Babe then committed one of the few egregious mistakes of his career. He lit out for second on a steal attempt and was promptly thrown out by catcher Bob O'Farrell to end the Series.

Overnight, the grizzled St. Louis pitcher with the oversized cap perched rather comically on his head became a national hero. His mano-a-mano duel with Lazzeri had instantly become baseball's version of Alexander Hamilton versus Aaron Burr or Jack Dempsey versus Gene Tunney. The dour Hornsby was proclaimed a genius for entrusting the decisive game to old Alex, and O'Farrell bolstered the quickly gestating myth by declaring that Alex was "the greatest clutch pitcher" of them all. "Lazzeri would have had to have been Houdini to get wood on that last pitch," he said.

A somber footnote to the Alex-Lazzeri confrontation was the strange fact that both players suffered from epilepsy, although neither man had apparently ever had a seizure on the diamond. In the years to come life was not kind to either of them. Lazzeri died in 1946, at the age of forty-three, after a heart attack that may have followed an epileptic seizure. He was posthumously elected to the Hall of Fame in 1991. Alex battled alcoholism, epilepsy, cancer, and short funds for the remainder of his life, sometimes appearing at flea circuses and sideshows to pick up a few dollars. When he went to Cooperstown in 1938 to become a member of the Hall of Fame, he was shabbily dressed and one ear was missing as the result of an operation. In 1950, at the age of sixty-

Lou Gehrig drove in 175 runs in 1927—more than Ruth, and more than everyone else in the majors. Despite the Bambino's home run record that season, Gehrig was voted the American League's Most Valuable Player.

three, he was found dead in a rented room in Nebraska.

Following the razor-thin loss to the Cardinals, the Yankees emerged in 1927 with a team that has been called, by many baseball savants past and present, "the greatest of all." It's hard to find substantial disagreement with this assessment anywhere.

They were seemingly a ball club without a weakness. Although some might deprecate the journeymen catching corps of Pat Collins, Johnny Grabowski, and Benny Bengough, the rest of the lineup was extraordinary. Their "Murderers' Row" of Babe, Lou, Meusel, and Lazzeri gave pitchers no respite. "They were all assassins of hurlers," wrote Paul Gallico, in the spirit of Roaring Twenties hyperbole. Wilbert Robinson, who once played for the Baltimore Orioles, insisted his old team couldn't compare with the 1927 Yankees. "They would have murdered us," he said.

Many argue that this team, the 1927 Yankees, was the greatest of all. Sitting in the front row (L-R): Wera, Gazella, Collins, Bennett (mascot), Bengough, Morehart, Thomas, and Durst. In the middle: Shocker, Dugan, Combs, O'Leary (coach), Huggins (manager), Fletcher (coach), Koenig, Ruether, Grabowski, and Pipgras. In the back row: Gehrig, Pennock, Lazzeri, Moore, Ruth, Miller, Meusel, Shawkey, Hoyt, Girard, Paschal, Styborski, and Woods (trainer).

As they went about destroying their opponents from the opening gun of the season, the Yankees also influenced the use of language. The press pronounced the Yankees as the team of "Five O'Clock Lightning," a reflection of the fact that games started at three in the afternoon, with late Yankee rallies usually getting under way after sundown. Out-of-town journalists, in awe of the Yankees all-around superiority, screamed "Break Up the Yankees!" But Ruppert loved every minute of the team's 110 victories (against only 44 losses); when the Yankees trounced the lowly St. Louis Browns in 21 out of 22 games, Ruppert was only sorry that his men didn't win all 22. In the end, the Yankees galloped off to a 19-game margin over the second-place Philadelphia Athletics, inspiring the *New York Times'* rhymester, John Kieran, to pen his tribute to Huggins's men:

There were mighty men in the good old days
When you and I were young
Yes, the Cubs were great in Chance's time
And the Pirates great in Wagner's prime
But I'll lay five bucks to one thin dime
There was never a team came crashing through
Like Ruth and the rest of the Yankee crew.

Woven into the months of that incomparable season were cultural and political spasms that created a melodramatic backdrop to the heroics of the Yankees ball club. Charles Lindbergh flew across the Atlantic to Paris in May, accompanied only by a couple of uneaten sandwiches (60 transatlantic flights had preceded him, by plane and dirigible, but Lucky Lindy, a nickname he despised, was the first to do it alone). The afternoon of Lindbergh's flight, Cleveland defeated the Yankees, one of their ten wins over the Yankees in 1927, the most of any team in the eight-team league.

When that other famous Ruth of 1927, the frosty blond, Ruth Snyder, was sentenced to die in New York on May 13 for the brutal dumbbell murder of her art editor husband, the Babe and Gehrig were in the second month of their home run derby. At the finish Lou was behind the Babe with "only" 47 round-trippers.

By the time that shoemaker Sacco and fish peddler Vanzetti went to their deaths in a Massachusetts electric chair in late August, the Yankees had piled up a 15-game lead over the Athletics. The next month, on the day that Gene Tunney won a decision over an aging Jack Dempsey in his storied Battle of the Long Count in Chicago, the Yankees licked Detroit, 8–7, on the Babe's two-run homer in the last of the ninth inning.

But the most exhilarating moment of the regular season was the Babe's sixtieth home run, hand delivered on September 30, one day before the end of the schedule. This Ruthian wallop, before only 10,000 at Yankee Stadium (the game was meaningless as far as the pennant race was concerned), went into the record books in the eighth inning of a tie game against the Senators. Southpaw Tom Zachary, who threw the pitch, swore until the day he died in 1969 that the ball, far up in the right-field bleachers and close to the foul line, was "foul by about four feet—but folks just won't let me forget it."

Why did Zachary want anyone to forget? After all, it's that pitch that people remember—and even

Earle Combs was an ideal leadoff man. He collected 231 hits and walked 63 times in 1927. Combs was responsible for the "Five O'Clock Lightning" rallying cry. Games began at 3:30 P.M. in those days, and late innings were played around 5 P.M. Whether the Yankees were ahead or behind, Combs would herald the home half of a late inning by shouting, "C'mon gang, five o'clock lightning, five o'clock lightning."

In 1925, playing for Salt Lake City in the Pacific Coast League, Tony Lazzeri hit 60 home runs and drove in 222 runs. Not surprisingly, the Yankees snapped him up, and for the next 12 seasons he was the team's regular second baseman. In six of his first eight seasons in New York he had more than 100 RBIs.

after Zachary came to the Yankees and had a fine 12–0 year in 1929, it's probably the only thing that his name is ever associated with.

Why did such magic attach to the Sacrosanct Sixty? After all, Ruth had banged 59 in 1921. So why the fuss about 60? Was it because the Babe had been the first to hit 30, then 40, then 50?

In the World Series of 1927 the Yankees lived up to their press notices. They faced the Pittsburgh Pirates, led by the Waner brothers, Paul and Lloyd, along with their Hall of Fame third baseman Pie Traynor. The Pirates had beaten out the Cardinals and the Giants in the last week of the season to win the National League race.

An everlasting myth about the Yankees' four-game sweep of the Pirates—in which Ruth and Gehrig knocked in 11 of the team's 19 runs, while the pitching staff limited Pittsburgh to a measly 10 runs—was that the New Yorkers had the Pirates beaten before a pitch was thrown. According to this pleasant fairy tale, prior to the start of the first game at Forbes Field in Pittsburgh, the Yankees' sluggers had put on such an eye-popping demonstration of power in batting practice that the Pirates almost conceded defeat on the spot. Huggins had supposedly ordered Waite Hoyt to throw softballs across the plate, so that the Yankee hitters could pump each pitch into the stratosphere. This makes an intriguing yarn but the truth is that Hoyt didn't throw batting practice that afternoon because he was the scheduled starting pitcher. The Yankees may have looked omnipotent, but it wasn't by Huggins's design. Certainly, the Pirates must have been impressed with those long Yankee blows. But they weren't rendered catatonic.

The outstanding pitching job of the Series was thrown by Pennock in the third game, played at Yankee Stadium before more than 60,000 fans. The Pirates had the reputation of being murderous on left-handers. But Pennock mowed down the first 22 Pirates before Traynor singled in the eighth inning to break up the no-hitter. This marked the finesse pitcher's fifth Series victory without a loss. "When I have control, I'm hard to beat," said the mild-mannered Pennock, who was addicted to understatement.

The next day the Yankees closed out the Series when Pittsburgh's pitcher, John Miljus, wild-pitched the winning run home. Ignominious for the Pirates, but in 1927, totally expected for the Yankees, who found it hard to lose.

Considering how high and mighty the Yankees were in the midst of the Jazz Age, it is astonishing to look at the salaries that Ruppert doled out at that time. The Babe, of course, was on another planet with his $70,000, the top figure in the game. The indomitable Gehrig, on the other hand, took home only

$8,000. The rifle-armed Meusel made $13,000, Combs earned $10,500, Poosh 'Em Up made $8,000, and his infield partner Koenig signed for $7,000. Pennock led the pitchers with $17,000, after having pitched in the majors for fifteen years. The 19-game winner Wilcy Moore made a grand total of $3,000. The batboy, Eddie Bennett, a little hunchback from Brooklyn, mostly depended on tips from the players. The Babe was generous with Eddie, who constantly provided him with hot dogs and a daily ration of bicarbonate of soda. Gehrig was parsimonious, because most of his salary went home to his parents.

In the flag marathon of 1928 the Yankees repeated. But all was not entirely well on the club. For one thing, Urban Shocker, their veteran spitball pitcher who had contributed handsomely in 1927 with 18 victories, was bothered by a serious heart ailment most of the year. Shocker had suffered for some time from the malady, and Huggins knew about it. In 1927 he had managed to work through 200 innings, despite pain and occasional fainting spells. But in 1928 he pitched in only two innings the entire season. His weight was down alarmingly and he had to retire early in the year. By the season's end, he was dead at thirty-eight. His passing was a shock to most of his teammates, many of whom were not aware of how desperately ill he was.

Meanwhile, Pennock, still a winning pitcher, had a chronic arm injury,

causing him to miss several games. In the World Series, Huggins was not able to call on Pennock for a single start. Joe Dugan, so dependable at third base for so long, had slowed up with a bad knee. He was a fine fellow to have around the clubhouse, for he was a convivial storyteller. But baseball, even on a winning team, can be a harsh business. Dugan was waived to the Braves after the season was over. Combs, bothered by a broken finger, also had limited playing time.

With 54 home runs, the Babe was again the chief igniter of five o'clock lightning, and Gehrig, with a .374 batting average, was almost as dynamic. How-

Tiny Miller Huggins managed the Yankees from 1918 through 1929, winning six pennants and three World Series. Infielder Joe Dugan said, "It wasn't an easy task to handle such monkeys as we had on the Yankees." Huggins handled them as best he could, even standing up to the Babe on a few occasions. He is seen here in 1928 with Athletics manager and owner Connie Mack, who was born three years before the end of the Civil War, and who would continue as manager of the Athletics for another 22 years.

ever, Lou's homer production fell from 47 to 27. At one stage of the race the Yankees were ahead by 13½ games. But the long season had tightened up by September, thanks to the crisp challenge made by Connie Mack's Philadelphia Athletics. Mack had assembled the last of his dynasties; his roster was packed with superb players, including Lefty Grove, perhaps the best southpaw of his time, Jimmie Foxx, Al Simmons, George Earnshaw, and Mickey Cochrane. In another year, the Athletics would dominate the American League the way the Murderers' Row club had in the twenties.

On September 9, the Yankees found themselves in a virtual tie for first place with the Athletics. The two teams then played a key doubleheader at Yankee Stadium before an overflow crowd of 80,000, which was the largest assemblage in the five years the structure had been open. The Yankees rose to the occasion, sweeping both games, with the help of Pipgras's shutout in the first contest and Meusel's grand slam in the second game. After that the Yankees were never headed; at the end they led the Athletics by 2½ games, a far cry from their margin in 1927.

The Yankees now had a chance at retribution against the Cardinals for their 1926 setback. The Cards had just been through a grueling race against the second-place Giants. But as the Series got under way the Babe was limping around with a charley horse and a sprained ankle, Lazzeri was nursing a sore throwing arm, Combs was ailing, and Pennock and Dugan were subpar. It didn't bode well for the New Yorkers.

But within less than a week the Yankees had literally blown open the St. Louis franchise, thanks to a devastating two-man show engineered by Ruth and Gehrig. Never before had a Series been so dominated by two men hitting back to back in the lineup. In the process, the Yankees overwhelmed Manager Bill McKechnie's team in four straight games, giving them eight consecutive victories in World Series play.

Always in the Babe's shadow, Gehrig may even have surpassed him in this Series. Lou hit .545, less than the Babe's .625 on 10 for 16, the highest batting average in Series history, but he hit four home runs and a double, while knocking in nine runs. Ruth didn't wait around for walks in this Series, as he'd done in 1926. But he did wait until the fourth and last game to unload three home runs at St. Louis's Sportsman's Park, the same venue where he'd hit three in 1926.

When Wee Willie Sherdel of the Cardinals tried to "quick-pitch" the Babe in that last game as Ruth turned around to swap a joke with catcher Earl Smith, umpire Cy Pfirman ruled that the Babe was right to protest. A strikeout against the Babe was reversed after a heated ten-minute squabble. Ruth then creamed Sherdel's next pitch out of the ballpark to settle the argument convincingly.

As the Yankees went about pounding the Cardinals, they also evened the score with their old nemesis Alexander. Now forty-one years old, Alex was no longer the pitcher he'd been two years before. He appeared twice in the 1928 Series and was touched up for 11 runs and 10 hits in only five innings.

The Series came to a fitting conclusion when Ruth made a one-handed circus catch of a foul ball in left field, where Huggins had placed him for each game in St. Louis.

As the 1929 season began the country was still riding along on its frenetic high. "The restlessness of New York approached hysteria," wrote F. Scott Fitzgerald, the laureate of the Jazz Age. The speakeasy

My All-Time Yankee Team

Selected by Donald Honig, baseball historian

1B	Gehrig
2B	Lazzeri
SS	Jeter
3B	Nettles
RF	Ruth
CF	DiMaggio
LF	Mantle
C	Dickey
P (Lefty)	Ford
P (Righty)	Ruffing
Mgr	McCarthy

LEFT: The Babe is moving forward in the batter's box as he watches his 60th home run of the 1927 season soar into Yankee Stadium's right-field grandstand. He hit it off the Senators' Tom Zachary, who threw, Ruth said, ". . . a slow screwball." In the locker room after the game he shouted, "Sixty, count 'em, sixty! Let's see some other son-of-a-bitch match that!"

Lefty Gomez is better remembered now for his bon mots than for his Hall of Fame pitching accomplishments. In 1934 he won 26 games, led the league in ERA, strikeouts, and shutouts. In five World Series he won six games and lost none. When he was told that he'd been elected to the Hall of Fame he shrugged and said, "It's only fair. After all, I helped a lot of hitters to get in."

The Great Engineer, Herbert Hoover, had succeeded Silent Cal Coolidge in the presidency. He agreed with his predecessor that "the business of America is business." His wife, Lou Henry Hoover, sent shock waves through the South when she invited a "colored lady" to the White House.

But the biggest shock was to come that fall when the cataclysmic stock market crash took place at a moment when few suspected that all hell would break loose in America. Millions soon lost their jobs, banks failed, and unbathed men sold apples on the street corners of New York City. The Yankees echoed the economic climate, too, as they succumbed to the pressure of the Athletics, a team that didn't have Babe or Lou—but seemed to have everything else. The signs were there—Gehrig had an off year at .300, the Babe hit only 46 home runs, Koenig wasn't making the plays at short any more, and Meusel was winding down his career in a Yankee uniform. On the pitching side, Pennock and Hoyt had become .500 hurlers. An added nuisance in the scheme of things was the incessant banter of a former pool hall hustler from West Springfield, Massachusetts, named Lou Durocher. A fancy-fielding shortstop, Durocher had come on to replace Koenig, but had be-

queen of Gotham, Texas Guinan, was getting laughs for her wisecracks and for calling her patrons "suckers." Gossip columnists like the fast-talking Walter Winchell titillated millions with his terse announcements of "blessed events," while the seductress Mae West was still inviting lonely young men to "come up and see me some time." One of the most sadistic incidents in crime warfare took place on St. Valentine's Day in Chicago when seven members of the Moran gang were lined up against a wall in their beer depot and riddled with machine-gun bullets.

come a hair shirt to the Babe. A story got around that Durocher, who was always short of money in those days, had stolen Ruth's watch. Durocher heatedly denied any such thing. "If I was going to steal anything from that big bum," Durocher said angrily, "I would have stolen his god-damned Packard." Outside of his distaste for Ty Cobb, Ruth disliked Durocher more than any other player in the game. (The following season the Yankees relieved the Babe of Durocher, when they sold Lippy Leo to Cincinnati in the other league.)

The Yankees, with all these difficulties, weren't exactly a basket case. But the Athletics just proved to be much better. Curiously, at the start of the season rumors percolated that the Yankees might try to trade Gehrig, presumably in an effort to restore some balance to the American League. This nonsensical notion failed to address the fact that Ruppert derived pleasure out of winning *all* the time. Never in a million years would he have been a party to such an act of equity. Gehrig, of course, stayed in New York, with the best part of his career still ahead of him.

It turned out that there was no need for anyone to "break up the Yankees" after they had won six flags in eight years. The Athletics did the job quite handily, thank you. And they would do it again in 1930 and 1931, with one of the best teams ever assembled. Connie Mack had presided over previous cycles of glory—in 1902–1905 and in 1910–1914; this was his third cycle.

Another melancholy event occurred in 1929 near the end of the season, plunging the team into gloom. One day late in September, Huggins, who had brought the man-child Babe into line a few years before, said he felt totally worn out. Before a game at the Stadium he asked to be taken home. In a few days he was dead at fifty, of complications resulting from an infectious skin disease. Many of the rambunctious Yankees, those lovers of Broadway's night lights, were truly saddened by his death, even those who had had their run-ins with the manager. The Babe said he had "always liked the little guy," while Gehrig regarded him as a surrogate father.

"I guess I'll miss him more than anyone else," Lou said. "Next to my father and mother, he was the best friend a boy could have. There was never a more patient or pleasant man to work for. I can't believe he's gone."

The search began for a new Yankee pilot, just as the Athletics were trouncing the Chicago Cubs in the 1929 World Series. The Babe, who had a hard time managing himself, had no reservations about putting forth his own candidacy for the job. But Ruppert never seriously considered "Root," which was how he always pronounced his slugger's name. Art Fletcher,

who had served as the Yankees' top coach since 1927, seemed the logical choice to succeed Huggins. But the lantern-jawed Fletcher, who had been a fine shortstop for the Giants as well as the team's captain, mysteriously turned down the job. Barrow then appointed Bob Shawkey to the post, judging that Shawkey's equable temperament and long record of service as a pitcher deserved reward.

The country was in the beginning stages of the Great Depression when Shawkey took over the job. As people had a new national anthem in "Brother, Can You Spare a Dime?," the Yankees' fortunes also plummeted. It was hard to blame Shawkey, for his pitching staff, once so dependable, had become weary. Pennock's arm continued to bother him, Pipgras no longer was a dominant hurler, and Hoyt decided he didn't like to listen to his manager's pitching hints. The result was that Hoyt was traded off to Detroit, along with Koenig. Meusel also was gone, traded to Cincinnati. It was once said of the reticent Meusel that he "had learned to say hello when it was time to say goodbye." Now he had said goodbye.

However, Shawkey did make one invaluable contribution to the Yankees' future. He encouraged Barrow to deal for Charlie "Red" Ruffing, a right-hander with four toes missing from his left foot as a result of a mining accident. Pitching for the hapless Red Sox, Ruffing had lost 47 games in 1928 and 1929. But Shawkey was convinced he could become a winner in New York. He turned out to be correct. Outfielder Cedric Durst was shunted off to Boston for Ruffing in another of those transfers that caused mass shudders in Beantown. Durst never played another game after the 1930 season.

After his blessed transition into a Yankee uniform, Ruffing won 15 and lost 5 in 1930, the start of a 16-year career in New York that eventually won him a niche in the Hall of Fame. However, the addition of Ruffing couldn't help the Yankees, or Shawkey, from finishing third, country miles away from Philadelphia's repeat champions.

At the season's end, when Shawkey entered Barrow's office to discuss a new contract for the 1931 campaign, he bumped into Joseph Vincent McCarthy, just as Joe was leaving the GM's lair. "I took one look and knew that was the end of my job in New York," said Shawkey, with some bitterness. His intuition was right on target, for McCarthy had just been hired to manage the Yankees in 1931. Barrow's net had spread to the National League, where McCarthy had managed the Cubs into the World Series in 1929. When his team ended up in second place in 1930, McCarthy was dumped.

McCarthy had a peculiar curriculum vitae for one so eagerly sought by Barrow. He had never played a second in the major leagues. But Barrow had long admired the Philadelphia Irishman's dedication, intelligence, and encyclopedic knowledge of the game. That had to be weighed against McCarthy's known proclivity for prohibition booze. In Barrow's mind, McCarthy's efficiency, which some later disparaged as nothing but "push-button managing," won out over any perceptible flaws.

The first thing that Barrow warned McCarthy about was his relationship with Ruth. This was going to be difficult, suggested Barrow, because the Babe, now thirty-five and bursting with desire to manage the Yankees, was not about to regard McCarthy as much more than a pretender. As baseball's biggest wage earner ($75,000 at this date), the Babe was the subject of a story, probably apocryphal, that was making the rounds. When asked why he should be making more than the president of the United States, Ruth supposedly answered that "I had a better year than he did." If Ruth could put Mr. Hoover down in such a dismissive manner, how would he deal with Joe McCarthy!

McCarthy's strategy was to let the Babe stew in his own juices. He didn't go out of his way to antagonize him. Neither did he try to ingratiate himself. There would be no public shouting matches with the Babe, no food fights in the kitchen. Instead, McCarthy worked at developing amicable relationships with Gehrig, Bill Dickey (the catcher who was also Gehrig's roommate), Pennock, Lazzeri, Ruffing, and Combs. These players appreciated McCarthy's attention to detail, including rigid dress codes—jackets and ties in the dining room, for example—and his de-

sire to instill the idea that there was something truly special about wearing the uniform of the Yankees.

McCarthy's mode caused his critics to sneer that rooting for the Yankees was like rooting for U.S. Steel. But McCarthy usually managed to have the last laugh. However, in the first season under his guidance, the Yankees didn't have enough to topple the Athletics. McCarthy ruled against any card playing in the clubhouse and insisted that all players keep themselves in prime shape. Such decrees couldn't prevent the Athletics from winning their third straight American League title. They beat the Yankees, ensconced in second place, by 13½ games, with help from Lefty Grove's 31 victories.

Both Ruth and Gehrig had splendid seasons in 1931, with the Iron Horse bursting out with a record 184 runs batted in. He tied the Babe at 46 home runs. Appearing in better shape than usual, Ruth put on quite a show with a .373 batting average and 163 runs batted in. In his second year with New York, Vernon "Lefty" Gomez became the southpaw successor to Pennock. Of Irish-Spanish extraction, Gomez quickly developed into one of the league's foremost hurlers, even as he won a reputation as one of the game's most engaging wits. Gomez, nicknamed "Goofy," was hardly that. He liked to attribute his success to "living clean and having a fast outfield." He also admitted that he often didn't know the score of a game in which he was pitching. "But I just knew how many runs I was ahead," he quipped. For the first time in years the Yankees also had a prolific base stealer in Ben Chapman, who led his league in 1931 with 61 thefts. Unfortunately, Chapman, who could play both outfield and infield, was a temperamental Southerner overtly hostile to a loyal segment of Yankee fandom—Jewish supporters. In a few years, Chapman was traded away, in part because of his foul mouth. (When black pio-

RIGHT: On June 3, 1932, in a game between the Yankees and the Athletics at Shibe Park, Babe Ruth had just clouted a home run in the top of the fifth inning. Lou Gehrig, offering congratulations, followed with a homer, his third of the afternoon. Two innings later Lou hit another ball out of the park, and in the ninth he barely missed hitting his fifth home run. The Yankees won the game 20–13. Mickey Cochrane is the Philadelphia catcher.

Pennants & Pinstripes *The New York Yankees 1903–2002*

neer Jackie Robinson arrived in the National League in the late forties, Chapman, then manager of the Phillies, was his chief tormentor, causing some fans to recall his behavior with the Yankees.)

The year of 1932 may well have been the worst phase of the Great Depression. Over 16 million were unemployed, 6 million banks had closed their doors, Hoovervilles had sprung up everywhere, one quarter of the population had no regular income, and street corner peddlers spit on five-cent apples to give them a shiny gloss. But under McCarthy's tutelage some of the gloom was lifted at Yankee Stadium as the club returned to the winner's circle. With a beleaguered country rallying to the urgings of the newly elected president, Franklin D. Roosevelt, the Yankees also responded with 107 victories.

In many respects 1932 added more to the legend of the Babe and Lou than any previous season. But as the Yankees finally caught up with Philadelphia, topping them by 13 games, two new men in the infield also contributed handsomely. Frank Crosetti was purchased from the San Francisco Seals in the Pacific Coast League to play shortstop, and he stayed around both as shortstop and coach for what seems an eternity. As an Italian American, the Crow was much in the tradition of Lazzeri, although he was never half the hitter Tony was. But he helped to stabilize the inner defense, along with diminutive Joey Sewell, who came over from Cleveland to play third base. Sewell may have possessed the darnedest batting eye this side of Ted Williams. In 1932 he struck out three times in 503 at bats. The next year he struck out four times in 524 appearances, which must have devastated the 5'7" Alabaman. Lefty Grove claimed he never feared Ruth or Gehrig, but it was Sewell who bugged him more than any other. "He'd just reach out with his bat—and ping!—there went a single over the shortstop's head." The pitching, coming from Gomez at 24–7, Ruffing at 18–7, and Pipgras at 16–9, was overpowering. A serendipitous plus came from the performance of Johnny Allen, at 17–4. Allen had previously been known for tearing up a hotel room or two after a difficult loss. His curbed temper helped the Yankees overcome the Athletics, who still had their sterling starting rotation of Grove, George Ernshaw, and Rube Walberg.

An unexpectedly low moment of the 1932 campaign took place in July. It involved catcher Bill Dickey, who, as Gehrig's primary pal, seemed to have inherited much of Lou's dignity and composure. However, Dickey suddenly lost his temper when Washington's Carl Reynolds crashed into him at home plate, spikes high, on a crucial squeeze play. Despite Dickey's staunch defense, Reynolds was pronounced safe. Knocked off his feet, Dickey sprang up and delivered a blindside blow to Reynolds's jaw. The jaw was broken and so was Dickey's reputation for being phlegmatic. Dickey was fined $1,000 (out of his $14,000 salary) and was suspended for thirty days. Later Dickey was repentant. "I thought he was going to hit me, so I defended myself," he said. "I'd have paid $1,000 more if I could have pulled back that punch."

But that year it was the inevitable tandem of the Babe and Lou that provided two of the most unforgettable days in Yankees history. On a blue sky June 3 afternoon at Philadelphia's Shibe Park, home of the A's since 1909, Gehrig reached his peak as one of the game's most fearsome sluggers. Until that day nobody in the twentieth century had crashed four home runs in a single game. Ed Delahanty of the Phillies had hit a quartet in 1896. Then came the drought.

Gehrig didn't pick on any slouches, either, for the starting pitcher that day was Earnshaw, who had captured 68 games in the three preceding years to go along with four World Series victories. In the first inning, Lou connected for a homer to right field, where the fence was some 331 feet away. In the fourth inning, he delivered again, also to right field. In the fifth inning, Lou smashed his third home run of the day to right field. Although he did not know it at the time, those three homers gave him a record—three home runs in one game four times.

Earnshaw was the victim of all three blows. After the third sock, Connie Mack had seen enough, so he removed Earnshaw to prevent further humiliation. In came another right-hander, Leroy Mahaffey. As Earnshaw settled uneasily alongside his manager in the dugout, Mack tried to soothe him. "Sit here for a few minutes, son," said Mack, at his avuncular best. "I want you to see how Mahaffey does it. You've been pitching entirely wrong to Gehrig."

In the seventh inning, Mahaffey, "demonstrating" for Earnshaw, threw a fast ball that Lou turned on and hit for his fourth straight home run. However, this one flew over the left-field wall. "I understand now, Mr. Mack," said Earnshaw. "Mahaffey made Gehrig change his direction."

Gehrig had chances in the last two innings to add to his collection. (No one in the game's history had ever hit five homers in a game.) In the eighth inning Lou grounded out. But as the Yankees kept hitting (they scored 20 runs that afternoon), Lou had a final opportunity in the ninth inning to hit a fifth homer. With the crafty Ed Rommel on the mound now for the A's, Gehrig blasted a tremendous drive to the most distant point of center field. Al Simmons, ordinarily not the most accomplished defensive man, made a desperate dash, followed by a last-second lunge, to capture the ball just before it was about to sail over the barrier. Years later, musing over his failure to hit that fifth home run, Lou said, "The last ball I hit was the hardest of all that day. But Simmons caught up with it. How do you figure it?"

But on Gehrig's most spectacular day, an event 125 miles away in New York City again pushed him

On the last day of the 1933 season, Babe Ruth pitched a 6–5 victory over the Red Sox. It wasn't an exemplary performance; he gave up 12 hits, but he also homered and managed to stem a Boston rally late in the game. His arm was so sore from the effort that he couldn't lift it after the victory.

into the shadows. The Giants were set to meet the Phillies that day, but it rained. So the angry, dyspeptic John McGraw stayed home, mulling over his managerial future. Embittered and ailing, at fifty-nine he had decided to quit, turning over the reins of the club to Bill Terry, the thirty-three-year-old first baseman of the Giants. Terry had long been Gehrig's rival as the most preeminent first sacker in the New York area. After 30 years and 10 pennants, McGraw's fierce competitiveness had at last burned out, causing him to distribute his valedictory announcement to the press. For one more day, John McGraw was the biggest news all over America. The *New York Times* splashed his resignation on its front page while radio commentators chatted about it all day. To learn that the diffident Lou had hit four home runs the day before, a *Times* reader had to turn to page 10 in the sports section. Once again, Lou had been upstaged. Usually it was the Babe who did the job. Now it was the old lion McGraw who had stolen the headlines from him.

In the bitter World Series that fall against the Chicago Cubs in which Gehrig whaled the hide off the ball (he accounted for eight runs batted in and scored nine times), it was Ruth again who seized the spotlight with one unforgettable bat.

For several days the Cub players had been riding the Babe unmercifully, picking on his bulging silhouette and questioning his ancestry. The Yankees, and the Babe, gave it back to the Cubs. They had learned that their former shortstop, Mark Koenig, who had joined the Cubs for the last month of a tight pennant race, had been voted only a measly half-share of Series money. This energized their bench to counter the Cub invective with their own gutter talk and barbs. (The rancorous atmosphere was hardly better outside of Wrigley Field; the Babe had been spat upon by Yankees haters.)

The Cubs' distemper was not improved by the loss of the first two games at Yankee Stadium. When the two teams moved to Wrigley Field for the third game, manager Charlie Grimm of the Cubs reacted just like his own name. Going into the fifth inning, the clubs were tied at 4–4, with the Babe stepping to the plate. Again he was greeted by Cub mouths in the dugout that pronounced him the most infamous bastard since Alexander Hamilton. Some of the Cubs, led by pitcher Guy Bush, who had been pummeled in the first game, ran out of their dugout to revile the Babe. Trying to stick to business, right-hander Charlie Root got two strikes and two balls on the Babe amid the cacophony. Then—and this is the moment that has since been the crux of controversy and endless argument—the Babe pointed somewhere in the distance. Following this gesture, or pantomime, he hit a tremendous shot off Root's next pitch that landed deep in the center-field bleachers. At the time it was estimated to be the longest home run ever hit in Wrigley Field.

Ruth, the ultimate vaudevillian, had played to the audience, even as they screeched their lungs out in disrespect. And, of course, he had delivered. "It was the Rashomon of all home runs," wrote Leo Trachtenberg. Over the years there have been varied interpretations of Ruth's supposed "called shot." Was he really informing Root and the crowd that he was about to hit one over the wall in center? Was he simply needling Root and the Cubs? Was he signaling to the world that it only takes one to hit it?

In Robert Creamer's biography of Ruth he reports that only one press witness concluded that the Babe pointed toward the outfield barrier. In the tempest of postmortems, many of the Babe's teammates insisted he pointed and hit it where he pointed. The loyal Gehrig, who followed the Babe to the plate, stoutly agreed that the Babe had pointed. Root, on the other hand, was angered that anyone would think he would have let Ruth get away with such insolence. McCarthy, never the most avid admirer of Ruth, wasn't willing to add to the folklore. "I didn't see him point anywhere," he said, a dissident voice ultimately drowned out by the believers.

As the Yankees now approached the 1933 season, they had stretched their consecutive World Series games victories to 12—four in 1927, four in 1928, and four more in the sweep against the Cubs in 1932.

In almost every respect—character, habits, temperament—Henry Louis Gehrig represented a dramatic counterpoint to his partner in mayhem, the Babe. A basically shy person, not particularly voluble—although he was fairly well read and a writer of nicely phrased letters—Lou suffered from a puzzling insecurity. Once he confided to a New York writer that he was concerned every day when he arrived at the ballpark that he'd never produce another base hit.

Ruth was Rabelaisian, a voluptuary. It would have been hard to invent such a figure. He did everything in excess. He drank, ate like a dinosaur, kept late hours, belched, cursed, roared with laughter, and generously tipped everybody in sight. The Babe smoked cigars, Lou sucked on his pipe. Gehrig was essentially an abstemious man who withdrew from outward displays of emotion. He projected a surface calm (which hid his anxieties) and, unlike the Babe, had difficulty ever asking the Yankee management for more money. Ruth, after all, was the Sultan of Swat, Gehrig was only the Crown Prince, the dimpled Boy Scout to the Babe's winking Falstaff. Historian Bruce Catton wrote that, "Ruth always took a host of Walter Mittys with him as he rounded the bases." But Lou rarely aroused such fantasies in his admirers.

Indomitable in his day-to-day pursuit of victory, Lou played every day through fifteen years. Until Cal Ripken, Jr., came along years later, Gehrig's consecutive game record was thought to be impregnable. He ignored the kinds of injuries that would have sidelined less committed men. He played with headaches, stomachaches, charley horses, broken fingers, chipped bones, torn muscles, severe lumbago attacks and returned to the lineup the day after a minor league pitcher beaned him. (Playing with a concussion, he hit three straight triples but the game and the triples were washed out.)

Strangely, this man who came to be known as the "Iron Horse" was raised on the grassless sidewalks of New York. Born in 1903 in the lower-middle-class section of Manhattan's Yorkville district, Lou was only one of four children who survived infancy. His parents were natives of Germany. His father, an art-metal mechanic, roamed the bars and turnvereins of Yorkville and Washington Heights, where the Gehrigs moved. But it was his mother, Christina, who became the dominating person in his life. Christina, an archetypical Brunhilde, worked as a cook, took in laundry, and washed dishes, making her the true breadwinner in the family. Although Lou's youth was not exactly Dickensian, the press later described him as a "product of the slums," a designation that infuriated Christina.

Lou often wore cast-off clothes, even in his first days as a professional ballplayer. Many of his teammates, even those who were fond of him, did not hesitate to say that he "had the first nickel he ever earned." But there was good reason for his behavior, for he had performed odd jobs to help out his mother before he had reached his teens.

Gehrig learned to play baseball and other sports within shouting distance of Hilltop Park, where the Highlanders-Yankees had played their first games. When he began to attend classes at the High School of Commerce in midtown Manhattan, Christina got a job as the cook in the Sigma Nu fraternity house at Columbia University.

In June 1920, when Lou was just seventeen years old, he traveled to Chicago with Commerce's baseball team to play Lane Tech High for the intercity championship. Already built like a Percheron, the piano-legged Lou emerged as the star of the game, which was won by Commerce. In the ninth inning, with Commerce ahead, 8–6, Lou crushed a long home run over Wrigley Field's right-field wall with the bases loaded. The New York papers immediately anointed him a "schoolboy Babe Ruth," which, in one way, was absolutely prophetic. It was also a foretaste of the fact that in the future he would always play second fiddle to his celebrated teammate.

Even as her son was being hailed, Momma Gehrig would have preferred that Lou study to become an engineer or an architect. She had little understanding of people who played baseball for a living and perceived

them as "bummers." But it wasn't long before the athletic authorities at Columbia encouraged Lou to come to Columbia. Oddly, it was as a football player that he was cherished.

After being admitted to Columbia, Lou was approached by John McGraw. He was invited to display his talents at the Polo Grounds while McGraw looked on. But McGraw, in one of his sullen moods, paid little attention to Gehrig and his beat-up first baseman's glove. What Lou had to settle for was an invitation to play with Hartford, in the Class A Eastern League, a team that had a working arrangement with the Giants. When Lou asked if playing for Hartford would prevent him from playing for Columbia, he was assured by the Giants' scout that it wouldn't make any difference. This happened to be poor advice and for the rest of his life Lou nursed a grievance against McGraw. At the time, Lou went ahead and played for Hartford under the assumed nom de first baseman of "Lou Lewis." The adoption of this poorly camouflaged name should have convinced Gehrig that he was engaged in some trickery. But badly in need of the few extra dollars he was making, he didn't think more of it. He played in a dozen games for Hartford that summer of 1921 without connecting for a single home run.

However, Andy Coakley, Columbia's baseball coach, who had been a pitcher for the Athletics, got wind of the fact that "Lou Lewis" was really Lou Gehrig. He made a trip to Hartford and persuaded Lou to quit. Coakley wanted to make certain that his talented prospect would get to play under him.

It became necessary for Gehrig to win back his good standing with Columbia and other rival schools if he hoped to play baseball and football with the Lions. Bobby Watt, Columbia's athletic director, was certain that Lou's mistake was an innocent one. He believed that Lou was deserving of more understanding from those colleges that booked Columbia on the athletic field. When asked by Watt if they would temper their collective judgment with mercy, Cornell, Dartmouth, Amherst, Williams, and other potential Columbia foes informed Watt that they would have no objection to Lou's resuming competition in both football and baseball in 1922.

Gehrig played in the backfield and on the line for a lackluster Lions 11 in 1922. The team lost more games than it won but Lou, called "the beef expert" by Paul Gallico, was a battler. When he played baseball in the spring of 1923, Lou hit some monstrous drives that convinced most witnesses that he was destined for stardom. One such witness was Yankees scout Paul Krichell. It didn't take long for Krichell to encourage Lou to sign a Yankee contract. Within months, Lou had started on his road to fame, baseball folklore, and ultimate tragedy. The "bummer" that his momma never wanted had become one of the game's heroes.

LEFT: Lou Gehrig's powerful physique is evident in this picture, taken in the early thirties. "Lou was the perfect team man," Tommy Henrich said. "He did what he was told, and in so doing set the example for the rest of us." Historian Bill James, who usually tends toward iconoclasm, wrote, ". . . not only did he reach a peak of performance that is as impressive as that of any first baseman in this century, but he sustained that peak for a decade of astonishingly consistent greatness."

1933–1942

I N 1933, NEW YORK WAS A CITY NUMBED BY THE GREAT DEPRESSION. IT WAS A PLACE WHERE SCHOOLCHILDREN OFTEN WENT WITHOUT MILK, WHERE UNLUCKY PEOPLE FORAGED FOR FOOD, WHERE SOUP KITCHENS DOTTED TIMES SQUARE, WHERE SKYSCRAPERS WENT UNFINISHED FOR LACK OF FUNDS, AND WHERE SUBWAYS WERE CROWDED WITH RED-EYED HOMELESS SLEEPING THROUGH THE NIGHT. ■ ELSEWHERE, TRAVELERS CROSSING AMERICA VIEWED A LAND OF STRIKING CONTRASTS: FOOD WAS PILED HIGH IN GRAIN

elevators while hungry people broke into grocery stores to steal an apple or a loaf of bread.

There were contrasts, too, in the men who had just come into power in the United States and Germany. The polio victim, Franklin D. Roosevelt, became a living inspiration to millions as he gallantly assumed the American presidency. He faced a country consumed with anxiety about its future, and boldly confronted the task by asserting that "the only thing to fear is fear itself."

In Germany, a mustached World War I corporal, Adolf Hitler, became chancellor in January. By the end of the summer, democracy was dead in that country after an orgy of paranoia, military rearmament, government-sanctioned anti-Semitism, and book burning. The jackboots of Hitler's storm troopers echoed ominously on the streets of the Third Reich.

Baseball, that nonideological institution, suffered, too, from the dismal economic conditions. In the early 1930s, ballparks were, for the most part, empty, dreary places, even if they represented a means of escape for fans. Many couldn't afford to buy tickets to games and clubs like the St. Louis Browns, Boston Braves, and Philadelphia Phillies often played to sullen crowds that numbered in the hundreds. Conditions became so bad that consideration was given to the notion that fans should return balls that were hit into the stands.

In the Southeast, where spring training took place,

OVERLEAF: One of the most potent Yankee lineups in the team's history. LEFT TO RIGHT: Frank Crosetti (shortstop), Red Rolfe (third base), Tommy Henrich (right field), Joe DiMaggio (center field), Lou Gehrig (first base), Bill Dickey (catcher), George Selkirk (left field), Myril Hoag (reserve outfielder), and Joe Gordon (second base). The picture was taken in 1938, Gehrig's last full season.

the sun still shone on baseball, but hearts were heavy. "Everywhere these cities seemed to be ravaged by an invisible enemy," wrote Rud Rennie of the New York Herald Tribune. "People seemed to be hiding. They wouldn't even come out to see the Babe and Lou when the Yankees were in town." At Yankee Stadium, attendance was down dramatically, sinking to under 750,000. That was still enough to lead all clubs at the gate.

In an effort to rescue baseball from the doldrums, the first All-Star Game between the two leagues was scheduled after a Chicago writer, Arch Ward, came up with the idea. The contest was staged on July 6, 1933, at Chicago's vast Comiskey Park. Befitting such a historic moment, the Babe, fading away in everything but poundage, hit the first All-Star home run off southpaw Wild Bill Hallahan of the St. Louis Cardinals. The blow turned out to be the margin of victory for the American League.

Over the course of the 1933 season the Babe's home run production dropped to 34, which put him second in the league to Philadelphia's big-muscled Jimmie Foxx, who had 48.

The Yankees finished seven games back of the pennant-winning Washington Senators in 1933, despite the fact that they fielded almost the same team that had won it all the preceding year. An indication of how much the Yankees had slipped was that they dropped 14 out of 22 games to the Senators, who ended up losing the World Series to the Giants.

The thirty-nine-year-old Babe was completing his twentieth big league season. So he arranged a celebration of sorts for himself and the club. He agreed to pitch the final game of the year against the Red Sox. After an explosion of advance publicity, 25,000 fans

In the early thirties a hardcover publication ran studio photos of all the major league players posing decorously in jackets and ties. In many ways the effect was reminiscent of a college yearbook. Even Leo Durocher, who got into squabbles with Ruth, looks like a studious undergraduate. Not all of the men in this grouping were playing for the Yankees in 1932, but all of them had at one time or another been standout performers for the New Yorkers. LEFT TO RIGHT, FROM THE TOP: Ben Chapman, Earle Combs, Frank Crosetti, Bill Dickey, Leo Durocher. SECOND ROW: Lou Gehrig, Lefty Gomez, Waite Hoyt, Mark Koenig, Tony Lazzeri. THIRD ROW: Joe McCarthy, Joe Sewell, Herb Pennock, George Pipgras, Red Ruffing. BOTTOM ROW: Babe Ruth, and Yankees' officials Colonel Jacob Ruppert, president; Ed. G. Barrow, business manager; Mark Roth, traveling secretary.

Yankees owner Jacob Ruppert, on the right, sharing a box seat with Giants owner Horace Stoneham for the opening game of the 1936 World Series. Two years earlier, in response to Ruth's request that he become the Yankees' manager, Ruppert told him, "How can you manage the team when you can't even manage yourself?" Ruppert's reign, from 1915 through 1938, encompassed eight pennants and seven world championships.

showed up at Yankee Stadium to witness a game that had no import outside of the Babe's mound appearance. But Ruth gave the fans their money's worth as he went all nine innings to win, 6–5. Naturally, he helped his own cause with a home run. He yielded 12 hits, 11 of them singles, but was able to reach back for a little extra every time the Red Sox threatened. Between innings, the Yankees' trainer ministered to the Babe's weary left arm and body. An hour after the game, when the Babe left the ballpark, his left arm was so sore that he couldn't wave to the fans. Instead, he tipped his cap with his right hand. There was no denying the fact that Ruth was very pleased with his tenacious performance. This farewell pitching triumph gave him a 94–46 career record. It also meant that he'd never experienced a losing season as a pitcher.

It also may have given him the impetus to return for still another season, after he had been dropping hints that he was going to retire. Of course, what the Babe really wanted was to get a phone call from Barrow making him the next Yankees' manager. But Barrow was not about to anoint the Babe. McCarthy was already working under a three-year contract, which would terminate in 1935, and Barrow was his strong advocate. Barrow kept hoping that either the Red Sox or the Tigers would sign Ruth as manager. But the Babe, his own worst adviser, kept yearning for the Yankees' job, even after Barrow offered him a spot as manager of the Newark Bears, the Yankees' talented farm club. But Ruth stubbornly resisted that idea. Here he was, baseball's savior, being shunted to the minor leagues. Hell, no!

So, despite all the ominous signs, Ruth returned to play for another year. It was a poor decision, turning out to be a painful finale for the Great Man.

In 1934 the Detroit Tigers suddenly emerged as the dynamic club in the American League, under the ignition switch of Gordon "Mickey" Cochrane, the former Philadelphia receiver who was now the playing manager of the Tigers. The Detroiters were loaded with G-Men that summer—first baseman Hank Greenberg, who might have signed with the Yankees if he hadn't suspected that Gehrig would last forever; silent second baseman Charlie Gehringer; and the veteran outfielder Goose Goslin. They had more than a little help from pitchers Tommy Bridges, Elden Auker, and Firpo Marberry, as well as Lynwood "Schoolboy" Rowe, who won 24 games, including a streak of 16 victories.

It was remarkable that the Yankees stayed as close to Detroit as they did. In the end, they finished in second place, seven games back.

In 1934 the Babe was a crumbling ghost of what he'd been. He hit only 22 homers and batted in 84, a pittance for him. Playing in only 125 games, he removed himself many times in the late innings to give his weary legs a rest. He ended up hitting .288, the only time that he failed to hit over .300, with the exception of his ruinous season of 1925.

Meanwhile, Gehrig was enjoying a marvelous season, with 49 homers (finally leading the Babe), 165 RBIs (runs batted in), and a .363 average. Under ordinary circumstances, Lou, with Triple Crown figures, would have picked off the Most Valuable Player designation. But the summer of 1934 was Mickey Cochran's season, even though Mickey's Tigers lost a rousing seven-game World Series that fall, succumbing to the dual wizardry of Dizzy and Daffy Dean of St. Louis.

As the Yankees made their last tour of the American League circuit in 1934, modest crowds came out to say farewell to the Babe. Many felt that they were getting a last chance to gaze at a living legend—although no one, at this stage, could be quite certain what road Ruth would take.

In the winter of 1935, the Babe publicly expressed his disaffection toward the Yankees, who now had a sticky public relations problem. If the club turned him loose without a concrete plan for his future, they would be regarded as being as heartless as many people suspected they were. In this instance, Barrow quietly contacted Emil Fuchs, the owner of the Boston Braves, in the other league.

"When in doubt, always throw a curve,"
Johnny Murphy replied when queried as to
the secret of his success. The Bronx-born
right-hander was a sterling relief pitcher and
spot starter for the Yankees for 12 seasons.
He won 12 games in relief in 1937, and in
1941 led the league in saves and recorded an
ERA of 1.98.

Red Ruffing was the muscle in the Yankees' pitching staff through the championship years of 1936–1939, winning 82 games in regular season play, and four more in World Series matches. He was a wonderful hitter, too, recording a lifetime batting average of .269. Bill Dickey said, "If I were asked to choose the best pitcher I ever caught, I would have to say Ruffing."

Fuchs's club had been losing games and fans at a furious pace. In the early twenties, Fuchs had hired Christy Mathewson, the former Giants pitching ace, for a front office job, believing that this gentleman of heroic dimensions would be bound to lure fans into the ballpark. Fuchs regarded the Babe in much the same way while choosing to overlook the Babe's comportment. So a deal was arranged for Ruth to join the Braves in a somewhat inchoate role of player, vice president, and assistant manager to Bill McKechnie. It soon became clear that the scenario was doomed to failure; the Babe still thought he should be managing the Yankees. While he pined for that role, he belted down one too many with the Braves' Rabbit Maranville, who could keep pace with the Babe any day—or night.

On May 25, the Babe huffed and puffed to the plate in a rousing Last Hurrah. Facing two tough right-handed pitchers, Red Lucas and Guy Bush, at Pittsburgh's spacious Forbes Field, the Babe connected for three long home runs. First he hit one off Lucas, then he teed off on Bush twice. Only a few years before, Bush had been the villain who had directed indecorous remarks at the Babe preceding the "called shot" in the 1932 World Series. Now he was victimized by the Babe's final home run. "It was the longest damn ball I've ever seen," said Bush. "The longest hit off me, or anyone else. There was no wind to help, either . . . it didn't need no help, no way."

It was always said the Babe was larger than life. His last belt against Bush was proof of that, if there had to be any proof. A few more than 10,000 people were on hand to witness the last of Ruth's 714 home runs—and his final base hit. He played one more game on May 30 in Philadelphia, then hung it up, his average of .181 writing a sad coda to his career. In all, he hit 730 home runs including 15 in the World Series and one in the All-Star Game.

As Ruth bowed out, the Yankees continued to play second banana to Detroit. That year the Tigers took the World Series over the Cubs. It's only fair to suggest that the Yankees did better than expected in 1935, with the Babe gone, Combs finished, and Gehrig knocking in "only" 119 runs. (Greenberg led the league with 170 RBIs, a whopping difference from Lou's output, which surely suffered from the Babe's absence in front of him.)

The noise level at Yankee Stadium was down, too, for attendance was off by over 200,000. The whole of the American League was down. The fans just didn't come out. The sting of the Depression was one reason; the main cause was the disappearance of Ruth.

Faced with developing a successor to the Babe, or a reasonable facsimile, McCarthy nominated a Canadian, George "Twinkletoes" Selkirk, to take over in right field. Myril Hoag had "caddied" for Ruth in previous seasons, but his lack of power caused McCarthy to favor Selkirk. This was hardly an enviable role to assume, as Selkirk was also given the Babe's old number 3 to wear. (The Yankees didn't retire Ruth's number until a decade later.) In time, the fans would come to appreciate Selkirk, who was a good defensive outfielder with a fluid swing that made him a .300 hitter.

"For some fans nothing that George could do was right," said McCarthy. "They booed him for a while but he didn't let it get to him. They got to like him just fine in a couple years."

But it wasn't left to Selkirk or a new third baseman, Robert "Red" Rolfe, a Dartmouth College product, to begin to set things right again for the Yankees. It fell to Joseph Paul DiMaggio to become the catalyst for another dominant Yankee era. For two years the New York press had been marketing the exploits of

this minor league outfielder. Just out of his teens, DiMaggio had become a California legend in the making by hitting in 61 straight games and knocking out a preposterous 270 hits for the San Francisco Seals.

Before DiMaggio ever set his spikes on Yankee Stadium turf, the advance flummery about him was staggering. Most normal athletes would have been smothered under such pressure. But DiMaggio proved to be equal to the task. Already it was said that he had Gehrig's commitment to excellence and the discipline that Ruth never acquired.

When he finally arrived in New York, after the Yankees doled out $25,000 plus five players ("The best deal I ever made," said Barrow) to pry him loose from the Seals, there was still some suspicion he was too susceptible to injuries. What also caused additional speculation and comment was Joe's temperament. From the start he exhibited a shyness and an aloofness that puzzled many observers. There developed an inscrutable aura about him that made people wonder if he was an introvert, a snob, or a dullard. Was he, they wondered, a man who was smart enough to keep his mouth shut because, in fact, he didn't have much to say? Or was he just an instinctive public relations genius? Did his seeming distrust of people come from an innate desire to preserve his privacy? And why, if he

BATTING ORDER
AMERICAN LEAGUE
TEAMS 1 2 3 4 5 6 7 8 9 10 11 12 R. H. E.
NATIONAL LEAGUE
TEAMS 1 2 3 4 5 6 7 8 9 10 11 12 R. H. E.
AT BAT
BALLS
OUTS
UMPIRES - PLATE
407 FT.

was such a private person, did he choose to spend his late hours in the company of those writers, professional gossips, and celebrity hangers-on who could be depended on to boast about sharing a table and a drink or two with him?

In the early days of DiMaggio's reign in New York, Arthur Daley of the *New York Times* wrote that he found Joe "silent and uncomfortable." He was correct in both assessments but DiMaggio's demeanor, whether one liked it or not, did not detract from his performance.

In his freshman year of 1936, DiMaggio displayed such velvety-smooth movements in the field and on the bases that the recently departed Combs was hardly missed. If Ted Williams insisted that he could read the signature inscribed on a major league baseball when it was pitched to him, DiMaggio, without being boastful, said that at the instant a ball was hit toward his domain in center field, he knew exactly where it would come down. And come down it would, into his waiting glove. At bat, Joe also had an unerring eye for the strike zone. There would be years when his home runs would exceed his number of strikeouts, an extraordinary ratio for any slugger. Perhaps his eye was not as good as Williams's. But you could get disagreement on that, too.

With his range of skills, DiMaggio became the key to the Yankees' drive to reclaim supremacy. Gehrig, the captain and still "as unvarying as a railroad track," as Don Honig so fittingly described him, was still around. With Lazzeri, he remained one of the stalwart holdovers from the charismatic team of the twenties. But it was to DiMaggio that Yankee fans now looked. Joe seemed to have been born for a Yankee uniform. He certainly looked better in it than the Babe and Lou ever had. He also always made a point of giving his best on the field, even when he wasn't feeling well. "There may be someone in the ball-

The Clipper's Debut

After hitting .600 in seven 1936 spring training games, rookie Joe DiMaggio burned his foot in a diathermy machine and didn't appear in his first regular season game until May 3. Playing against the St. Louis Browns before a Yankee Stadium crowd of 25,000, DiMaggio reached first on a fielder's choice in the first inning. But in the second inning he singled, in the sixth he tripled, and in the eighth he singled again. He also scored three times and drove in a run.

Manager McCarthy placed Joe third in the line-up, right ahead of Lou Gehrig, ensuring some good pitches for him. Ben Chapman was the incumbent center-fielder, so DiMaggio played left field, where he handled one routine fly ball.

"The only time I felt anything like a flutter around the heart was when I stepped up to bat for the first time," he said. "Guess that was only natural." McCarthy added, "Yes, sir. He came through like a real money player. He lived up to my expectations."

park," he explained, "who has never seen me play before." The remark epitomized his attitude about playing professional baseball.

With DiMaggio leading the way, the Yankees embarked on another era of excellence, with the much-maligned McCarthy deftly maneuvering the chess pieces. Lazzeri was at second, Rolfe at third, and the Crow at shortstop, a cohesive infield that Dickey stared at every day from his perch behind the plate. The latter experienced a 1936 season that put other catchers to shame: he batted .362, an all-time high for the position.

The pitching was as strong as any other staff in baseball, even with the emergence of the Van Meter, Iowa, wunderkind, Bob Feller, in Cleveland. Ruffing was as durable as ever, with 20 victories, and Monte Pearson, obtained from Cleveland, won 19. Gomez was at 13–7 and Bump Hadley, acquired from Washington, was very effective, with a 14–4 mark. The

By 1938, his third season in a Yankee uniform, Joe DiMaggio was drawing praise from his teammates. Red Ruffing said, "You saw him standing there and you knew you had a damn good chance to win the baseball game." From the beginning the expectations he placed on himself were unrelenting. "A man is never satisfied," he said. "You go up there and get four hits and you want five so bad you can taste it."

Yalie, Johnny Broaca, and relief pitcher, Johnny Murphy, rounded out the corps.

There was no officially recognized Murderers Row on this Yankee team. But the hitting produced by this club—an average of seven runs a game—was good enough to bring the Yankees home 19½ games ahead of the Tigers. The Yankees were inadvertently helped by Hank Greenberg's broken wrist, which sidelined him for most of the season, and a mental breakdown suffered by manager Cochrane of Detroit. But with five players—Selkirk, Dickey, Lazzeri, DiMaggio, and Gehrig—all batting in over 100 runs, nothing short of

an earthquake in Yankee Stadium could have halted this club. With his 49 homers and 152 RBIs, Gehrig was awarded the Most Valuable Player honor. But true to Lou's tradition of constantly dwelling in some-body's else shadow, this time it was Lazzeri who played the trick on him. One afternoon in May, Tony hit two home runs with the bases loaded and drove in 11 runs as the Yankees butchered the Athletics, 25–2. Lazzeri came within one run of Sunny Jim Bottom-ley's National League record of 12 RBIs in a single game.

Returning to the World Series against the Giants, their ancient foes, the Yankees walked off with the postseason competition in six games. Seeking their thirteenth consecutive Series triumph, the Yankees came up short in the opening game at the Polo Grounds. They were defeated by southpaw Carl Hubbell, the screwball wizard who had come into the game with 16 straight victories, which established him as the dominant pitcher in the National League. However, when the Yankees faced Hubbell for a sec-ond time he was less of a mystery; they topped him, 5–2, with the help of a Gehrig home run.

The Yankees had considerably less trouble against the other members of the Giants' staff, winning two games by lopsided margins of 18–4 and 13–5. In the 18–4 rout it was Lazzeri, the blacksmith's son, who set the pace with a grand slam homer, the second in Series history. Seated in a flag-bedecked box seat at the Polo Grounds, President Roosevelt, about to rout the Re-publicans' Alf M. Landon in the fall election, looked on approvingly with 43,000 others. As usual, Gehrig was a prominent Series performer, with his two homers matching Selkirk's two. For the first time in Series play, however, Lou's batting average dipped below .300.

In his initial season, DiMaggio ended up with a .323 average and 206 hits. When 1937 came around, it was "déjà vu all over again." This time it was Joe's in-fected tonsil that kept him out of the lineup until May 1. When he did get back into the game, his bat ex-ploded. In his first game, he signaled he was prepared for another electrifying campaign by banging three hits off Boston's Rube Walberg. As the season grew old it was apparent that DiMaggio's frosh season was no flash in the pan. Each day at Yankee Stadium either his bat or his glove did something to bring roars of approval from his fans.

The contest between the Yankees and the Tigers in 1937 was nip and tuck until a near-tragic accident took place that dimmed the lights for Detroit. On May 25 at Yankee Stadium, while 15,000 fans looked on anxiously, Bump Hadley, the Lynn, Massachusetts, right-hander known for poor control (in each of seven seasons prior to 1937 he had walked over 100 batters; in 1932 he passed 171 batters), unleashed a 3–1 pitch to Mickey Cochrane that hit the player-manager on the head with a sickening thud. More than likely, Mickey had lost the ball in the white-shirted center-field background. The feisty Cochrane went down as if he'd been picked off by a sniper's bullet as the ball ricocheted off his head and back to Hadley on the mound. "My pitch sailed. I don't know why, it just did," said a saddened Hadley.

There were no protective helmets in those days and Cochrane hovered between life and death for almost a week. When he finally recovered from a badly fractured skull, he was forced to retire at the age of thirty-four. Mickey's life had been saved but the Detroit season, already bedeviled by Schoolboy Rowe's sore arm, was in ruins. The Yankees proceeded to spread-eagle the field as they ended with 102 victories and a 13-game margin over a struggling Detroit team.

There were slight changes in the Yankees front line in 1937 but, for the most part, it was the unremitting power of Gehrig (37 homers, 159 RBIs, and a .351 average), DiMaggio (46 homers, 167 RBIs, and a .346 average), and Dickey (29 homers, 133 RBIs, and a .332 average) that left all other teams in the rear. One of the new hands was Tommy Henrich, once a Cleveland prospect, who had been ruled a free agent by Commissioner Landis. The good judge did the Yankees an enormous favor when he found that Cleveland had dealt unethically with Henrich, thus permitting Tommy to sign with the Yankees for $25,000. In a few years Henrich became one of the Yankees' most popular players. In the process, he won the nickname "Old Reliable." He also developed into one of the players most accessible to the New York press corps, a quality not to be ignored in the steamy media environment of the big city.

With Selkirk out a good part of the season and Jake Powell, a racist hothead (oddly, acquired in an exchange for another hothead, Ben Chapman, in 1936), bothered by illness, Henrich and Hoag got a chance to fill in in the outfield. Tommy originally aspired to play first base but after taking a look at the Iron Horse he made a judicious decision to become a Yankee outfielder.

For a second straight year the Yankees wound up in the World Series against the Giants. Once this interborough rivalry pitted the indomitable personalities of the Babe and McGraw against each other. But now it was DiMaggio and Lou versus the estimable Hubbell and the little slugger from Louisiana, Mel Ott. With the presence of these stars New York once again became the center of the baseball universe. Interest had reached the boiling stage when the clubs opened the Series at Yankee Stadium. For the first two games, over 120,000 fans jammed the Stadium. The Yankees rewarded their supporters with two easy wins, both by the score of 8–1, a result that surely must have confounded numerologists. Only Hubbell managed to rescue the Giants from another four-game sweep by the Yankees. His freakily twisted southpaw arm won the fourth game for the Giants at the Polo Grounds, despite a Gehrig home run.

My All-Time Yankee Team

Selected by David Halberstam, author of *Summer of '49* and *October 1964*

1B	Gehrig
2B	Randolph
SS	Jeter/Rizzuto
3B	Nettles
RF	Ruth
CF	DiMaggio
LF	Mantle
C	Berra
P (Lefty)	Ford
P (Righty)	Reynolds
Mgr	Stengel/Torre

". . . but my favorite Yankee of all is Tommy Henrich."

Gomez, who had taken two games from the Giants in 1936, repeated that performance in 1937. He had become a remarkable clutch pitcher, even if he occasionally broke his concentration—and the equanimity of McCarthy—by delaying a game to watch planes flying overhead. (By the time his Yankee career ended in 1942 he had won six games in the World Series, and lost none.)

As the 1938 season approached, the world champion Yankees—now happily called "The Window Breakers"—seemed in need of additional talent about as much as McCarthy needed the Babe as an assistant manager. Yet Barrow was never content with the status quo. He let the veteran Lazzeri, one of the first heroes in the Italian market, drift away to the Chicago Cubs,

following his unconditional release by the Yankees. Called up to take his place was a twenty-two-year-old second baseman from the Newark Bears, Joe Gordon, who stepped in immediately as another power hitter in an already power-packed lineup. In his first year Gordon banged 25 home runs and showed the leadership potential that ultimately won him several jobs as a big league manager.

Having earned $15,000 in his second year, DiMaggio decided to ratchet up the discourse about his pay in 1938. He steadfastly maintained, through various official and unofficial representatives (Joe Gould, the cigar-smoking manager of the former heavyweight champ Jimmy Braddock, did a good deal of the talking for DiMaggio), that he was worth

New York Mayor Fiorello LaGuardia greeting Joe DiMaggio before the first game of the 1938 World Series. A politician showing up for a World Series game is not an uncommon event; what is interesting is that LaGuardia had traveled to Chicago for this game. DiMaggio and his mates rewarded the mayor's loyalty with a four-game sweep of the Cubs.

Pennants & Pinstripes *The New York Yankees 1903–2002*

$40,000. Barrow angrily rejected such a figure, saying the Yankees would offer him $25,000, no more, no less. During the widely publicized haggling, Barrow pointed to Gehrig's $39,000 salary, suggesting that Joe had the effrontery to ask for more than Lou was being paid. DiMaggio countered by saying that what Gehrig was making should have no bearing on his own pay scale. By implication, Joe was criticizing the loyal, insecure Lou who had always been reluctant to ask Barrow for more money. When the season began in April, the rebellious Joe remained unsigned. Later in the month, the holdout came to an end, with Barrow docking DiMaggio some $2000, representing eleven days pay. In signing DiMaggio for $25,000, Barrow had broken down Joe's resistance by portraying him as an ungrateful malcontent, a message of negativism that seemed to go over well with the fans, who booed Joe when he finally returned to the lineup.

Joe regained his stride in short order as he methodically helped to drive his team to a third straight flag. Joe's RBI production of 140 led the Yankees, but it was noticeable that Gehrig was "down" to 114. With all the good things that happened, it was still a strange summer for both the Yankees and Gehrig. As Lou passed his 2000th consecutive game in June, only scant attention was paid to this watershed event. As was the case many times before in Gehrig's career, he found himself relegated to the backseat thanks to a wildly fast southpaw named Johnny Vander Meer. In that same month of June, Vander Meer pitched two straight no-hitters for Cincinnati, the second one against the Brooklyn Dodgers in the first night game ever played at Ebbets Field. Thus, Vander Meer became *the* baseball story of the summer, while Lou went on sturdily performing

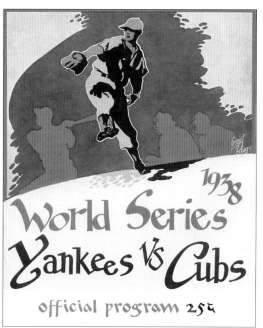

The cover of the 1938 World Series program. On the strength of their four-game sweep of the Cubs, the Yankees became the first team to win three world championships in a row.

his quotidian duties, then going home to his wife, Eleanor.

Gehrig—and all of the other Yankees—were overshadowed again on the night of June 22 at Yankee Stadium. The heavyweight champion of the world, Joe Louis, stepped into the Stadium ring that night and destroyed Max Schmeling in less than one round of boxing. The fight was a sports event that transcended sports, for Louis, a black man, had been cruelly stigmatized by Adolf Hitler as an inferior human being. Schmeling, whether he accepted the role or not, had become Hitler's designated Aryan. An enormous crowd of over 80,000 watched in astonishment—and with schadenfreude—as Schmeling collapsed in a heap under Louis's furious assault. Louis's fists had spoken for the despised and ignored of the world. Soon, like millions of other Americans, Louis would be in uniform as part of a citizen army that would unravel Hitler's hopes for world conquest.

The World Series that fall between the Yankees and the Chicago Cubs had to be anticlimactic in such a summer. The Cubs' pitching failed to stop the Yankees, who took four straight over them again—making it eight times in a row that McCarthy had beaten his former team in Series competition. If ever a man had been vindicated, it was McCarthy. Yet there were still those who disparaged his managerial acumen. The single dramatic game in the Series was game two, when the aching-armed Dizzy Dean, who had lost about everything except the ability to draw chuckles, contained the Yankees for seven innings. Then Crosetti hit a two-run homer off of one of those slow curves, followed by DiMaggio's two-run homer in the ninth. That was the end of Dizzy as an effective starting pitcher.

Manager Joe McCarthy is probably not making a rude gesture toward Bill Dickey, despite the Yankee catcher's apparent violation of McCarthy's strict decorum standards. The setting is Chicago's Comiskey Park in 1939, and the Yankees are on their way to one of the 1460 victories of McCarthy's New York tenure. McCarthy never had a losing season during his 24-year managerial career, and was 30–13 in World Series play.

January that Colonel Ruppert had died at the age of seventy-two. The torch was passed to Barrow, who became president in charge of everything.

At spring training in 1939 Lou worked almost desperately, the sweat pouring from his body. But he looked feeble and poorly coordinated. One day DiMaggio stood behind the batting cage and watched in gloomy fascination as Lou missed 19 pitches in a row in practice. In the clubhouse on another day Lou fell down trying to pull on his pants. Others noticed, as they tried to look away, that when Lou walked he appeared to shuffle his feet. "God, it was sad to see!" said pitcher Wes Ferrell, who had joined the Yankees in 1938.

McCarthy kept hoping that his eyes were deceiving him. But having always made it his business not to miss anything on a ballfield, he knew something was not right with his favorite Yankee. The manager never put sentiment first in his dealings with his men. But in this instance, his heart ruled his mind: Gehrig would open the year in the lineup, for his 2,123rd consecutive game.

By April 30, 1939, Lou had appeared in eight games, with a bleak ledger to show for it. He went hitless in five of the games, had a total of four singles, one run batted in, and no homers. Oddly, he had struck out only once in 28 times at bat, but that might have been because he was swinging at pitches early in the count. On May 2, when the Yankees were in Detroit, Gehrig went to McCarthy's room in the Book-Cadillac Hotel. He told McCarthy to remove him from the starting lineup. "It's for the good of the team, Joe," said Lou. "The time has come for me to quit."

"You don't have to quit," said McCarthy. "Take a rest for a week or so. . . . You'll be back." But McCarthy knew that Lou had to get out of the lineup be-

A dominant Series player in times past, Gehrig did little more against the Cubs than show up every day. He hit only four singles and had no home runs or runs batted in, as he relinquished his cleanup position to DiMaggio. This disappointing performance was an omen of things to come in Lou's life. But most observers chose to chalk it up to Lou's advanced baseball age of thirty-five.

In the off-season Gehrig tried hard to get his body into shape for his seventeenth year in a Yankees uniform. He adamantly refused to believe that there was anything wrong with his legs, his back, or his general health. The long streak would go on, he thought, and he would continue to contribute, as he always had. But the truth was that during the creeping mystery of the 1938 summer something had gone radically wrong in every phase of Lou's game. His bat flailed at pitches that he had once pounded for line drive home runs. His legs appeared rubbery, his reflexes were almost catatonic. Puzzled by his own sudden decline, Lou (and all of the Yankees) heard the lugubrious news in

fore he was badly hurt by a pitched ball. It was painful for him to think such things, but McCarthy knew that Lou's chances of ever getting back were slim. He had seen too much of the physically debilitated man, even if he didn't know exactly what was the matter with him.

McCarthy named Ellsworth "Babe" Dahlgren, a slick-fielding San Franciscan, to replace Gehrig, something he never thought he'd have to do. Two months later, Gehrig underwent tests at the Mayo Clinic in Rochester, Minnesota. Within a week, the clinic issued its report, in the bloodless idiom of medical public relations. It was found, said the clinic, that Gehrig was "suffering from amyotrophic lateral sclerosis, an illness involving the motor pathways and cells of the central nervous system . . . the nature of this trouble makes it such that Mr. Gehrig will be unable to continue his active participation as a baseball player . . ."

Baseball and the Yankees had suffered a wrenching body blow. Gehrig was through. On July 4, 1939, surrounded by many of his tough old squadron from the Murderers' Row club of 1927 (though he was estranged from Lou, the Babe was there, too, looking tanned as a lifeguard), Gehrig told 62,000 hushed fans at Yankee Stadium that he was "the luckiest man on the face of the earth . . . I might have had a bad break, but I have an awful lot to live for." The speech, delivered by Lou without notes, has since been acclaimed, with minimal sarcasm, as baseball's Gettysburg Address. "The words are nearly as familiar to Americans, with even the remotest sense of history, as 'four score and seven years ago,'" wrote Ron Fimrite in *Sports Illustrated*.

In July, the annual All-Star Game was played for the first time at Yankee Stadium. McCarthy didn't shrink from starting six of his own Yankee players, in-

On July 4, 1939, Yankee Stadium was bulging with more than 62,000 fans there to honor Lou Gehrig, the mighty Iron Horse, who had recently been diagnosed with a terminal disease that ended his career. Teammates and opposing players alike stood in hats-off reverence as speeches were delivered. Gehrig's famous valedictory included, "Look at these grand men. Which of you wouldn't consider it the highlight of his career just to associate with them for even one day? Sure I'm lucky."

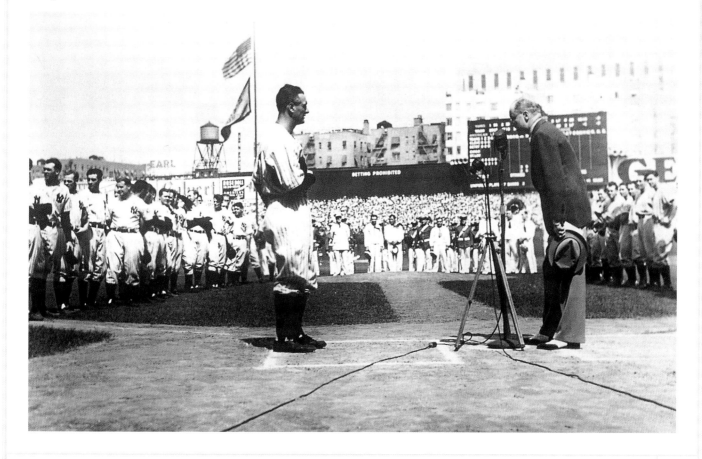

cluding the pitcher Red Ruffing. "After all," said McCarthy, with a mischievous wink, "I've got to play my best men." One of his best, DiMaggio, connected for a home run, as the Yankees-American League defeated the National League, 3–1, before 63,000 admiring fans.

Even with Gehrig benched forever, the Yankees were still too good a team to lose. They won 106 games, leaving the Red Sox far in the rear. They had even added another crushing bat in the hands of Charlie "King Kong" Keller, who played left field alongside DiMaggio in center and Selkirk in right. In his rookie season, Keller, whose gentle manner belied his fierce nickname, batted .334. DiMaggio led the American League with his highest-ever batting average of .381, signaling he was just getting warmed up for what was to come in two years. Ruffing posted his fourth 20-victory season in a row, benefiting from a lineup that gave opposing pitchers no surcease. (Ruffing probably could have been a starting player for many teams, for he was one of the greatest hitting pitchers of all time. In a 1–0 10-inning shutout that he pitched against Washington some years before, he hit the game-winning home run.)

As the second team in history to win four straight pennants (the Giants did it from 1921–1924), the Yankees thought that they would have tougher competition than usual in the World Series. Cincinnati had a sound team, with a solid-hitting first baseman, Frank McCormick, and two pitchers, the converted third baseman Bucky Walters (27–11) and Paul Derringer (25–7), who had led the way to the Reds' first flag since they "defeated" the Black Sox in the 1919 World Series. The Reds' lineup also included the ponderous catcher Ernie Lombardi, who might have led his league forever in hitting if he'd been able to leg out base hits. It was no exaggeration

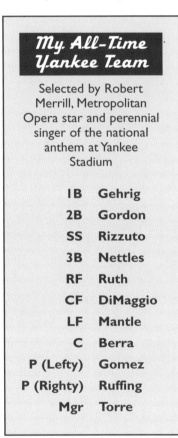

My All-Time Yankee Team

Selected by Robert Merrill, Metropolitan Opera star and perennial singer of the national anthem at Yankee Stadium

1B	Gehrig
2B	Gordon
SS	Rizzuto
3B	Nettles
RF	Ruth
CF	DiMaggio
LF	Mantle
C	Berra
P (Lefty)	Gomez
P (Righty)	Ruffing
Mgr	Torre

that third basemen invariably played out in short left field when Ernie was at bat—and they still managed to throw the poor fellow out.

Nobody expected that the Yankees would again sweep the World Series, as was their custom. But Ruffing won the first game and Monte Pearson took the second with a two-hit shutout. Hadley relieved Gomez in the third game and got credit for the victory. The fourth game featured a three-run, game-winning tenth inning by the Yankees that cast Lombardi in a Pagliacci-like role. Keller had stormed into him at home plate, kicking the ball loose and knocking the Reds' catcher into a state of utter confusion. Spying the dazed Lombardi sprawled on the ground, the ever-alert DiMaggio lit out for home and made it. The Yankees had won their record fourth straight world title, with Keller's three homers and six RBIs emerging as the primary batting story of the games. Again, the shrill cry of "Break up the Yankees" echoed throughout baseball land. But Lombardi's "snooze," an unfair characterization if ever there was one, remained the one episode in the Series that fans preferred to remember.

Scarcely noticed in the tumult following the Series victory was the presence of Gehrig in the locker room. He had dutifully stayed with the club, a mournful dugout spectator, for the whole season. On the train trip to Cincinnati, Gehrig spent time chatting with New York's feisty mayor, Fiorello LaGuardia. As a result of this relationship, Lou was offered a post on the city's parole board, which he accepted.

Would anything put a stop to the Yankees hegemony? The answer was simple and unexpected. Detroit, led by Greenberg, Charlie Gehringer, Rudy York, and the remarkably durable pitcher Bobo Newsom, beat out both Cleveland and a faltering Yankees team in a tight race for the 1940 pennant. On a club that had shattered the fences for four years, DiMaggio kept shattering. But he was pretty much alone in his efforts. For the second year in a row Joe was the American League's batting leader. However, Keller suffered from a sophomore letdown, Dickey sank to .247, Crosetti dwindled to .194, Gomez had a sore arm, and even the dependable Ruffing failed to win 20 games. In short, almost everyone had the miseries in a year in which McCarthy had fully expected to shepherd his team to a fifth straight title.

There is never any certainty in baseball. The Yankees learned that in 1940, despite the fact that the team was constantly nourished by a productive farm system under the supervision of George Weiss. Weiss, a stern and rather humorless man, who had been named to his job by Barrow seven years before, was inspired by the example of the pioneering Branch Rickey, who had built the St. Louis Cards' farm system. Top farm teams in Kansas City and Newark (the latter club was considered sufficiently talented to play in the big leagues), provided the continued muscle for McCarthy's roster. Six years later, Rickey broke down baseball's color barrier and fans witnessed the courageous performance of Jackie Robinson. But Weiss

Until Graig Nettles established his claim, it was generally accepted that the best third baseman ever to play for the Yankees was Robert "Red" Rolfe. Rolfe joined the Yankees organization after graduating from Dartmouth College in 1931. In the 1936 World Series against the Giants he hit .400, and in the Series a year later he hit .300. An exacting professional, he also led an exemplary private life. It was once said of Rolfe that his idea of a wonderful evening was to play bridge with three other guys who didn't talk.

failed to emulate Rickey in that shameful chapter of baseball history.

In spring training of 1941, DiMaggio, eager to get to work on time, received a traffic ticket for speeding. As things turned out, it was probably the only time all year that Joe was stopped. As America edged closer to entry into World War II, the game produced a blend of heroics, from Ted Williams and his .406 batting average to others like the young Pete Reiser in Brooklyn, who was forever challenging outfield fences with his body. But it was DiMaggio, now twenty-six years old, who rose to new heights that summer of 1941. Playing for $37,500 while other mortals in the game barely reached $7,000, DiMaggio put on a show that proved his credentials as the successor to the Babe and Lou.

It is astounding to look at what DiMaggio achieved with his bat under day-to-day stress. He projected a comfortable image under intense pressure. Yet his large consumption of cigarettes, at a time when people were not educated about them, revealed much about his internal tensions. In spring training, Joe warmed up to his task by hitting in 19 straight games, then he added eight official games at the start of the regular season. That was followed by a brief slump. DiMaggio was human, even in that season.

On May 15, on a muggy day at Yankee Stadium, Joe connected for a first-inning single against Edgar Smith, a journeyman southpaw. Not a soul suspected it at the time, but baseball's most inviolable streak had been launched. Not until two months later did the tapestry of daily consistency come to an end.

Throughout the rest of May and early June, Joe's bat kept up the daily tattoo of base hits. By now Americans everywhere were captivated by DiMaggio's achievement, even as the news from abroad had become increasingly grim. One day newspapers and

Yankees scout Bill Essick watched Joe Gordon play at the University of Oregon and promptly wired General Manager Ed Barrow, "At his best when it meant the most and the going was toughest." Barrow wired back, "Sign him." Essick did so, and after some minor league grooming, Gordon reported to the Yankees in 1938 and was their peerless second baseman for seven seasons.

radio carried the story of Rudolf Hess's unscheduled aerial adventure to Scotland in a stolen plane. Was Hitler's henchman trying to broker a peace with the British?

DiMaggio's fellow slugger Hank Greenberg played the first three weeks of the 1941 season, then became the first major star to be drafted into the army. His salary went from $55,000 a year to the GI's humble 21 bucks a month.

Alan Courtney, a songwriter, celebrated Joe's gestating streak with lyrical tribute, "Joe, Joe DiMaggio, we want you on our side." Each summer morning, as Robert Creamer relates in his book, *Baseball in '41*, people around the country asked, in coffee houses, diners, barber shops, school rooms, on farms, and at subway stops, "Did he get one yesterday?" And there was never any need to explain who "*he*" was.

On the night of June 2, Joe hit safely again, but the melancholy news the next day was that Gehrig, the mighty oak of 2,130 straight games, had died, three weeks short of his thirty-eighth birthday. Lou had lost his two-year battle against a disease that was subsequently named after him. DiMaggio's streak reached 30 on June 17, an all-time Yankee mark that put him ahead of Roger Peckinpaugh and Earle Combs. That same night, Joe Louis retained his heavyweight crown when he knocked out the converted light-heavyweight from Pittsburgh, Billy Conn, in the thirteenth round at the Polo Grounds. A spectator at the fight, Joe was applauded thunderously as he entered the ballpark.

Just ahead for DiMaggio was the American League mark of 41 games set by George Sisler in 1922 and the major league record of 44 set by Wee Willie Keeler in 1897. How much longer could Joe keep it up? Would opposing pitchers continue to give him good pitches to hit? Would the official scorers elect to give Joe a break on batted balls that might be chalked up as errors rather than basehits? In truth, DiMaggio didn't need help from anybody, either pitchers or scorers, for he was in an incredible groove. Over one stretch he connected for 24 hits in 44 times at bat, signaling that he was in no mood to end his assault.

Before a midweek crowd of 52,000 at Yankee Sta-dium, he tied Keeler's 44 on July 1 with hits in both games of a doubleheader against the Red Sox. When the Lou Gehrig center-field monument was unveiled on July 6 at the Stadium, DiMaggio crashed six hits in still another doubleheader with Philadelphia. (A profusion of scheduled twin bills made Joe's daily accomplishment even tougher.) He reached 48 in his streak with a crowd of 66,000 on hand to honor both Gehrig and DiMaggio. He reached 50 straight with four hits against the Browns on July 11 and then went to 53 in Chicago's Comiskey Park on July 13, as 50,000 Windy City partisans cheered for their enemy.

Luck, which had played a minimal role up to this point, came to Joe's aid on July 14, when his dribbler wormed its way through the White Sox infield. On the same day, Hollywood producer Samuel Goldwyn, who admitted knowing practically nothing about baseball (though he said he'd heard of DiMaggio!) announced that he would film the life story of Gehrig. Mentioned as a candidate to play Lou was a former baseball broadcaster named Ronald Reagan. But the laconic Gary Cooper eventually won the part, with the Bronx-born, sweet-faced Teresa Wright assigned to play Eleanor Gehrig.

The streak hit 55 on July 15 against Ed Smith, the same gentleman who had fed Joe the pitch that inaugurated the DiMaggio deluge back in mid-May. The next day, in Cleveland, DiMaggio banged three hits to run the skein to 56. By this time it appeared that fans in "foreign" cities were rooting more for Joe's base hits than for a home team win.

On the night of July 17, another swollen crowd of 70,000 jammed Cleveland's Municipal Stadium to see if Joe could keep the miracle going. But finally the gods went against him. Ken Keltner, one of the league's best fielding third basemen, made two brilliant plays on hard ground balls hit by DiMaggio. When Joe walked in the fourth inning many in the crowd hissed pitcher Al Smith. (There were times during the streak that DiMaggio swung at 3–0 pitches, with the endorsement of McCarthy, who might have assassinated any other Yankee batter who tried to do the same thing.) In the eighth inning, with Jim Bagby pitching, Joe came up with the bases loaded. Again, he hit a hard ground ball, but shortstop Lou Boudreau gobbled it up and turned it into a double play, as many in the crowd moaned. The streak was over at 56 games. During the two-month siege on the American League's pitchers, DiMaggio hit safely in 29 games at home and 27 on the road, an equitable distribution. The accumulation of hits included 15 home runs, 16 doubles, four triples, and 56 singles.

"I wanted it to go on forever," Joe said wearily after the game, puffing on his inevitable Camel. The owners of other clubs would have liked it to have gone on, too, for thousands had come out to their ballparks to cheer for Joe. With the streak at an end, attendance was down by half.

When Joe left the ballpark, accompanied by his teammate Phil Rizzuto, he informed Phil that the Heinz 57 people had promised him $10,000 if he had gotten a hit that night. "Tough luck," said Rizzuto. Then, having forgotten his wallet, Joe borrowed several dollars from Rizzuto and waved goodnight to the shortstop.

However, DiMaggio's hot hand had been quelled only temporarily, for at once he put together another batting streak—this one for 16 games. If Keltner hadn't thwarted him on the night of July 17, DiMaggio would have had a run of 73 straight contests with a hit.

Meanwhile, the Brooklyn Dodgers, without a World Series appearance in 21 years, were clawing their way to a National League pennant. Their summer-long skirmish with the Cardinals, who brought up Stan Musial late in the season to help them in their bid, ended with them facing the Yankees in the postseason. The Dodgers' manager, Leo Durocher, one of the game's ineffable provocateurs, had bullied a club that was full of tough, brassy, hard-drinking athletes, sort of a mix of the original Baltimore Orioles and the Gashouse Gang. Men like Dixie Walker, the marbles-playing shortstop, Pee Wee Reese, Joe Medwick, Billy Herman, and the ex-Cubs first baseman, Dolf Camilli, were no slouches, especially when they were supported by a pitching staff consisting of Whitlow Wyatt, Curt Davis, Fat Freddie Fitzsimmons, Kirby Higbe, and the rubber-armed reliever, Hugh Casey.

The Yankees knew they'd be in for a battle, and when the Dodgers won the second game of the World Series to tie the classic at one all, it looked like it would be a donnybrook to the bitter end. But then

Frankie Crosetti played for the Yankees from 1932 through 1948, then coached for another 20 years. He played or coached in a total of 122 World Series games. The sight of Crosetti waving runners home from his third-base box was nearly as familiar a sight at Yankee Stadium as the rooftop frieze. His nickname "Crow" seems to have derived less from his surname than from his constant chatter and chirping on the field.

fate intervened to propel the Yankees to victory. In the third game at Ebbets Field, Fitzsimmons, once a Giants favorite, pitched seven shutout innings, until his knee got in the way of a line drive hit back to the mound. The forty-year-old Fitz had to be removed from the game. The Yankees then went on to win with two runs in the eighth off Casey.

But it was the fourth game at Ebbets Field that long-suffering Dodger fans would never erase from their memory. The outlook *was* brilliant for the Dodger nine that day, to paraphrase "Casey at the Bat" (mark that name Casey), for Reiser had slugged a two-run homer to give Brooklyn a 4–3 lead going into the ninth inning. Now it was up to Casey, who had

lost one game already in the Series, to retire three Yankees to give Brooklyn the win.

Casey got Johnny Sturm and Red Rolfe to ground out quickly and only had to retire Henrich to bring about a two-all deadlock in the Series. With a count of three balls and two strikes on Henrich, Casey unleashed a wild pitch—could it have been a squishy spitter?—that Old Reliable Tommy swung at dly and missed. Years later Henrich told author David Halberstam that, "Casey simply reached back and put too much on his curve and the ball broke too much." But the Dodgers' catcher, Mickey Owen, who hadn't committed an error all year, also missed. The ball tore through his grasp, even as the right arm of umpire Larry Goetz was raised in the air signaling a third strike. Turning his head to watch Owen scramble after the ball, Henrich raced to first base. The chemistry of the ball game had changed in that mad instant. Already on the way to their postgame showers, the Yankee players returned to the bench. A game seemingly beyond recall had taken on new life. In quick succession, as Durocher and his men watched dumbfounded, a despondent Casey gave up a single to DiMaggio (who, until this point, had had a mediocre Series), a double to Keller, a walk to Dickey, a double to Joe Gordon, and a walk to Rizzuto.

When the ninth-inning slaughter ended, the Yankees had won, 7–4, after one of the most startling rallies in Series history. In an anticlimax the next day, the Yankees sewed up the Series, behind the blimpish Ernie Bonham. In the borough of Brooklyn the fans tried to console themselves with the tired refrain, "Wait 'Til Next Year."

In a postmortem about the missed third strike, Owen said, "I'm only sorry about one thing. I should have called time and stopped the game, giving Casey and myself a chance to get over the shock. I've always kicked myself for not doing that.'" (Ten years later, Casey, only thirty-seven years old and supposedly depressed over a broken marriage, shot himself to death.)

Two months after the World Series was over the Japanese rained bombs on the Hawaiian island of Oahu. This sudden attack, on the large U.S. base at

Charlie Gehringer said, "Dickey certainly made catching look easy." Bill Dickey was a bulwark behind the plate, and his .362 average in 1936 remains the highest single season average ever recorded by a catcher. After a fistfight with an opponent in 1932, he was fined $1,000 and suspended for 30 days. He celebrated his first day back with three singles and a grand slam homer.

Pearl Harbor on December 7, 1941, a place generally not well known to most Americans, cost 2,280 American lives and wounded more than a thousand. The next morning, President Roosevelt, citing "a date that will live in infamy," declared war on Japan.

Recalling that time, the author William Manchester, who would fight with the marines in the Pacific, wrote, "It had been a fine, golden autumn, a lovely farewell to those who would lose their youth, and some of them their lives, before leaves turned again in a peace-time fall."

With a nation at war against Japan, Germany, and Italy, a pertinent question now arose. Should a pas-

time like baseball, which some might regard as frivolous, be permitted to play its games while young men were going off to fight on bleak islands in the Pacific and against Hitler's supermen in Europe? When DiMaggio asked for a raise following his magnificent 1941 season, Barrow, ever the penny-pinching patriot, reminded Joe that men like him were dying for just a few dollars a month. If Barrow's intent was to embarrass DiMaggio, he may have succeeded, for Joe signed for $43,000, less than he requested.

"Losing Pitcher" Hugh Mulcahy of the Phillies was the first major leaguer to go into the service. But stars like Greenberg and Feller, who enlisted in the navy, were also among the early birds to join up. For the most part, though, ballplayers were no more anxious than anybody else to shed their baseball uniforms for GI fatigues.

President Roosevelt, who had happily thrown out first balls at Washington Senators games, was asked by Commissioner Landis if baseball should carry on. FDR answered that he thought that baseball provided recreation when people needed a release from the tensions of war. "I honestly feel that it would be best for the country to keep baseball going," he wrote to Landis. "There will be fewer people unemployed and everybody will work longer hours and harder than ever before. That means they ought to have a chance for recreation and for taking their minds off their work even more than before."

Such a pronunciamento did not mean that Roosevelt thought that able-bodied players should avoid serving. To the contrary, they should go, he announced. In time, 350 major leaguers were in uniform, including DiMaggio, who went into the army air force in 1943, and his brother Dom, who enlisted in the coast guard. Joe's batting rival, Ted Williams, became a flier in the navy. There were some big leaguers who faced tough combat, including pitcher Warren Spahn of the Boston Braves, Buddy Lewis of the Senators, and Bob Feller. But many, like DiMaggio, wound up playing baseball for the army or navy, which wasn't a bad way to spend the war years.

Before going into the military service, Joe played

through the 1942 season. His life had been complicated by his marriage to Dorothy Arnold, a blond movie actress he had met some years before at the Biograph Studio in the Bronx. The tabloids typically characterized the relationship as "tempestuous," and the marriage ultimately ended in the divorce courts. In addition, DiMaggio's ulcers were a constant annoyance. All of these distractions forced him to pay a price at home plate: he ended the 1942 season with a .305 batting average and 21 home runs, the lowest figures of his career up to that point.

One of the highlights of the first wartime season was a specially arranged confrontation between the forty-seven-year-old Babe and the legendary strikeout pitcher Walter Johnson, then fifty-five. On August 23, the Army and Navy Relief Fund raised $80,000 as

70,000 people paid their way to watch the Babe swing at some 20 pitches thrown his way by the once-invincible Johnson. The idea was to let Ruth smash a few out of the ballpark. Johnson, who hadn't thrown a pitch in anger for half a dozen years, was willing to play his role. The Babe did bang several far and high out of Yankee Stadium but by the end of the mano-a-mano he was puffing like a wounded bull. It marked the last time these two Hall of Famers ever appeared together in a baseball park. Johnson died four years later and the Babe was gone in 1948.

Not burdened by many personnel losses to the service (Henrich went into the coast guard and Johnny Sturm left for the army), the Yankees won the pennant again in their relentless fashion. They won 103 games, topping Boston by nine games. Their key

In the fourth game of the 1941 World Series, umpire Larry Goetz has indicated that Tommy Henrich is out on strikes, but doesn't see the ball squirting away from Brooklyn catcher Mickey Owen. Badly fooled on the pitch, Henrich thought, "If I'm having this much trouble with this pitch, maybe Mickey is too." He reached first safely, and the Yankees, down 4–3 with two out in the ninth, went on to win the game 7–4.

player was Joe Gordon, who played well at second base all season and won the league's Most Valuable Player Award. Gordon hit .322 and was a potent batter in the clutch, with 103 runs batted in.

On the mound Bonham experienced a fine year, with 21 victories and only five losses. (Sadly, Bonham would die in 1949, at the age of thirty-six, after an appendectomy.) Ruffing, who seemed to have been around since the Stadium opened, had a 14–7 record at the age of thirty-eight. The fiercely competitive Spud Chandler, once an all-around athlete at the University of Georgia, posted a 16–5 mark, and Hank Borowy, a local hero from the Fordham campus, compiled a 15–4 record.

Few could anticipate that the St. Louis Cardinals, who had barely survived a grueling pennant struggle against the Dodgers, would give the Yankees much of a challenge in the World Series. But having edged out the Dodgers on the final day of the season, the Cards remained razor sharp and hungry. Their starting lineup in the World Series of 1942 averaged about twenty-six years of age—the youngest ever in Series history—and their manager, Billy Southworth, a Nebraskan who had once been an able outfielder in the National League, was adept at handling such youthful talent. Enos Country Slaughter, Terry Moore, Marty Marion, and Stan Musial were the standouts on the Cardinals, and they had two 20-game winners in freshman Johnny Beazley and Mort Cooper. Walker Cooper, Mort's brother, was the catcher, and the blond third baseman, Whitey Kurowski, often came up with key hits.

"They might not be so hot at the plate," observed Casey Stengel, then managing the Boston Braves, "but they sure got a lot of strength in their ankles."

Ironically, though the Cardinals lost the opening game of the Series, they showed their true mettle. It should have been a warning to the Yankees that the Cards were not going to roll over and play dead. Ruffing was pitching a no-hitter until two were out in the eighth inning of that first game, when Moore singled. Then, in the ninth, Ruffing had two outs on the board when Southworth's kids awakened from their slumber and put together enough hits and walks to score four

Spurgeon "Spud" Chandler turned down a better offer from the Cubs in 1932 to sign with the Yankees. In 1943 his record was 20–4, with a 1.64 ERA, the lowest since 1919. He had a career winning percentage of .717, but did not pitch in enough games to qualify for the record book.

runs. With the tying runs on the bases, Chandler, Ruffing's reliever, came in to put down the rally. The victory was Ruffing's seventh Series triumph, the most recorded by any pitcher until Whitey Ford ambled along in a later Yankee generation.

In the locker room, Slaughter promised that the Cards would come back to haunt the Yankees. "We sure gave 'em one helluva scare," he said. He was right in both assessments. In a mystifying turnaround, the Cardinals won the next four games, even licking Ruffing in the final game. On the way to their astonishing victory, the Cardinals had the usual imperturbable New Yorkers bellyaching about umpire decisions, a sure sign that they were a badly beaten team. In the third game, Ernie White shut out the Yankees with his southpaw pitches, the first time the Yankees had suffered such ignominy since Jesse Haines whitewashed them in the 1926 Series. The coup de grace came in the ninth inning of the fifth game at Yankee Stadium before 70,000 shocked fans, when Kurowski unloaded a two-run home run to break a 2–2 tie.

DiMaggio batted .333 in the Series but failed to hit a homer. Keller had two homers, and Rizzuto, not known for his power, had one. But the big winner was Kurowski, who was a radio guest on Fred Waring's show and received $25 for the appearance.

Now, as the country faced its "rendezvous with destiny" (President Roosevelt's mystical phrase), an increasing number of players marched off to war to face fear, death, misery, boredom, crap games, smelly, crowded troopships, and Betty Grable and Rita Hayworth cheesecake grinning at them from their barracks walls.

In 1939, his rookie year, Charlie Keller outhit another rookie, Ted Williams, .334 to .327. He joined Joe DiMaggio and Tommy Henrich to form one of the best outfields in baseball history. Management's insistence that Keller change his all-fields batting style to become a pull hitter probably took at least 30 points off his lifetime batting average. "King Kong" was Keller's nickname, but no prudent person used it in his presence.

Joe DiMaggio

It would be hard to make the case that Joseph Paul DiMaggio, a man of Italian descent, had as difficult a time assimilating in the baseball world as Hank Greenberg, the first Jewish superstar baseball player, or Jackie Robinson, the sorely harassed pioneer black player. Yet DiMaggio's travails should not be underes-

timated. He played in a time when even major publications such as *Life* magazine resorted to ugly stereotypes in portraying him. "Instead of olive oil or smelly bear grease, he keeps his hair slick with water," said *Life* in 1939. "He never reeks with garlic and prefers chicken chow mein to spaghetti." The magazine also

Joe DiMaggio hitting against the White Sox in 1946, his grace clearly in evidence. Ted Williams was always complimentary about Joe. "It is probably my misfortune that I have been and will inevitably be compared with Joe DiMaggio," he said.

reminded its millions of readers that Joe could actually speak English without an accent, even if he had learned Italian first. (Only a few years before, the New York tabloids referred to Tony Lazzeri as the "Walloping Wop.")

Such unpleasantness must have contributed to DiMaggio's general demeanor. Cognizant of his role as one of the first Italian-American heroes, he chose to behave properly in every way, including how he dressed, what he said—or didn't say—and how he comported himself on the diamond. Joe's sensitivity about his Italian heritage must have been an issue with him. After all, even President Roosevelt had once been quoted as saying that Italians were "a nation of opera singers."

Author Robert Creamer said of DiMaggio that "he was a product of the Sicilian mystique—keep your mouth shut." From the start of his career with the Yankees, DiMaggio chose to be aloof, removed, almost icy to most people, including those he played

with. Such was Joe's desire for privacy that one of his fellow Yankees said of him that he "led the league in room service." He had an almost paranoid wariness of the press, which is odd, considering that many in the New York press corps wrote reams of worshipful copy about him, almost from the day he arrived. Joe remained suspicious of them, as well as others who would have liked to have been regarded as pals and admirers. He never seemed to have close friends and those he did cultivate were mainly business associates who could be expected to do favors for him, give him advice, buy him meals, or sit silently with him at Toots Shor's.

After Joe left baseball, he was constantly referred to as "baseball's greatest living former player" (a felicitous phrase that he relished, though it might have been legitimately challenged by others). He also managed to develop a social patina and an innate sense of theater. For example, he insisted on always being introduced last at Yankee Old-Timers' Day, and with his expensive tailoring and carefully tended white hair, he had the appearance of a United Nations dignitary. Even when he had been an army sergeant during World War II, Joe's uniform was always carefully pressed and custom made.

DiMaggio was the son of a fisherman, Zio Pepe. He was born in Martinez, California, in November 1914. Martinez was a tiny fishing village about 25 miles from San Francisco, the same city that had already sent so many baseball-hungry youths to the big leagues. Lazzeri, Crosetti, Lefty O'Doul, and Ping Bodie all hailed from San Francisco. "I knew I'd be lonesome in New York," said Joe, before he came to the Yankees. "But O'Doul told me not to be afraid of the big city. He called it 'a friendly city.' That turned out to be true."

Joe turned out to be the best ballplayer in a family of ballplayers. His brother Dom, considerably smaller than Joe, was for years a mainstay of the Red Sox outfield and less remote from the press than his older brother. Vince was the first to play professional baseball, with the San Francisco Seals. But his vulnerability to the strikeout caused him to be a journeyman. Still another brother, Tony, once showed promise as a player but gave up his career in the sport in order to help his father in the fishing business.

Baseball was everything to Joe. It was what he worked at, what he knew, what he wanted. By the age of seventeen he had made it to the Seals in the Pacific Coast League, under manager Ike Caveney. Seals owner Charles Graham paid Joe $250 to sign a contract and no entrepreneur ever got more for his money.

By the time Joe got to the big leagues he could do everything well. He excelled at every phase of the game, including running the bases. McCarthy said of Joe that he never saw him thrown out on the bases. That might have been managerial hyperbole, but it reflects the impression DiMaggio left on those who followed the game closely. Branch Rickey, that keen judge of baseball talent, called DiMaggio "an artist." Stengel insisted Joe was simply "the best." Most baseball men might have agreed that he was the game's Mona Lisa, an inscrutable, almost unknowable person.

As author Robert Smith put it, Joe appeared to operate "under a thin shell of disdain."

Another less puzzling part of DiMaggio's story was that during his entire career he was cursed with injuries, some of which less spartan athletes would have had trouble dealing with. These ailments proliferated with each passing season. His reputation as injury-prone was well earned; he conducted frequent well-publicized battles with swollen knees, bone spurs on his heels, body germs, and a hypersensitive stomach. The latter affliction may have revealed more about Joe's inner tensions than anything he ever said.

Three years after his retirement in 1951, DiMaggio met and married Marilyn Monroe. The union probably was doomed from the moment they exchanged vows in San Francisco's City Hall. Columnist Jimmy Cannon, who prized Joe's friendship above all others who played games for a living, nominated them as "America's Sweethearts," the successors to Mary Pickford and Doug Fairbanks, Sr. But Cannon must have conveniently forgotten that Mary and Doug's marriage foundered.

The tabloids devoted an inordinate amount of space to trivial details of the DiMaggios' marital life, hardly a development that appealed to the reclusive Joe. He also turned out to be a possessive and jealous husband, who resented Marilyn's flirtatiousness and the roles she played on the screen. He was as uncommunicative with Marilyn as he had been with most people.

Marilyn's sad and unstable life had been full of unhappy episodes with other husbands and lovers, even as she attempted to establish her credentials as a serious actress and comedian. Constant fights with Joe wore down her resistance, causing her to seek a dissolution of the marriage. After only nine months of marriage—only a bit longer than a major league season—the two were divorced in October 1954. Marilyn later married the playwright Arthur Miller, a marriage that also ended in divorce.

When Marilyn died after an overdose of drugs in 1962, Joe arranged for her funeral and was her chief mourner. For years afterward he decorated her grave with roses, a gesture that drew widespread comment and sympathy.

1943–1952

IN 1943 AMERICANS WERE MORE CONCERNED WITH THE WAR THAT WAS RAGING IN EUROPE AND ASIA THAN THEY WERE WITH THE DEPLETED ROSTERS OF BIG LEAGUE BALL CLUBS AND THE MEDIOCRE STANDARD OF WARTIME PLAY. BUT LIFE DID GO ON, AND SOME MINOR ATTENTION WAS PAID TO THE TRIVIA OF DAILY LIFE, SUCH AS CHARLIE CHAPLIN'S MARRIAGE TO THE TEENAGE OONA O'NEILL OVER THE HEATED OBJECTIONS OF HER FAMOUS PLAY-WRIGHT FATHER, EUGENE. OTHERS SOUGHT MOMENTARY PLEASURE BY VIEW-

ing Rodgers and Hammerstein's *Oklahoma* on Broadway, or by reading Betty Smith's *A Tree Grows in Brooklyn*.

But Hitler's "scorched earth" policy in Russia, the beginning of the Allies' crushing around-the-clock bombing of Germany, and angry race riots in several American cities were events that transcended batting averages and pennant races.

Because of travel restrictions, spring training that year became an event that chilled the bones of ballplayers. Since Judge Landis had decreed that teams should train north of the Mason-Dixon line, the Yankees went through their preseason warm-ups at Asbury Park, New Jersey, on a high school diamond. The Dodgers took orders from manager Durocher at a West Point facility, and both Chicago teams trained in the state of Indiana, where the temperature usually hovered in the thirties. The Phillies stayed close to home in Hershey, Pennsylvania.

By the time the 1943 season opened for the Yankees, DiMaggio was wearing another uniform, as were first baseman Buddy Hassett, Rizzuto, Ruffing, and Henrich. In the reshuffling of their lineup the Yankees made a deal for first baseman Nick Etten of the Phillies. Owner Gerry Nugent of the Phillies paid $10,000 and received four players for Nick. Soon after, Nugent was replaced as owner by William D.

OVERLEAF: **Casey Stengel looks a bit wary as he addresses the Yankees for the first time in a 1949 spring training session. Amusement registering on some of the players' faces suggests that the new manager has begun his tenure with a choice bit of Stengelese. Many of the veterans, including Joe DiMaggio, thought Stengel was a bit too jocular. Some felt that he was not the right man to lead the team.**

Cox, although losing Etten had little to do with his leaving. Other Yankee additions came from the minor league "feeder" in Newark. Johnny Lindell, a policeman in the off-season, was converted into an outfielder with the unenviable job of replacing DiMaggio. Bud Metheny, also from Newark, took over for Henrich, and Billy Johnson was assigned to third base. Another Bear, George "Snuffy" Stirnweiss, shared the shortstop post with the veteran Crosetti. George Tucker Stainback had been with Detroit the previous season and the Yankees got him to play part time in the outfield.

But there were still enough old-timers on the Yankees to make them resemble the Yankees and not a minor league club. Dickey was behind the bat, Gordon remained at second base, and the big bat of Keller was available in the outfield. The pitching was still very sound, with Chandler, at 20–4, easily winning the Most Valuable Player Award. Bonham and Borowy helped out Chandler, while the lantern-jawed Johnny Murphy trudged in from the bullpen enough times to keep the opposition at bay. At the finish, the Yankees were 13½ games ahead of the Senators.

In the National League, the Cardinals repeated, this time by 18 lengths over Cincinnati. But they had been weakened by the departure of outfielders Moore and Slaughter. Coming into a repeat performance of the World Series against the Yankees, they were further disadvantaged by Judge Landis's ruling that the first three Series games had to be played at Yankee Stadium because of travel restrictions.

The Yankees were determined to even the score against St. Louis—and they did, as they played to three packed houses at the Stadium. In the first game

The Babe had a cameo appearance in <u>The Pride of the Yankees,</u> the 1942 film based on the life and career of Lou Gehrig. Teresa Wright played Eleanor Gehrig, and admitted to not knowing much about baseball at the time. In the late 1990s, she was invited to sit in George Steinbrenner's box as a reward for becoming an enthusiastic Yankees fan.

The Yankees waged many memorable battles with the Giants and Dodgers over the years, and on one occasion played both interborough rivals at the same time. This unprecedented exhibition took place at the Polo Grounds on June 26, 1944, on behalf of the War Bond Sports Committee, and raised nearly $6 million. Yankee Stadium would have held more spectators, but the game was scheduled for 7 P.M., and lights would not be installed in the Bronx ballpark for another two years.

As it was, 50,000 fans attended and were treated to pregame hitting, throwing, and running contests, musical performances introduced by comedian Milton Berle, cavorting by baseball's "Clown Prince" Al Schacht, and an appearance by former Mayor Jimmy Walker, who introduced a group of old-time New York and Brooklyn stars to the strains of "Auld Lang Syne." Presiding Mayor Fiorello LaGuardia threw out the first ball, then, in the spirit of the occasion, threw out two more.

The "game" itself was anticlimactic. Brooklyn batted first, with the Yankees in the field, and the Giants in their dugout. The Dodgers scored a run before they were retired, then they took the field while the Yankees batted. In the second inning the Dodgers were matched against the Giants while the Yankees sat down. This alternating scheme continued until each team had six chances at the plate. The format was devised by a mathematics professor from Columbia University. When nine "innings" were completed the Dodgers had five runs, the Yankees one, and the Giants none.

Since there were only two dugouts, two squads had to coexist at various times. When the Yankees and Dodgers occupied the same dugout, managers McCarthy and Durocher, not exactly kindred spirits, sat at opposite ends of the bench.

Chandler defeated southpaw Max Lanier, thus cracking the string of four straight defeats that the New Yorkers had suffered in the 1942 Series.

The Cardinals bounced back in the second game behind Mort Cooper, who pitched under considerable emotional distress. Just hours before the game began his father died suddenly. Cooper refused to step aside, starting and finishing a 4–3 victory over Bonham. The situation was remindful of Detroit's Bobo Newsom in the 1940 World Series, when he also took the mound despite the loss of his father.

But Cooper's courageous victory was all the Cards could reap, as the Yankees smothered them in the last three games, taking the Series four games to one. It marked the Yankees' tenth world title. In the fifth game, Dickey delivered a two-run home run to defeat Cooper and give McCarthy his seventh and final New York championship. "It felt real good beating them," said Dickey, who was usually reserved in victory or defeat.

Following their triumph, many of the Yankees packed up their caps and sent them to Marine air ace Pappy Boyington in the South Pacific. Pappy had promised to give one to each of his fliers who had knocked a Japanese Zero out of the air.

By now, in the wartime years of 1944 and 1945, baseball's teams were almost bankrupt of first-rate talent. The needs of the military had siphoned off most of the game's star players, as well as the journeymen. If a man was a 4F—a player with a chronic health condition that would defer him from the draft—his service was eagerly sought. And a conscientious search went on for overage players who still had a hit or two in their bats. A one-armed outfielder named Pete Gray (real name: Peter Wyshner) played for the St. Louis Browns while Bert Shepard, who lost a leg over Germany's skies, actually pitched for Washington in a game in 1945. The thirty-year-old Gray could muster little power from his left arm but he managed to bat .218, with two triples, six doubles, and no home runs among his 51 hits. His determination had to be admired but he was not invited back to the majors after 1945.

Like all other clubs, the Yankees suffered from the talent drought. They didn't have any Pete Grays or Shepards on their roster, but they had a veritable Coxey's Army on hand, including Snuffy Stirnweiss, whose .309 mark in 1945 was enough to lead an impoverished American League. With a tatterdemalion crew—players like Oscar Grimes, Mike Milosevich, Mike Garbark, Russ Derry, Hersh Martin, Don Savage, Larry Rosenthal, Rollie Hemsley (a catcher in his seventeenth season), and the forty-year-old Johnny Cooney—McCarthy wasn't able to do better than third in 1944 and fourth in 1945.

Near the end of the 1944 season, a familiar Pittsburgh Pirate from the 1927 World Series, Paul Waner, was added to the Yankees ensemble. At forty-one, bespectacled and prone to hoist one too many, Waner, a Hall of Famer, played in nine games and got one hit. One day a fan shouted at Waner, "Hey, Paul, how come you're in the Yankee outfield?" To which Waner replied, "Because DiMaggio's in the Army!"

Those in the peanut gallery who had repeatedly questioned McCarthy's abilities as a manager might have found some support for their mischievous views in these subpar seasons. But, in all fairness, McCarthy didn't have much to work with, which underlines a point made by historian Charles C. Alexander. "The willingness of major league clubs to employ one-armed or one-legged players, while refusing to tap abundant talent from the Negro leagues," wrote Alexander, "more than ever highlighted the absurdity and injustice of baseball's persistent color barrier."

Remarkably, in 1944, the traditionally inept St. Louis Browns won their first American League pennant (also their last) but were defeated in an all-St. Louis World Series by the Cardinals.

In 1945, after Detroit defeated the Chicago Cubs in a seven-game World Series, led by Hank Green-

My All-Time Yankee Team

Selected by Suzyn Waldman, Yankee announcer

1B	Gehrig
2B	Richardson
SS	Rizzuto
3B	Boyer
RF	Ruth
CF	DiMaggio
LF	Mantle
C	Berra
P (Lefty)	Ford
P (Righty)	Reynolds
Mgr	McCarthy

berg (who had just emerged from the air force) and southpaw Hal Newhouser, the most momentous news regarding the Yankees occurred off the field. The heirs of Jacob Ruppert—Mrs. J. Basil Maguire, Helen Wyant, and Mrs. Joseph Holleran—completed the sale of the ball club to a colorful triumvirate. The price was $2,800,000, a mere pittance compared to what one would receive for the Yankees in today's bullish market. What distinguished the new ownership from the past patroons who had overseen the Yankees was their unpredictability. This was especially true of Leland Stanford "Larry" MacPhail, the leader of the group.

MacPhail was a well-advertised two-fisted drinker with a loud voice and an almost uncontrollable temper. But he was also a brilliant baseball man, who did not shun change or innovation. When he headed the Cincinnati Reds franchise in the 1930s, he introduced night baseball to that city in 1935, despite opposition from the game's Luddites. He was a strong supporter of broadcasting his team's games over the radio, again bucking those who feared "giving away" the product. In time MacPhail's bellicosity soured the folks in Cincinnati and he left town. When he made his departure, he was snapped up almost at once by the Brooklyn Dodgers, who were indisputably in need of several blood transfusions. MacPhail more than provided that with his energy and dynamism. "There's a thin line between genius and insanity, and Larry's case is pretty thin," said Leo Durocher, who was installed as the Dodgers manager by MacPhail.

MacPhail immediately went to work to change the image of Ebbets Field and the team that played in it. He brought in a number of hustling athletes, practically made over the broken-down old ballpark with a fresh coat of paint, hired a non-Brooklynite Southerner, Red Barber, to handle the radio broadcasts, and repaired the dugouts, restrooms, and locker facilities.

The inventive and irascible Larry MacPhail was a co-owner of the Yankees for three tumultuous years, 1945–1947. He brought night baseball to Yankee Stadium in 1946, staged archery competitions and foot races before games, and thoroughly alienated co-owners Del Webb and Dan Topping, and most of the players. He is pictured here regaling the New York press corps, none of whom seems especially enthralled.

Crowds flocked to Ebbets Field to see another broken-down institution, Babe Ruth, who was hired to play traffic cop at first base. Would anyone pay to watch a first base coach? MacPhail proved that they would. By the time that MacPhail left to join the service as a fifty-two-year-old lieutenant colonel, the Dodgers had become winners. During World War I MacPhail supposedly had helped to kidnap the kaiser. In World War II he didn't try to do the same thing with Adolf Hitler—but the thought must have occurred to him. Coming to the Yankees, it was clear that he would be calling the shots.

However, the others in the new Yankees triumvirate weren't exactly pallid flowers. Handsome Dan Topping, a captain in the army, was a man with Anaconda Copper millions who appeared to own squatter's rights to the oft-used newspaper description, "playboy sportsman." When he wasn't playboying he also owned the Brooklyn Dodgers pro football franchise, which was hardly a roaring success. The third man in the mix, Del Webb, was an Arizona construction magnate who had a very sincere interest in money. Both Webb and Topping relied on MacPhail to make all baseball decisions.

By 1946 baseball was returning to a reasonable facsimile of "normalcy" following the 1945 World Series between the Tigers and the Cubs. Detroit managed to win, after jaundiced observers clucked that they didn't think either team of fat, slow old codgers could end up ahead.

Now, as the Yankees' boss-of-all-things, MacPhail

was determined to enter the postwar era by modernizing the whole Yankee environment. When it was discovered during World War II that the lights of Ebbets Field and the Polo Grounds could reveal ships in New York harbor at night, the Yankees elected not to proceed with the construction of a lighting system at the Stadium. But MacPhail moved ahead with the installation, and the first night game took place on May 28, 1946. His finger on the throbbing pulse of postwar consumerism, MacPhail built the first Stadium Club behind the grandstand, with a members-only restaurant and seats going for as much as $150 each. For the first time, too, MacPhail, with visions of being a baseball version of Phineas T. Barnum, staged fashion shows and track-and-field events, all of which helped to set the turnstiles merrily humming. A record 2,265,512 fans, a million more than the Yankees had ever attracted before, flocked to the Stadium. This was a minor miracle, considering that the club didn't perform particularly well.

If MacPhail was visionary about most matters, he was behind the times on the explosive issue of bringing black men into the game. He remained a stubborn holdout, even as Branch Rickey, his antagonist with the Dodgers, was preparing the way for Jackie Robinson to join his club.

The 1946 Yankees were full of familiar faces. DiMaggio rejoined Henrich and Keller in the outfield, giving it that prewar look. The infield, with Gordon at second base and Rizzuto at shortstop, included

Etten at first base. Third base was handled by Johnson and Stirnweiss. The major share of the catching fell to Aaron Robinson, who swung from the left side, and the veteran Dickey. Chandler was the top hurler, with a 20–8 year. He was aided by Bill Bevens and the bullpen expert, Johnny Murphy.

But the Yankees were not ready to return to glory. Even DiMaggio experienced a subpar year, as he batted under .300 for the first time in his career. Most of the bats creaked from lack of use, causing the club to trail the Red Sox (who ended a pennant famine of 28 years) by 17 games. It is not easy to accept the fact that the Yankees' third-place finish was partly attributable to trouble in the front office. But it was a contributing factor. Bothered by a rebellious gall bladder, McCarthy was bothered even more by MacPhail. He couldn't stand MacPhail—and the feeling was mutual. McCarthy had had a free hand under

Cookie Lavagetto is still dazed from the events of the day before when his pinch hit in the ninth inning of the fourth 1947 World Series game ended Bill Bevens's chances for a no-hitter. Bevens seems to have recovered.

On May 28, 1946, the Yankees played their inaugural
night game at Yankee Stadium; nearly 50,000 fans
attended. The evening also marked Bill Dickey's first
home appearance as Yankees manager. Unfortunately, the
Bombers lost 2–1 to the Washington Senators.

Ruppert and Barrow. But with both of these men gone, he had to deal with the abrasive MacPhail. And it didn't work out.

Thirty-five games into the season (the Yankees won 22 of them), McCarthy announced that he was resigning and would return to his farm near Buffalo, New York. The newspapers recited McCarthy's accomplishments: he'd won more games—1460—than any Yankee manager in his 15 years at the helm, while winning eight pennants and seven world titles. To assuage the hurt of Yankees fans, MacPhail named the thirty-nine-year-old Dickey, at the end of his active career, as the successor to McCarthy. Dickey, the longtime roommate of Gehrig, was popular and knowledgable, but he turned out to lack the stomach for on-field leadership. By September he'd had enough of the job and quit. In the final weeks of a chaotic year, coach Johnny Neun took over the managerial reins. Three New York managers in one season was a record, albeit a discordant one.

However, the year could not be counted as a total disaster, for two new players were added to the scene. Vic Raschi, a right-handed pitcher from the Pacific Coast League, joined the cast late in the year, in time to pitch in two games. He would ultimately become one of the fine hurlers of his era.

The other late-season addition was a young man named Lawrence Peter "Yogi" Berra. A veteran of the Normandy invasion in World War II, Yogi Berra may have been the most identifiable Yankee since the Babe. To look at him, with his happily homely face, a gap between his front teeth, and a body only slightly higher than a fire plug, was to provoke smiles of pleasure in anyone around him. He also proved to be a kind, decent fellow with no apparent large ego in an ego-driven business. He also possessed a potent southpaw swing that was made to order for the Stadium's right-

field porch. When he opened his mouth, Berra enriched the language with unending pearls of malaprop wisdom. No doubt, once the writers had tuned in to some of his inadvertent maxims— "It ain't over 'til it's over," "It's deja vu all over again"—they worked diligently to put other words into his mouth. It was only fair game. But none of it was malicious. It was all good, clean fun and typical of Berra. It's possible that Yogi earned his universal appeal more for his sayings than for his superb two decades in the Yankee batting order as both outfielder and catcher. But that assessment would be doing this Yankee a grave disservice, for he was truly one of the greatest of all Bronx Bombers.

In the winter of 1946 the Yankees further fortified their pitching corps by dealing for Allie Reynolds, a Cleveland right-hander. An ugly rumor had persisted about Reynolds, who, like most players of Indian lineage, was known by the uninspired nickname of "Chief." The rumor insisted that when the chips were down, or the game was on the line, Reynolds did not usually rise to the occasion. Whatever the source of the story, when Yankee fans heard of the trade for the capable Joe Gordon, they didn't take kindly to it. However, in swift order Allie became half of the best right-handed pitching tandem— along with Raschi—that the Yankees had had in years. Over the next eight seasons Allie never posted a losing docket. And in World Series play he was almost as unbeatable as were his predecessors Lefty Gomez and Herb Pennock. To round out the changes in 1947, George McQuinn, always a steady hand at first base, was acquired to take over that position.

After the three-manager year of 1946, the Yankees settled on Stanley "Bucky" Harris as their new leader. Harris had spent a lifetime in the game, after a youth in Port Jervis, New York. In 1924, when Bucky was

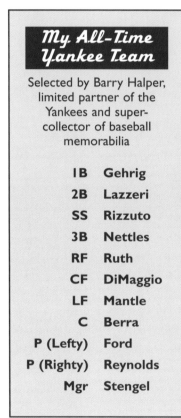

My All-Time Yankee Team

Selected by Barry Halper, limited partner of the Yankees and super-collector of baseball memorabilia

1B	Gehrig
2B	Lazzeri
SS	Rizzuto
3B	Nettles
RF	Ruth
CF	DiMaggio
LF	Mantle
C	Berra
P (Lefty)	Ford
P (Righty)	Reynolds
Mgr	Stengel

only twenty-seven years old, owner Clark Griffith of the Washington Senators plucked him out of his infield ranks and made him the "boy wonder manager" of the club. Harris led Washington to a seven-game World Series triumph over the Giants that year, establishing him as something of a genius. He even connected for two homers in that Series. The Senators won the American League flag again in 1925 but lost the World Series to Pittsburgh, again in seven games.

Subsequently, Harris managed the Tigers, Red Sox, and Phillies, always with an easy, affable manner. Coming to the Yankees at the age of fifty-one, he was in command of a team that was set to trample on the rest of the American League.

On a Sunday in April of 1947, another watershed moment in Yankee annals took place at the Stadium, when a debilitated and almost unrecognizable Babe journeyed from Florida for a day in his honor. Suffering from a painful tumor affecting his larynx, the man who had rescued baseball from the Stygian gloom of the Black Sox scandal struggled through a brief speech before a packed house. His voice was hoarse and the sad croak brought tears to the eyes of thousands.

"The only real game, I think, is baseball," said the Babe. "You've got to start from way down, when you're six or seven years old . . . you've got to let it grow up with you, and if you're successful and try hard enough, you're bound to come out on top."

In another year the Babe would be gone forever.

The game's greatest icon had said farewell. But a new, blazing icon emerged that same year in Brooklyn's Jackie Robinson. Subduing his private rage and playing with controlled fury, Robinson smashed baseball's color barrier with an all-around talent that could dominate a ball game. Since he played in the National League, Robinson didn't get to face the Yankees until that fall in the World Series. But the Yankees heard enough about him to realize that this man's presence would change the sport. While other teams would quickly follow suit and add black players to their rosters, the Yankees remained stuck in a time warp as they continued to reject the potential of black athletes. It would be another six years before the Yankees finally signed a black man to play for them.

A revivified Yankee club, led by the laid-back Harris and aided immeasurably by a new bullpen specialist, Joe Page, had little trouble capturing the American League pennant in 1947. They showed the way to Detroit by 12 games and were never in jeopardy. At one point they won 19 straight games. Of the team's 97 wins, Page corraled 14 victories while saving 17 games, in 54 appearances. Page never seemed to take life too seriously, a prime ingredient for a relief man. Left-handed and hard-living, Joe Page was a tonic for DiMaggio, often bringing a smile to Joe's face. DiMaggio rebounded for a fine year, winning the Most Valuable Player Award for the third time, while others, like Rizzuto and Henrich, also experienced comeback years. Reynolds, now called Super Chief, had his customary good season with 19 victories, while a new arrival, Connecticut Yankee Frank Shea, contributed 14 wins against only five losses.

The late A. Bartlett Giamatti, baseball's seventh commissioner, once said that "baseball is designed to break your heart . . . it's a reminder of how slight and fragile are the circumstances that exalt one group of human beings over another." The eloquent Giamatti might have had the 1947 World Series between the Yankees and the Dodgers in mind.

To begin with, there was a level of excitement surrounding this fall classic that exceeded almost all others that had gone before. Some good reasons can be offered. Was it the presence of the dramatic Robinson, or the singular role of DiMaggio? Was it the heat generated by the excellent lineups fielded by the interborough rivals? Was it the simmering hostility between MacPhail and Rickey, which had led to the one-year suspension of Dodger manager Durocher? Or was it that baseball had now settled into its postwar posture, with New Yorkers of all backgrounds relishing the chance to release their emotions?

Whatever the cause, this reunion of the Dodgers and Yankees in the Series produced one of the most exciting postseason set of games ever staged, and, in the process, underlined the validity of Giamatti's words.

The Series was ultimately captured by the Yankees in seven turbulent games. The contests were seen on television for the first time, although on most sets the picture was murky. Over two million dollars came in at the gate, a record, and each game at the Stadium and antiquated Ebbets Field drew packed houses.

The first game, played at Yankee Stadium, was going the Dodgers' way until the Yankees exploded for five runs in the fifth inning. The twenty-one-year-old right-hander Ralph Branca, a 20-game winner that year, had retired the first 12 Yankee hitters, then the bottom fell out for him. The Yankees took the game, 5–3.

"DiMaggio started the inning with an infield hit to deep short and my inexperience hurt me because I started pitching in a hurry," Branca told writer Peter Golenbock. "I was grabbing the ball and throwing it and not taking my time."

In the second game the Yankees bombed Dodger pitchers for 15 hits in a 10–3 victory. Everyone but Berra joined in the attack, as Reynolds pitched the entire nine innings. With Brooklyn rooters on the verge of nervous collapse, the Dodgers reversed things in the third game with a 9–8 victory at Ebbets Field. A six-run second inning nourished the Dodgers in a game that went three hours and five minutes, the longest Series game played to date. Hugh Casey, still surviving in the Brooklyn bullpen, was the winning pitcher, gaining a measure of revenge for the doleful events of 1941.

But it was the fourth game at Ebbets Field

that produced a level of melodramatics rarely seen in any championship sports event. By the ninth inning of this game, the Yankees' Bill Bevens, unsung for most of his career, was nursing a precarious 2–1 lead, in what passed for a no-hitter. He had kept the bases clogged with eight walks through eight innings. But he was still bidding for Series immortality. Dodger fans had learned to tolerate World Series misadventures—Bill Wambsganss's unassisted triple play for Cleveland against Brooklyn in 1920 and Owen's missed third strike on Henrich in 1941. Now they anticipated a third indignity at Bevens's hand.

To start the last of the ninth Bruce Edwards flied out. Furillo then worked Bevens for a walk, the ninth for Brooklyn. McQuinn grabbed Johnny Jorgensen's foul pop for the second out, putting Bevens on the brink of the oddest no-hitter in Series history. But Burt Shotton, the bespectacled favorite of Mr. Rickey, who became Brooklyn's manager following the tumult over Durocher, began to improvise. He sent Al Gionfriddo, just another roster player on the Dodgers, in to run for Furillo, and Pete Reiser, despite a broken bone in his ankle, was chosen to pinch-hit for pitcher Casey. Plagued by ill luck that deprived him of recognition as one of the game's premier players, Reiser was

Two days after Cookie Lavagetto's heroics, another part-time player, Al Gionfriddo, secured his own place in World Series history. After a long, weaving run he stuck his glove above the bullpen fence and converted a three-run homer hit by Joe DiMaggio into an out. The Dodgers won the game 8–6, extending the 1947 Series to a seventh game.

Gionfriddo's miraculous catch has prompted the only photographed show of emotion by the usually stoic DiMaggio. When asked how he maintained his poise on the field, he replied, "I am a ball-player, not an actor."

field. It was much too high for Henrich to catch. "Those were a few seconds I could have lived without," Henrich said later. As the ball bounced crazily off the wall, Gionfriddo and Miksis scampered around the bases. As the tying and winning runs came home on the first and only Brooklyn hit of the afternoon, Ebbets Field turned into a madhouse. Bevens had lost his no-hitter and the Series was all tied up at two games each. An ironic footnote to this scenario was that Bevens never pitched in a regular season big league game again, while the sudden hero Lavagetto never batted again in a regular season game.

The Yankees had always been enterprising in tamping down premature celebrations in Brooklyn. In the next game they performed their magic again by defeating the Dodgers, 2–1, behind Shea. Shotton tried to replicate the ending of the fourth game by sending up Lavagetto in the ninth inning with two out and a runner on base. But this time Cookie wasn't up to the task of saving Brooklyn. He struck out, even as Henrich, standing close to DiMaggio in the outfield, heard Joe say, "For Christ's sake, say a prayer." After the game was over, DiMaggio conceded that he'd been praying. "I just wasn't sure it was getting through," he said.

But the Dodgers weren't ready to throw in the towel. In game six, before 74,065 at Yankee Stadium (the largest Series crowd in history), the Dodgers took a lead of 8–5 into the bottom of the sixth inning. With two out and two Yankees on the bases, DiMaggio, with two Series homers already under his belt, tagged one some 415 feet, within inches of the left field visitor's bullpen. This time the irrepressible Gionfriddo,

still regarded by Bucky Harris as a potent threat. When Gionfriddo proceeded to steal second base, that left first base open. In defiance of baseball orthodoxy, Harris ordered Bevens to walk Reiser, thus putting the winning run on base.

"He can still swing that bat," explained Harris, rationalizing the strategy.

Hardly able to run, Reiser was replaced at first by Eddie Miksis. But Shotton was not through making his chess moves. This time he pointed in the dugout to Harry "Cookie" Lavagetto. "Go up there for Stanky," commanded Shotton. To some this seemed foolhardy, for Stanky had the reputation of being an excellent contact hitter. But within a few precious seconds, Shotton had turned into an unmitigated sorcerer. With one strike against him after a late swing, Lavagetto, at thirty-four years old and slightly over the hill, ripped the next pitch high and far to right

Bon vivant Dan Topping, on the left, was co-owner of the Yankees for 20 years, beginning in 1945, and presided over 15 pennants and 10 world championships. A large degree of that success can be attributed to Ed Barrow, whom Lou Gehrig called ". . . the builder of baseball's greatest empire." Barrow was named Yankees' general manager late in 1920; three years later the New Yorkers claimed their first world championship.

sent into the game only moments before as a defensive replacement, sped to the railing and, with a do-or-die stab, grabbed the ball before it could fall in for a game-tying home run.

Convinced he had a home run, DiMaggio was stunned to see the 5'6" Gionfriddo come up with the catch. As Joe approached second base, he kicked at the dirt, an out-of-character expression of frustration. "In all the years I played with Joe I think that's the only time I ever saw him get mad," Phil Rizzuto said. Wilfrid Sheed regarded Joe's gesture as a "gentle contemplative scuffing of the ground with the foot," which puts Sheed at odds with others on the vehemence of the gesture. When he walked out to his center-field position, DiMaggio was still talking to himself.

The Dodgers held on to win that afternoon, sending the Series into a seventh game. Considering what had already transpired, the last game was anticlimactic. With Page pitching five airtight innings in relief, the Yankees won, 5–2, for their first world title since 1943.

As if there hadn't been enough heart palpitations

for the week, a teary-eyed MacPhail suddenly announced in the Yankees clubhouse during the wild post-Series shivaree that he was selling his one-third interest in the club to Messrs. Topping and Webb. As he shouted out his alcoholic valedictory, MacPhail erased much of the luster of the Yankees victory. But his two co-owners were not saddened in the least. They were astute enough to appreciate MacPhail's contributions during his 33 stormy months. But now they yearned for some quiet time. The first thing they did was to install George Weiss, the chief of Yankee farm operations, as general manager. Weiss was as colorless as MacPhail was flamboyant. He was a Yale man who had earned the nickname of "Lonesome George." But few questioned his baseball acumen. MacPhail went home to his Maryland farm, far from the Bronx and certainly far enough removed from Weiss, who could now run things in a more controlled way.

In June 1948, the Yankees celebrated their twenty-fifth year at Yankee Stadium. A dying Babe Ruth showed up to stamp the epiphanic moment with his presence. For one last time the Babe would hear the roar of a Stadium crowd.

"I'm gone, Joe," he whispered to his 1927 teammate Joe Dugan. Two months later the Babe was dead at fifty-three, and his body was laid out in the rotunda of Yankee Stadium, an edifice that his 42-ounce bat had built. Over 200,000 mourners—Irish, Italians, Jews, blacks, Latinos, Germans, rich and poor—queued up to bid the Babe farewell.

In that same summer of 1948, Weiss didn't get a winner in his first year, even though DiMaggio crashed home 155 runs and the Yankees' three big pitchers—Reynolds, Raschi, and southpaw Eddie Lopat—combined to win 52 games. It didn't prove to be enough, for the American League race that year

On June 1, 1948, Babe Ruth, frail and fatigued, stepped onto the Yankee Stadium grass for the final time. The Babe's appearance was part of the festivities celebrating Yankee Stadium's twenty-fifth anniversary. As usual, he stole the show, with a gravel-voiced salute to baseball and all the young men who played it.

had three teams, including New York, competing until the end. The Yankees were edged out next to the last day, leaving Cleveland to lick the Red Sox—now managed by Joe McCarthy—in a one-game playoff for the pennant. As soon as Cleveland beat the Boston Braves in the World Series, Weiss convened a press conference at New York's 21 Club, ordinarily more famous for its expensive hamburgers than as a venue for startling baseball announcements. But this time Weiss did have something startling to say: Charles Dillon "Casey" Stengel would be the next manager of the Yankees, replacing the dismissed Bucky Harris.

Well along in life at fifty-nine, and carrying the baggage of many failed summers as manager in varied ports, Stengel had earned a reputation as a buffoon. The New York press found it hard to believe that this man, the bandy-legged warrior of the Giants and Dodgers in the 1920s, was being unveiled as a successor to Huggins and McCarthy. Wasn't this the same fellow who over two decades before had crazily circled the bases for an inside-the-park homer against the Yankees in the World Series, causing the humorist Will Rogers to crack, "I never saw a man run faster than that, unless he was running away from the sheriff!"

On August 17, 1948, flags atop Yankee Stadium were at half-staff in tribute to Babe Ruth, who had died the day before. Thousands filed reverently past his bier at the Stadium over the next two days. Yankee fans and Yankee haters alike mourned his passing.

Pennants & Pinstripes *The New York Yankees 1903–2002*

Third baseman Billy Johnson hit .285 and knocked in 95 runs in 1947. When Casey Stengel took over the team in 1949, Johnson bridled under Stengel's platooning. "I believe if you're hitting good it doesn't matter who's pitching," he said.

Wasn't this the same double-talking Casey whose rambling, often slyly caustic phrases, tended to hide his failures as a manager of the lowly Dodgers and Boston Braves? He invented and employed Stengelese, a muddled and garbled form of English, but wasn't that mainly to deflect defeat and win the affection (which it did) of a doting press? Casey's idiosyncratic idiom would one day make its way into the Congressional Record, but at that point his teams had never made it into the winner's circle. A man who loved practical jokes, as long as the jokes weren't on him, Casey was known as the guy who once unleashed a scrawny little bird from under his baseball cap.

Yet, it was acknowledged that Casey was a keen student of the game, with an insight into players' psyches. He also had a remarkable memory for almost everything—except the names of his players. The clowning, as author Donald Honig pointed out, was "a calculated sort of clowning."

Born in Kansas City, Missouri (thus his nickname, joining the K and the C to make Casey), Stengel had started out in life to be a dentist, but he abandoned that profession because he didn't think people wanted to have their teeth pulled out by a southpaw.

In his previous managerial assignments Casey had never been concerned about winning popularity contests among his players, some of whom resented him. He would find, as he started his first season as Yankee chief, that many of the Yankees regarded him as ill-equipped for the job. They shared the feelings of most people around New York that Weiss, who had known Casey well years before, had made a horrendous mistake in hiring the man. But these naysayers would wind up with egg on their faces. In the next twelve years, starting in 1949, he would wave his wand through 10 pennants and 7 world championships.

At his first spring training camp with the Yankees Casey projected a vulnerable image. When he told his players to "line up in size place, alphabetically," the tone was set for his reign. Some of the veterans, like DiMaggio, looked askance at this strange, deeply lined creature. "He's bewildering," said Joe. "He doesn't seem to know what it's all about."

But the doubters would learn that Casey knew much more than they thought he did. In time, he would even earn the flattering nickname, "The Old Professor."

In 1949 Stengel had to contend with a ball club that wasn't quite in the tradition of the transcendent 1927 team. It hardly had an all-star cast. To make matters worse, so many of Casey's personnel wound up on the infirmary list that he might have been forgiven for thinking he was back managing the Braves. Of course, Casey had inherited DiMaggio. But this was an aging DiMaggio. At thirty-four, his body was constantly vulnerable to the pounding of daily performance. His aching heel, full of painful calcium deposits, had caused him to miss the first two months of the cammen—seven—alternated at first base during the year, with Henrich winding up there for 52 games. Berra was shifted to catcher from the outfield, after taking instruction from Dickey about the finer arts of receiving. And the little shortstop Rizzuto became the team's unlikely "iron man" by coming to work every day without first reporting to trainer Gus Mauch. Faced with such a staggering hospital list, Stengel resorted to day-to-day improvising. He shuffled players in and out of the lineup so constantly that he may have forgotten, from one game to the next, who had been penciled in the previous day. Harold Rosenthal, the *Herald Tribune* sportswriter, was the first to describe Stengel's modus operandi as "platooning." The term stuck, just as "push-button manager" became a permanent putdown of Joe McCarthy.

Not having played an inning until late June, DiMaggio woke up one morning, put his rebellious

ABOVE: In 1946, many years before serving a term as president of the American League, Bobby Brown was a rookie shortstop at the Yankees' training camp in St. Petersburg. With Phil Rizzuto standing in his way, Brown switched to third base, and in the 1947 World Series pinch hit three times and collected a single, two doubles, and three runs batted in.

RIGHT: "He doth bestride the narrow world like a colossus," Cassius said of Caesar, and the same could have been said of Joe DiMaggio as he plundered American League pitching during the 1948 season. He hit .320, and led the league with 39 homers and 155 runs batted in. By then his fame had grown so large that he rarely appeared in public places. "It got so that the only place I could relax was at the ballpark," he said. "Being there was like a haven. That was the best place to hide. Nobody could catch me there."

paign. But he rarely complained, choosing to play with pain because he was always concerned about how people would regard him.

Stengel needed Joe, his best player, and he relied on him to tell him the truth about his condition and when he'd be ready to play. DiMaggio may have possessed certain serious character flaws, but he was never a malingerer. To the contrary, he ached to play every day, even when he couldn't.

There were others on the team who also fell victim to injuries and ailments. An astounding number of

foot on the floor, and, for once, there was no pain. By this time the Yankees' season had turned precarious. They had managed to hang in, but they badly needed their big man. With a crucial three-game set coming up with the Red Sox at hostile Fenway Park, DiMaggio told Casey he was ready to play. What Joe accomplished during those three days is what continues to make normally rational people into obsessive baseball fans. "DiMaggio's return had become, day-by-day, an occasion of national drama," David Halberstam wrote in his book, *Summer of '49*. There is no other way of reporting it: DiMaggio powered the Yankees to three straight victories, causing millions to shake their heads in disbelief.

In the first game Joe hit a single and a home run. In the second game he hit two home runs. In the third game he hit his fourth home run in three games. In all, DiMaggio drove in nine runs and scored five times. His bat, which had previously carved the unmatchable 56-game hitting streak, had now added another glowing chapter. In addition, he had cooled off the Red Sox to such an extent that everyone knew that the Yankees and Red Sox would inevitably battle each other to the end of the pennant race. Somehow, the schedule had magically arranged for a climactic pair of games between the two bitter rivals at Yankee Stadium.

So on that last weekend of the season the Red Sox invaded Yankee Stadium to defend their one-game margin over the New Yorkers. All year long the Red Sox had fared well at home. On the road it had been a different matter—and Yankee Stadium was not only "road" but the lair of the indomitable Yankees.

Prior to these two final games the atmosphere in the Boston dugout was not too optimistic. Even Ted Williams suspected that the Yankees derived an edge

A trace of a grin shows on Joe DiMaggio's face as he crosses the plate at Fenway Park on June 30, 1949, registering his fourth home run and ninth run batted in in three games. It was his first appearance of the season after recovering from a heel injury. A Boston writer complained after the second game, "We used up all our adjectives last night." Stengel shook his head and said, "He makes big league baseball look simple. It isn't that simple."

because they would probably deny him any good pitches to hit, since he was the only left-handed slugger in the Sox lineup. Also, it wasn't news to anybody who made a living traveling to ballparks that Yankee Stadium, in September and October, was a place full of mysterious shadows. Williams had been concerned about it for a long while, and so were some of the other Red Sox hitters. "They should turn on the Goddamn lights," Teddy Ballgame would growl. To the Yankees, who had enormous respect for Williams, it was nice to know that he found the Stadium disconcerting.

On the other hand, Stengel relished the chance to play these two games and come out ahead. What a glorious opportunity for the grizzled old guy to show all those detractors what kind of a manager he was. He had his two dominant right-handers, Reynolds and Raschi, set to go. They would face Boston's two best pitchers, Mel Parnell, a southpaw, and Ellis Kinder, a right-hander. Between them they had won 48 games, while losing only 12. They would be a tough matchup for the Yankees. If the final game on Sunday would be decisive, McCarthy felt that Kinder would be able to handle the pressure.

On Saturday, October 1, Yankee Stadium was the place to be. With 69,000 Yankee fans screaming their support, the Yankees came out on top, 5–4, on a home run by Johnny Lindell in the eighth inning. Reynolds held the Red Sox in check until Joe Page could trudge in from the bullpen and wrap up the decision. The two teams were now in a flat-footed tie for first place, setting the stage for the Sunday game, which would decide the pennant.

It was Raschi versus Kinder, with baseball fever in New York at a peak. The crowd that assembled that afternoon hadn't the slightest idea that Kinder had spent a good deal of the night before the game "on the town," which means he'd been drinking pretty hard. He was a throwback to the days when baseball men didn't train very hard and still managed to perform well. In this case, Kinder was, remarkably, up to the task. He gave up a run in the first inning to the Yankees, when Williams, in left field, lost Rizzuto's drive in the sun. The ball fell for a triple and Phil scored on Henrich's infield out. After that, Kinder was untouchable. But so was Raschi.

With the game standing at 1–0 in favor of New York, McCarthy removed an angry Kinder for a pinch

After three lackluster seasons as a starter, Joe Page was sent to the bullpen in 1947 and responded with 14 relief wins and a 2.48 ERA. In the seventh game of the 1947 Series he relieved in the fifth inning and gave up one hit the rest of the way. Eddie Lopat said, "When he came in the other team was dead." The photograph shows Page entering a game in 1949, a year in which his 60 appearances and 13 relief wins were indispensable to the Yankees' pennant drive. Bullpen catcher Charlie Silvera said, "He had a strong arm and a strong heart."

hitter in the eighth inning. With Kinder, who had beaten the Yankees four times during the year, finally out of the game, the Yankees jumped on Parnell and Tex Hughson in the bottom of the inning for four runs, aided by a bloop double by Jerry Coleman. To their credit, the Red Sox fought back in their final at bat. They scored three runs. It made the score close, at 5–3. But Birdie Tebbetts popped out to Henrich for the final out— and the season was over for Boston. The Yankees had won two marvelously tense and exciting games, eating the hearts out of Boston supporters and sending Yankee fans home deliriously happy.

There were many more triumphs to come for Stengel, but this pennant had to be the sweetest of all for him. It was even accomplished in those last two games without a fully healthy DiMaggio, who played with a high fever. If there really was a curse on the Red Sox stemming from the day that Boston let the Babe come to New York, then the Sox had dutifully played out the script, much to the pleasure of Casey.

Brooklyn had survived a scary National League race to emerge on top; they won it on the last day of the season, just as the Yankees had. In a sense, it was just like old home week for Casey, since he had once played for the Dodgers and had also managed them in the years when they had solidified their reputation as "Bums."

As the Yankees prepared to face the Dodgers again in the World Series, both clubs could have been forgiven if they offered the alibi of total exhaustion. That's what a tight-to-the-finish pennant race can do to men. The first eight innings of the opening game at Yankee Stadium buttressed that suspicion. Reynolds totally baffled the Dodgers through the top of the

TOMMY HENRICH

"Old Reliable" Tommy Henrich carried the Yankees during the first three months of the 1949 season, compensating for the absence of DiMaggio. He delivered 18 game-winning hits and 16 homers, 12 of which decided the game's outcome. He also fielded well at first base and in right field. Regarding defense, he made a clear distinction between business and pleasure. "Catching a ball is a pleasure," he said. "But knowing what to do with it after you catch it is a business."

ninth, yielding only two hits and striking out nine, while the prognathic-jawed Don Newcombe, the twenty-three-year-old National League Rookie of the Year, was equally overwhelming in stymying the Yankees through eight innings. Newcombe, the pioneer among black power pitchers, regarded batters as his mortal enemies; the fact that most of these hitters were white men only added to his desire. This sunny afternoon he was pitching the game of his life. Then came the bottom of the ninth with Henrich the first man up. Newcombe let Tommy get ahead in the count, two balls and no strikes. On the next pitch, Henrich pulled Newcombe's fast ball over Carl Furillo's head in right field for a home run. That was it, a 1–0 win for the Yankees, and quick despair for Brooklyn. Old Reliable had finished off Newcombe in as good a game as the Dodger had ever pitched. Reynolds proved to be just a smidgen better.

The next afternoon Preacher Roe, as smart a hillbilly as you could find on a major league roster, dupli-

The first game of the 1949 World Series was a scoreless match between the Yankees and Dodgers until the last of the ninth inning, when Tommy Henrich drilled a Don Newcombe curveball into the lower right-field grandstand. "They didn't call him 'Old Reliable' for nothing," Newcombe said later. "Mr. Handricks," Casey Stengel said. "He was a great player."

cated Reynolds's effort, with a 1–0 triumph over the Yankees. The single run scored on a Gil Hodges single after a Robinson double. The teams then journeyed to Ebbets Field for the third game. But this time apple-cheeked Johnny Mize, obtained late in the year from the Giants, mainly for pinch-hitting chores, did his job to perfection. Inserted in the ninth with the bases loaded, Mize singled, the first of many October pinch hits he would produce under Casey's aegis. The single broke a 1–1 tie and gave the Yankees a victory. In games four and five the Yankees simply outbelted the Dodgers. Newcombe failed in one game, as Bobby Brown, a future president of the American League, hit a bases-loaded triple. In the other game the Yankees

pounded six Brooklyn pitchers early and often for a 10–6 victory. (In coming years, Newcombe kept losing to the Yankees, causing some to accuse him unjustly of failing "in the clutch." His color had more to do with this accusation than reality.)

With the Yankees' Series victory, Casey the Clown had evolved into a baseball Rodin. But he kept his role in proper perspective. "I just get more help now," he said.

By 1950, halfway through the twentieth century, the other Joe McCarthy, this one the Republican Senator from Wisconsin, was dominating the news considerably more than the former Yankee manager who bore the same name. In his frenzied hunt for Reds,

McCarthy told President Harry S. Truman that the State Department had more Communists than the Kremlin. His highly publicized but undocumented search made it virtually impossible to cheer for the despicably named Cincinnati Reds, to dye your hair red, or to spread Russian dressing on your lettuce and tomatoes. The Yankees even stopped flying a red flag to indicate that the team had lost that day (a blue flag signaled victory). "The club had received numerous politically motivated phone calls about the red flag," wrote William Marshall, in his book, *Baseball's Pivotal Era: 1945–1951*.

Such goings-on were part and parcel of the Cold War, which got hotter when Truman sent troops to Korea in the face of the infusion of Soviet-equipped soldiers into the area. In the midst of such turmoil, which disturbed the tranquillity of the country, the apolitical Stengel approached his second year as the Yankees' chief.

This time it was the Detroit club, managed by the former Yankees' third baseman Red Rolfe, that tried to put a dent in New York's winning ways. For more than half of the season the Tigers remained in first place as the Yankees played cat and mouse with them. However, by the end of August, Stengel's men took the lead, ultimately copping the flag by three games over the Tigers.

There were some key additions to the Yankee cause in 1950, chief among them a young pitcher named Edward "Whitey" Ford, as blond as he was cocky, and with a sneaking resemblance to the actor Jimmy Cagney. Nurtured on the sidewalks of New York (East 66th Street in Manhattan), Ford had been signed by the Yankees a few years before for the bargain basement price tag of $7,000. The Red Sox and Dodgers had taken a look at him and decided to pass. At 5'10" and 175 pounds, Ford appeared small on the mound; maybe that had discouraged other teams from signing him. In the minors Ford had posted fine records. But nobody could have anticipated how successful he would be after joining the rotation of Raschi, Reynolds, Lopat, and Tommy Byrne. Ford had a tendency to throw ground balls, which were gobbled up by an infield spark-plugged by Rizzuto. It turned out to be Rizzuto's best year with the Yankees, as he hit .324 and was picked as the American League's Most Valuable Player. Meanwhile, for his half year's toil, Ford went 9–1, as he was helped along by his battery mate Berra, who hit .322 with 24 home runs.

That season also marked two significant developments in the Yankees' chronology. For one, Billy Martin, an infielder with the cockiness of Ford, arrived with the Yankees. Martin would not rate inclusion in any pantheon of Yankee greats. But for the next few years he became a brash, bellicose presence on the field and off it.

The extent to which a manager's success depends upon the skills of his players was addressed by Casey Stengel at the end of the 1949 season, his first with the Yankees, when he said, "I am the same manager I always was, but nowadays I seem to get a little more assistance from my help."

During the bumpy course of the 1949 season, when so many Yankee players were benched with injuries, Phil Rizzuto missed only one game. He played every game in 1950, hit .324 with 200 hits, and won the Most Valuable Player Award. "You want to know the key to our team?" Billy Johnson asked. "It's that little guy there. Without him we're just another team."

In a game against the Indians in 1950, the Yankees put a runner on third with one out in the last of the ninth with the score tied. Phil Rizzuto was the batter and everyone in the ballpark, including Cleveland pitcher Bob Lemon, knew what was coming. Lemon aimed his first pitch at the bill of Rizzuto's cap, but Phil lifted his bat to eye level and bunted perfectly, scoring the winning run. "Only Rizzuto could have bunted that ball," Stengel said.

He had experienced a tough boyhood in California and his aggressiveness and excessive drinking were frequently attributed to that background. He fought with foes, and sometimes with his own teammates. In time he became a favorite of Casey, who felt that Martin got the most out of his talent.

The other development was on the lugubrious side. DiMaggio, at thirty-five, was plagued with injuries to his knees—and at one stage Casey actually benched him for his weak hitting. Joe's resilience was now in question. His .301 average was not up to his usual standard, though he did end up with 32 home runs. Many observers felt DiMaggio might be playing out the string. However, when Joe's bat came alive in September, with a 19-game hitting streak, these same folks had to bite their tongues.

One of the highlights of the season was a day put aside to honor the mellow-voiced Yankees broadcaster, Mel Allen. Mel was a boy who grew up to study law in Alabama, but then surfaced in the camp of the Damn Yankees. Over 50,000 fans showered the popular Allen with gifts and cash. In keeping with his generous persona Mel contributed the money to Columbia University for a Lou Gehrig Scholarship Fund and also for a Babe Ruth Scholarship Fund in Alabama. Allen, who arrived in the Yankees booth in 1939, often told the story of how a dying Gehrig had once confided to him that "your broadcasts have helped to keep me going."

In the World Series of 1950 the Yankees showed no mercy to Philadelphia's Whiz Kids, who had won the National League pennant (the team's first since

1915) by defeating the Dodgers on the final day of the season. Manager Eddie Sawyer, a well-educated man who taught biology in the off-season at his alma mater, Ithaca College, had handled his youthful up-starts (average age: twenty-seven) superbly. But when they faced the Yankees they were dead tired from the rigors of a tense pennant race. Not even the surprise opening game pitcher, Jim Konstanty, who relieved all year for Sawyer, could faze the New Yorkers. The Yankees took four straight from the Phillies, limiting the Whiz Kids to five runs and 26 hits. DiMaggio's home run in the tenth inning of the sec-ond game accounted for a 2–1 Yankees victory, also serving notice that his bat was not moribund.

But as the 1951 season got under way, it was clear that DiMaggio had seen his better days. In spring training he was more gloomy than usual. His legs hurt, his heels hurt, and his pride hurt. Then, when the sea-son played itself out, his overall performance—12 homers, 71 RBIs, and a .263 average—was proof that his preseason melan-choly was justifiable.

In spite of DiMaggio's de-bilities, and his unease with Stengel, the Yankees still man-aged to march on to their third consecutive flag. Most of the way they had stiff competition from Cleveland, which boasted one of the league's best pitching staffs in history. Rapid Robert Feller won 22, Mike Garcia won 20, as did Early Wynn, and Bob Lemon was hardly a slouch, with 17 victories. But with all of that pitching, the Indians still couldn't make it to the top. The Yankees put the pressure on in September and led Cleveland at the end by five games.

Overshadowing New York's victory was the re-tirement of DiMaggio. The Yankees had wanted Joe to stay on but his timing, always impeccable in the past, caused him to make another crucial decision about the rest of his life. All 116 games that he had played in in 1951 were painful efforts. "It hurt him just to get in and out of taxicabs," said Phil Rizzuto. So refusing to accede to sentiment and the substantial raise offered to him by the Yankees, the thirty-seven-year-old DiMaggio bid farewell to his sport. In the past, when the Babe's powers had diminished, there was Lou, and when Lou became terminally ill, there was Joe. Now, waiting in the wings was the nineteen-year-old kid named Mickey Charles Mantle.

Mantle had been signed by the prescient Yankees scout Tom Greenwade for $1,000 in 1949. Soon he would domi-nate the hopes and dreams of a postwar generation of Yankees fans. Born in Spavinaw, Okla-homa, Mantle weighed in at 200 pounds and was six feet tall. His muscles bulged like pontoons and his legs ap-peared as sturdy as mighty oaks. His grin was as wide as the Grand Canyon and his face "was as open as the part of America that he came from," wrote the late Leonard Shecter. Mickey's dad, Mutt, had lived for baseball, so he named his son Mickey after Gordon Stanley "Mickey" Cochrane, the fiery Hall of Fame catcher for the Philadelphia Athletics and the Detroit Tigers. Not lacking in ingenuity, Mutt also raised his blue-eyed boy to hit from both sides of the plate.

After Mantle had jumped from Class C to the Yankees, in no time at all he was being hailed as the successor to DiMaggio. This was before he had even faced an enemy pitcher in Yankee Stadium. Casey took one squinty look at Mickey and announced "he can hit over buildings." Other admirers said that when Mickey "hits the ball it even sounds different."

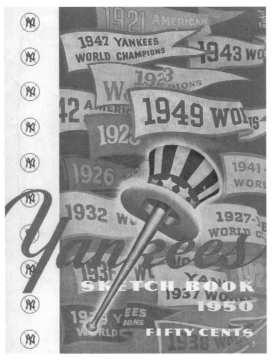

The first Yankee yearbook, called a Sketch Book in 1950, displayed the world championship flags won by the team's illustrious predecessors.

In one of those intriguing coincidences that have marked big league baseball, Willie Mays, another wunderkind of a center fielder, had reported that same year to the New York Giants. It wasn't long before Yankees and Giants fans heatedly debated who was better, Mickey or Willie—and Dodgers fans threw their own nominee, Duke Snider, into the cauldron.

That first year Mickey's immediate canonization suffered a slight hitch. In midsummer, succumbing to the pressure and his own doubts about his ability to play in the majors, Mickey was sent back to Kansas City for a decompression session in the minors. Not only was Mickey battling the demons of overhype, but his young father was also dying of Hodgkin's disease. Within a short time, Mickey was again with the Yankees, ready to become Ruth and DiMaggio all wrapped into one guy called Mantle. Mickey was sent to right field, while DiMaggio stayed in center.

While the Yankees and their fans responded to the dramatic ups and downs of Mantle, another Oklahoman, Allie Reynolds, finally put to rest—if he really ever had to—those ugly rumors that he lacked heart. Within a span of ten weeks Reynolds pitched two no-hitters. The first was against Cleveland in July, the second against the Red Sox in September, in front of 40,000 spectators. Only Johnny Vander Meer, the Cincinnati blazeballer, had ever pitched two no-hitters in one year—and Vander Meer's feat in 1938 came back-to-back, a record that has never been equaled.

Allie's second no-hitter was particularly special because he did it without the cooperation of his normally dependable catcher, Berra. With two out in the top of the ninth inning and his no-hitter on the line, Reynolds faced Ted Williams. The crowd thrilled to such a dramatic confrontation. Ted watched the first

In 25 preseason games in 1951, Mickey Mantle hit .402, belted nine homers, many of them Homeric, and drove in 32 runs. But Casey Stengel was uncertain where to play him. He told a group of reporters, "He definitely ain't a shortstop, and he ain't an outfielder yet. You writers did this to me. I gotta bring him into New York." Mickey began the season in right field in the same year that Willie Mays arrived with the Giants.

The first few weeks of Mickey Mantle's rookie season in 1951 were a nightmare of strikeouts and frustration. He's seen in this photograph returning to the dugout after fanning in a game against the White Sox. After a brief stay in Kansas City, Mantle returned to the Yankees in August and put on number 7. He gradually sharpened his outfielding skills, and in 1952, with Joe DiMaggio in retirement, moved to center field. He told a reporter, "I've still got so much to learn it scares me."

pitch go by for a strike. On the second delivery Williams's bat produced an innocent-appearing foul pop behind home plate. Yogi seemed to have it in sight all the way. But as he stuck out his big mitt, the ball plunked off the end of Yogi's glove. The crowd emitted a collective sigh that could have been heard all the way to Times Square. But Reynolds remained the coolest man in the park. He rushed over to Yogi to lend him moral support. "Don't worry, we'll get him again," the pitcher said reassuringly, though perhaps not totally believing his own words.

On the next pitch, it was deja vu all over again, as Yogi himself might have commented. Williams swung, and another towering foul rose over Yogi's head. They

insist there are no second acts in American life but Yogi defied that hoary maxim. He surrounded the ball, then hugged it firmly in his catcher's mitt, providing a Pearl White finish to Reynolds's second no-hitter. Later Allie confessed that he'd thrown nothing but fast balls to Ted, who was reputed to eat them for breakfast. "It gave me a terrific charge to do that," he said. "Each pitch had to be more unexpected than the one just ahead of it."

Notwithstanding the Yankees' ever-glorious home run tradition, the single home run that seized the attention of millions in 1951 was not hit by a Yankee. It was the handiwork of the Giants' Bobby Thomson, who brought heartaches to Brooklyn

ABOVE LEFT: "Feller had a good fastball," Eddie Lopat said, "but on a given day for three, four innings Allie Reynolds could throw the ball harder than anyone I ever saw." Reynolds was a mainstay starting pitcher, but also worked unselfishly from the bullpen when needed. He won seven World Series games in his career, saved four more, and in four October showdowns with the Dodgers limited Jackie Robinson, Gil Hodges, Roy Campanella, and Duke Snider to a combined average of .124.

ABOVE RIGHT: The Yankees acquired Eddie Lopat in 1948. He was nicknamed "the Junk Man" due to his repertoire of slow, slower, and slowest curves, screwballs, and sliders. He was most effective against free-swinging power hitters. Slugger Walt Dropo said, "I like to see them go up there and try to figure out what Eddie Lopat is doing to them." In 1951, Lopat registered his best record: 21 wins and a 2.91 ERA.

LEFT: Amiable Yogi Berra dreaded mound conferences with Vic Raschi. Raschi's greeting was usually on the order of "Gimme the damn ball and get the hell out of here." He won 98 games from 1948 to 1952, then dropped to 13 wins in 1953, at which point George Weiss cut his salary by 25%. When Raschi protested, Weiss traded him to the Cardinals. Casey Stengel was distressed by the loss of his big right-hander. He told a reporter that to win one big game his choice was Raschi.

homes with his ninth-inning blast off a stunned Ralph Branca, to capture the decisive third game of the National League playoff. That blow transcended the cold statistics of the game's record books to enter the realm of folklore. To this day millions will remind you of where they were and what they were doing when Bobby connected. Though there were only 34,000 at the Polo Grounds at the time, millions imagine they were there to witness Thomson's "shot heard 'round the world."

Yes, the World Series *did* take place that autumn. But after Bobby's homer everything was anticlimactic. The Giants managed to carry their late-season magic through the first Series game against the Yankees at Yankee Stadium. Monte Irvin, who might have been baseball's first black player if Branch Rickey had chosen differently, went on a tear, cracking a triple and three singles and stealing home in the first inning

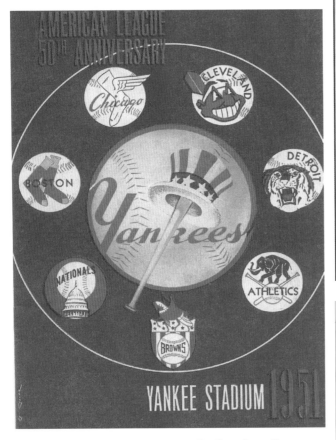

The 1951 scorecard sold at Yankee Stadium for a dime. Starting lineups were imprinted the night before in the centerfold, which often resulted in crossed-out names and scribbled entries.

Scouting Report

Pennant-contending teams routinely assign scouts late in the season to follow likely World Series opponents and detail their strengths and weaknesses. In 1951, the Brooklyn Dodgers, seemingly on their way to the National League flag, sent scout and former infielder Andy High to spy on the Yankees over the last month of the campaign. When the Giants' Bobby Thomson derailed Brooklyn's pennant express, the Dodgers turned High's report over to the Giants, a surprising gesture given the teams' mutual distaste.

After the World Series the report was acquired by *Life* magazine reporter Clay Felker. Here are some excerpts from High's "skinny." Mantle: "Play him straight away and deep. Wrist action is not good. Left-handed pitchers can pitch him overhand fastballs inside for a strike." Berra: "Don't throw him a strike on the first ball. He is a good hitter and you can't throw him two similar pitches in succession." Rizzuto: "Very good fielder. He can push, bunt, or hit the low pitch."

The most damning commentary, however, was reserved for the aging DiMaggio: "He can't run and won't bunt. His reflexes are slow and he can't pull a good fastball at all." Joe did struggle in the first four games of the Series, but in the fifth game he belted a home run at the Polo Grounds, sparking a Yankee victory.

Close friends of DiMaggio felt the report confirmed Joe's inclination to retire. "I'm just not Joe DiMaggio any more," he said.

against Reynolds. It helped to add up to a Giants triumph. Would Durocher, the Giants' manager, who had played with the Babe and Lou, be able to pull off another miracle?

The Yankees' response was a second game win behind Lopat, the soft-balling southpaw, tying the Series at one game each. Again, the Giants surprised the Yankees by besting Raschi in the third game. The contest was highlighted by the Giants' combative second baseman, Eddie Stanky, "dropkicking" the ball out of the glove of Rizzuto. This controversial maneuver set off a big inning for the Giants, who moved ahead of the Yankees in the Series.

But from that point on the Yankees' hitters took charge. DiMaggio homered, in a last frisson of glory, to burnish a Yankee victory in game four. The final two games featured the thunder of Yankee bats and the general failure of Durocher's pitchers. The year, thus, belonged to Bobby Thomson—but the world championship went to the Yankees. However, it was a painful moment in the second game that would have a lasting effect on both the Yankees and Mantle. As Mickey chased a fly ball into right center field—as

DiMaggio looked on—he stepped into a drain cover. (Incidentally, the ball was hit by Willie Mays, Mickey's effervescent rival.) His right knee was sprained so badly that Mantle was forced to sit out the rest of the Series. It marked the first of a sad clutch of leg injuries that damaged Mantle's body and dampened his spirit.

The Supreme Commander of the Allied Forces in Europe in World War II, Dwight David Eisenhower, known to songwriter Irving Berlin and the world as Ike, was elected president of the United States in 1952. Rocky Marciano, from Brockton, Massachusetts, upended Jersey Joe Walcott that year to become heavyweight champion of the world. But the more

The clubhouses at the Polo Grounds were located in a building set between the distant center-field bleachers. Players entering and exiting did so within easy voice range of the spectators. Phil Rizzuto is seen here, leading his teammates onto the field prior to the start of the third 1951 World Series contest. Phil's grin, as well as Hank Bauer's, suggest that some zesty suggestions were being offered by Giants' fans that day.

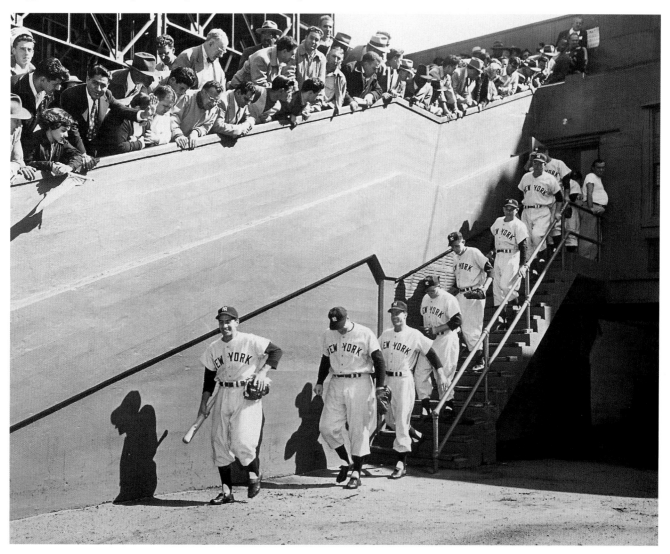

things change, the more they stay the same: in baseball, the Yankees won the American League flag for the fourth straight time under Stengel.

Before the 1952 campaign got under way Stengel knew it wasn't going to be easy. DiMaggio was history and the new kid in town, Mantle, was cavorting in Joe's center-field spot. But by midseason Mickey's bat was banging out tape measure home runs, to the astonishment of all—especially the New York press. Mantle's nightclub-prowling sidekick, Billy Martin, had made his claim for squatter's rights to second base. Gone from the scene were Jerry Coleman and the accomplished pinch hitter and fill-in man, Bobby

Brown. Both of them had gone into military service as a result of America's involvement in war-torn Korea. Gil McDougald took over third base, possibly the best guardian of that position since Red Rolfe left some years before to coach the baseball team at Dartmouth, his alma mater.

Led by Mantle, the outfield was solid. Gene Woodling, from Akron, Ohio, a fine defensive player and a steady hitter, was a .300 batter with great competitive instincts, and the tough former marine, Hank Bauer, could play on anybody's ball club. Berra had become a tower of strength behind the plate, handling a superior staff of Reynolds, Raschi, Johnny Sain (for-

In the fourth game of the 1951 World Series, played at the Polo Grounds, Joe DiMaggio slugged the last home run of his career, a two-run shot that helped the Yankees beat the Giants and tie the Series at two games apiece. He announced his retirement several weeks later. "Right after the 1951 season I realized I couldn't take it any longer," he said. "I could not recuperate from things as quickly as I did when I was younger."

merly of the "Spahn and Saik and pray for rain" duo of the Boston Braves), and Lopat. Still in service at the time was Ford.

The Indians may have had three 20-game winners in Lemon, Wynn, and Mike Garcia but the Yankees still topped them in the American League dogfight. At the end the New Yorkers were two games in front of the frustrated Clevelanders, whose manager, Al Lopez, a Hall of Fame catcher, seemingly made a career out of finishing as a runner-up to Casey.

It is worth mentioning here that Reynolds remains one of the unsung pitchers of any era. At the age of thirty-seven (he might possibly have been older, just as Tommy Henrich was probably older than the age listed in the record books), the Superchief was better than ever. He won 20 games and lost 8, becoming the oldest pitcher in over 30 years to capture 20 games. He also led his league in ERA, shutouts, and strikeouts. And just in case anyone thought he wasn't contributing enough, Allie would go down to the bullpen when late-inning help was needed. Eddie Lopat once told Reynolds he shouldn't volunteer for such duty, but Allie did it anyway, saving six games in 1952.

When the Yankees met the Dodgers again in the World Series, Reynolds was primed, as usual, to take care of the Boys of Summer (which is what the Dodgers were named a few years later by writer Roger Kahn). But after Allie lost the opening game at Ebbets Field, Brooklyn rooters, long accustomed to their dirge of defeat—"Wait 'Til Next Year"—began to think that "next year" had finally arrived.

However, the enterprising Stengel was not about to throw in the towel at this point. Using Johnny Mize

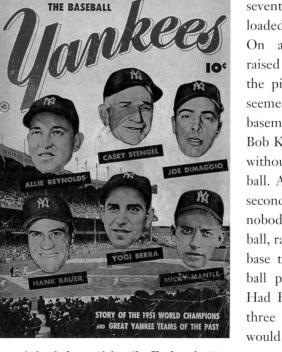

A comic book dramatizing the Yankees' 1951 championship year was published shortly after the season ended.

both as a pinch hitter and substitute for Joe Collins at first base (Johnny hit three homers in the Series), Casey rallied his troops from a one game deficit to sweep the last two games. Both of those games were staged at Ebbets Field, with Reynolds winning the decisive seventh game in relief of Lopat.

The Yankees won their fourth straight world title to match the 1936–1939 club, but this did not come without tremors of the heart. In the last game, with the Yankees in front, 4–2, in the seventh inning, the Dodgers loaded the bases with two out. On a 3–2 count, Robinson raised a tantalizing pop fly near the pitcher's mound. For what seemed like an eternity, first baseman Collins and pitcher Bob Kuzava stared up at the sky without moving to catch the ball. At the last millimeter of a second, Martin, realizing that nobody was going to catch the ball, raced in madly from second base to grab it just before the ball plunked into the ground. Had Billy not made the catch, three Dodgers almost certainly would have come around to score, thus putting Brooklyn into the lead. As it turned out, Martin's take-charge lunge, with his cap flying off à la Willie Mays, saved the game and the Series for New York.

Following the game, as the Yankees celebrated and the recidivist Dodgers sulked, Martin explained that "no one was calling me off the ball . . . I didn't think my play was so much until I got to the dugout and they were all slapping me on the back . . . then, when I saw the films of the play, I realized how far I had come."

The Dead End Kid from the West Coast had always had a special appeal to Casey. Now the Old Man couldn't find words enough to extol him.

ABOVE LEFT: The Yankees paid the Oakland Oaks $65,000 for two players in 1950: Jackie Jensen and a throw-in named Billy Martin. "I suppose if you play to win all the time you can't exactly be a sweet guy," Martin said, in defense of his bellicose playing style. Casey Stengel always liked Billy. "That fresh kid has got it here in his heart where it counts," he said.

ABOVE RIGHT: Billy Martin making the sensational catch in the seventh game of the 1952 World Series that averted an embarrassing disaster for the Yankees. A year later he was a larger thorn in the Dodgers' side, hitting safely 12 times, with two homers, two triples, eight runs batted in, a .500 average, and the Series-winning hit in the sixth game. "If you get Mantle and Berra out," Roy Campanella said, "and Martin comes up and hits a little bloop that beats you, that's tough."

LEFT: Johnny Mize, "the Big Cat," had six hits in the 1952 World Series, three of which were home runs. He was thirty-nine years old at the time, three years older than he was when Leo Durocher pronounced him too old and too slow and put him on waivers. He won home run titles for both the Cardinals and the Giants during his National League years, and ended his career with a lifetime .312 average.

My All-Time Yankee Team

Selected by Yogi Berra, Hall of Fame Yankee
("Only players I played with")

1B   Skowron
"Had real good power, especially the other way."

2B   Martin/Richardson/Coleman
"Billy and Bobby, geez, they were real good. Jerry Coleman helped us win five World Series in a row, so how can I leave him off?"

SS   Rizzuto
"Phil and Pee Wee Reese were as good as they come."

3B   Clete Boyer/Gil McDougald/ Bobby Brown
"Clete was the best fielder. Gil could play everywhere and Bobby got a lot of big hits."

RF   Tommy Henrich/Roger Maris/ Hank Bauer
"Tommy, a great guy, great teammate, and great in the clutch. Maris a better all-around player than he gets credit for. Bauer helped us win a lot of World Series, then he got traded for Maris."

CF   DiMaggio
"Joe Di, who else?"

LF   Mantle
"Mickey."

C   Elston Howard
"He knew how to work with pitchers. A real good guy, a real good friend."

P (Lefty)   Ford
"Whitey was the best!"

P (Righty)   Allie Reynolds/Vic Raschi
"DiMaggio loved playing behind Allie. They both came up kind of late but they were great."

P (Relief)   "Geez, Luis Arroyo, he wasn't bad. Spec Shea, Joe Page. We had some good ones."

Mgr   Stengel
"Who else?"

"Picking this team was more painful than my knee replacement."

Yogi Berra is the kid from the wrong side of the tracks who made it as an American folk hero. Like a Dempsey punch or a Ruthian swat, Yogi has become part of the popular culture of America. Yes, he is known for his malaprops ("I never said half the things they said I said"—), but Yogi has also come to stand for integrity and his own incomparable dignity. He has evolved into a symbol of what can be so good about the game. Truth be told, baseball can always use someone without a monstrous ego or a case of distemper. Yogi's humility has stood the test of time. He doesn't need press agents. He's there for all to see and appreciate.

When Yogi first joined the Yankees one unfeeling observer said that he "looks like the bottom man on an unemployed acrobatic team." Equally unkind references compared him to simians and monkeys. "Aw, nobody wins games with their face," was his rebuttal to all demeaning remarks. But, all the while, the squat little fellow (no more than 5'7") was becoming one of the greatest catchers of any era. Once Bill Dickey took Yogi in hand, there was no stopping his progress as a fine defensive receiver. "He taught me his experience," said Yogi about the learning process with Dickey. Ultimately, Yogi passed along his own experience to Elston Howard.

If the Babe, Lou, DiMaggio, and Mantle were all transcendent Yankees, Yogi was the bulwark of 14 World Series teams, and the catcher in 15 All-Star Games. In 1952 he finished fourth in the Most Valuable Player voting and the next year he was second to Cleveland's third baseman, Al Rosen. But in 1951, 1954, and 1955 he was the MVP, an extraordinary accomplishment for a once-awkward player who was bypassed early in his career by the sagacious Branch Rickey. "Berra might have been the most respected player in the game during the period in which he played," wrote Rob Neyer in his book *Baseball Dynasties*.

In the eyes of Stengel, Yogi was "my assistant manager." Casey knew that Yogi had a keen knowledge of the weaknesses of batters and could always be

depended on in a pinch. Stengel was very fond of Yogi. At a time when some of his charges liked to spend the late hours whooping it up at New York's flashy nightclubs, he knew he wouldn't have to go looking for Berra in such locations.

Of all of the well-remembered tales emerging from the Berra catalogue, perhaps the most classic is the one involving Bobby Brown. Bobby and Yogi had roomed together when they played for the Newark Bears. It was not unusual for Brown to burn the midnight oil reading weighty medical textbooks, for he was a medical student at the time. He later became a cardiologist. Night after night, Yogi would watch as Bobby perused his books. Not wishing to disturb his more cerebral buddy, Yogi immersed himself in his own favorite reading matter, comic books. One night, not able to contain his curiosity any longer, Yogi asked Bobby, "Did you finish it?"

"Yep," replied Bobby.

"How did it come out?" Yogi asked, in all innocence.

Notwithstanding his bon mots, Yogi has also been responsible for some of the game's most thoughtful comments. Prior to an All-Star Game, several of Yogi's fellow American Leaguers were mulling over the problem of how to pitch to Stan Musial, an eternal pain in the neck to all hurlers. When it came for Yogi to deliver his opinion, he said, "The trouble with you guys is that you're trying to figure out in ten minutes something nobody has been able to figure out in 15 years."

It took only a few years for Yogi to become one of the most feared hitters in baseball. He quickly won a reputation as the game's best "bad ball hitter," beating out the Cardinals' Ducky Medwick for that honor. The venerable black pitcher, Satchel Paige, who, it is rumored, started his baseball career when Warren Harding was president, declared that the best lefty batter was Ted Williams, and the best righty was DiMaggio. But, Paige added, "The greatest bad ball hitter ever invented was Yogi." Fred Hutchinson, who pitched against Yogi when he was with Detroit, agreed that Yogi was a great bad ball hitter. "But don't ever throw him a *good* one," he added.

In 1949, after Yogi's first good year in New York, he married Carmen Short, an attractive brunette. Joe Garagiola, the catcher and talker, was his best man. When a reporter observed that Carmen was so pretty, while he was such a homely guy, Yogi bristled. "I'm human, ain't I?" he retorted.

Yogi has never been anybody but himself. He's the boy from The Hill in St. Louis who could play any sport you can name—and hooky, too. He never took much to the classroom or schooling. So it must have come as a surprise to him and to millions of Yogiites when a Yogi Berra Museum opened in Montclair, New Jersey, several years ago. At the dedication ceremony at this little jewel box of a museum, Yogi, always in character, said, "Usually when you get one of these you're dead or gone." When he said it his brown eyes shone and a wide smile creased his face.

1953–1962

AT SPRING TRAINING IN 1953 YOU WOULD HAVE HAD TO SEARCH HARD FOR A WRITER WHO DIDN'T THINK THE YANKEES WERE GOING TO WIN AGAIN. THIS PLACED A HEAVY BURDEN ON CASEY, SINCE HE WOULD HAVE PREFERRED THAT THE "EXPERTS" WOULD PICK HIS CLUB FOR LAST PLACE. "WELL," INTONED CASEY, "THERE COMES A TIME IN EVERY MAN'S LIFE AT LEAST ONCE, AND I'VE HAD PLENTY OF THEM . . . IF MANTLE COULD PLAY GREAT I KNOW HE'D BE BETTER THAN LAST YEAR . . . MARTIN HELPED ME MANAGE

the team a lot last year. He made some suggestions I vetoed and that made me look good."

After the writers tried to untangle that typical convoluted Casey oration, they concluded that Stengel was as confident as they were that the Yankees were about to win for the fifth straight time. After all, as Robert Creamer reminds us in his biography of Stengel, Casey really was out to surpass Joe McCarthy, with his four straight with the Yankees, and John McGraw, who had guided the Giants of an earlier time to four straight triumphs.

Within a couple of months, the Yankees moved into first place. At one point Casey's men racked up 18 consecutive wins—one short of the American League record held by the Yankees of 1947 and the White Sox of 1906. The all-time mark was 26 straight set by the Giants of 1916. Fourteen of those victories took place in the West.

But all good things come to an end. Suddenly the Yankees plunged into a nine-game losing streak. And although they kept their spot at the top of the league, Casey went into a funk. "During that streak Casey grew surly with the press," wrote Creamer. "He barred reporters from the clubhouse after games, but paradoxically he was quiet and patient with the players." Of all people, Casey should have been familiar

with slumps. After all, he had managed the lowly Braves and Dodgers in the thirties.

Inevitably, it seems, the Yankees went on to win, by 8½ games over Cleveland. They did it with the help of Whitey Ford, just back from military duty, and the other usual suspects—Raschi, Reynolds, Sain, and Lopat. Curiously, Mantle had only a so-so season, with a .295 average, 21 homers and only 92 runs batted in. Most of the time he seemed bothered by his various leg disabilities, as he participated in just 127 games. One of Mickey's homers, however, was a monstrous blast at Washington's Griffith Stadium off Chuck Stobbs. It was officially recorded at 565 feet, a longitudinal thrust exceeded these days only by Mark McGwire and Sammy Sosa.

Once again, the Dodgers had a chance to upend the Yankees in the World Series. Just how many times could this splendid team of Robinson, Snider, Reese, Campanella, Newcombe, Furillo, Erskine, Reese, Cox, and company lose to the Stengel club? Certainly the Dodgers had come close in previous postseason games, but something always seemed to happen, whether it was a Mize, a Kuzava, or a Billy Martin, to shut the door. In 1953, the Yankees won the first two games, one on a two-run homer by Mantle, then lost the next two. The last two games went to the Yankees, with Reynolds, always such a combative pitcher, winning the decisive game, to give the Yankees a stunning fifth world championship title in a row.

Stengel's favorite bad boy, Martin, turned out to be the hero of the week, as he enjoyed six games that placed him in the same class as such headline-grabbing Series icons as Christy Mathewson, Pepper Martin, the Babe, and Lou. Billy won the last game

OVERLEAF: George Weiss, who served as Yankees' general manger from 1948 to 1960, was admired as the brains behind the dynasty but he was disdained for his penny-pinching approach to player salaries. Allie Reynolds once left a session with Weiss and told a reporter, "We finally got together and I got my raise. But it was like dating a scorpion." Years later a researcher discovered that Weiss received a percentage of any salary decreases he was able to exact.

Bad-ball hitter Yogi Berra was notoriously unselective at bat. Early Wynn said, "One time I bounced a curve six inches in front of the plate and he slammed it for a double." Yogi's answer was, "A bad pitch isn't a bad pitch anymore when you hit it into the seats." No pitcher enjoyed the prospect of facing him. The Dodgers' Clem Labine said, "Yogi has to be the toughest hitter I ever faced in my life."

from harlequin to genius in five easy lessons. Could the Yankees do it again in 1954? Casey, savoring these consecutive championships, thought they could. "These guys are just growing into greatness," he predicted. "We'll win again."

But something happened on the way to six in a row and it turned out to be Cleveland's remarkable pitching staff. Even the redoutable fireballer, Bob Feller, with 13 victories, was just an also-ran on the Indians' staff. Bob Lemon and Early Wynn both had 23 wins, Mike Garcia took 19, and Art Houtteman won 15. The relievers Don Mossi and Ray Narleski were as good as any other tandem in the league. All this added up to a total of 111 victories for the Indians, which was one more than the great Yankees of 1927 had accumulated.

In the face of such dominant Cleveland pitching, Stengel goaded his men all year. He badly wanted to win and also didn't think very highly of manager Al Lopez's team. As the Yankees took on the Indians for a crucial double-header in Cleveland in early September, Casey still thought his team could turn it around. But with the biggest, noisiest crowd in baseball history (86,000) showing up to embrace its team, the Yankees fell twice. That put an end to Casey's hopes for a sixth straight pennant. His team didn't take it very benignly either. As the Yankees ran off the field after the double defeat, several of the players brushed aside the photographers. And Casey, usually so pleased at photo opportunities, shouted that he wanted the door to the locker room shut. In the end, the Yankees did win 103 games, which under normal circumstances would have been enough to win the pennant. With Martin in the service, Rizzuto, at thirty-six, having a subpar year, and

with a ninth-inning single that put the finishing touch on his rampage against the Dodgers' pitchers. He ended up with 12 hits, including two homers, two triples, a double, seven singles, five runs, and eight RBIs. When Billy's adrenaline was put to constructive use he was a tough man to put down.

So the Yankees had five straight flags and five straight World Series victories, transforming Casey

Gene Woodling, Johnny Mize, and Hank Bauer in 1953. Woodling and Bauer both hit over .300 that year, and the forty-year-old Mize hit safely 19 times in 61 pinch-hit appearances to lead the league.

Raschi sold off to the Cardinals after an acrimonious salary dispute with the front office, Casey still managed to keep his team in contention. In this losing year, he may have done his best managing.

The ultimate irony was that the Indians then went to the World Series against the Giants of Leo Durocher, Mays, Irvin, Johnny Antonelli, and an inspired pinch hitter named Dusty Rhodes, and lost it in four straight. Heavily favored, Cleveland couldn't survive Mays's game-saving, over-the-head catch in the first game. Many suspected that the Yankees would have done better, and Casey was part of that group. "Those Indians are nuthin' but a one-shot," Casey growled. He turned out to be correct.

A disappointed Yankees club, with a pitching staff growing old, faced 1955 with some trepidation. But the front office knew this was no time to stand pat. So in the winter of 1954 an 18-player supermarket deal

was arranged that sent outfielder Gene Woodling and a host of others to Baltimore for a handful of players. Two of the men that the Yankees received were right-handers Bob Turley and Don Larsen. Both of them would have a profound impact on the future of the team. If anyone could have predicted what Larsen, a 21-game loser, could do for the Yankees, he would have been laughed at. But Casey seemed to see something in the big guy—even when others saw no there there.

In addition, the Yankees, on the prowl for a slugging first baseman since Gehrig left the picture, elevated Bill "Moose" Skowron to the job. A muscular fellow with football credentials from Purdue, Skowron made Yankee fans forget such obscure names as Dick Kryhoski, Fenton Mole, Don Bollweg, Frank Leja, and others who had aspired to cover first base, but without much success. Along with Mantle and

Gene Woodling

Berra, Skowron gave the Yankees impressive home run punch. Tommy Byrne rejoined the pitching rotation, which was sorely in need of resuscitation.

Perhaps the most significant addition to the Yankees roster in 1955 was a dignified, talented black man from St. Louis, Elston Howard. When he made his appearance as the first African American on the club, Elston was originally ticketed for the outfield. But in time he became one of the finest catchers in the game. It had been almost a decade since Jackie Robinson had broken baseball's infamous color line, but the Yankees had remained intransigent on the issue. Other clubs, aside from Tom Yawkey's Red Sox, the Tigers, and the Phillies, had integrated their rosters, but George Weiss hadn't budged. Weiss had never been a social activist; he had relied on the cynical excuse that the Yankees were a winning ball club *without* the contribution of black men. That was a lame excuse for such inaction, especially when so many black stars had begun to dominate every department of major league play.

ABOVE: **Gene Woodling played for the Yankees from 1949 to 1954 and his timely hits earned him the nickname "New Reliable." During one week in August 1951 he came to bat 23 times and had 17 hits, for a .739 average. He committed one error in 1952, and just one in 1953, playing most of his home games in Yankee Stadium's difficult left field. This photo is from the Yankees' picture pack, a popular souvenir sold at the Stadium during the late forties.**

RIGHT: **"This little fellow with the knickers and the small boy's cap" was how writer Robert Creamer described Edward "Whitey" Ford. The baby-faced southpaw only looked like a high schooler. Pitching coach Jim Turner said he was the oldest twenty-one-year-old he had ever seen. On his return to the Yankees in 1953 after two years in the army, Ford joined Allie Reynolds, Ed Lopat, and Vic Raschi to form what Branch Rickey called ". . . the best balanced pitching staff in the history of baseball."**

The 1953 Yankees, the team that set an unprecedented and unmatched record of five consecutive world championships. LEFT TO RIGHT; front row: Schallock, Ford, Martin, Rizzuto, Berra, Kraly, Crosetti (coach), Stengel (manager), Dickey (coach), Turner (coach), McDougald, Noren, Woodling, and Silvera. Middle row: Mauch (trainer), McDonald, Miranda, Coleman, Kuzava, Miller, Gorman, Renna, Triandos, and Raschi. Back row: Mize, Lopat, Carey, Mantle, Bauer, Houk, Sain, Bollweg, Reynolds, and Collins. The batboys are Carrieri and Manzidelis.

Yankee Stadium in the 1950s

Those with crystal memories of Yankee Stadium in the 1950s recall a much bigger ballpark than today's incarnation. Perhaps it's because we were smaller then, and awed by the towering grandstand crowned with the curving copper frieze. The outfield was a vast sweep of green, extending far beyond the limits created for the renovated ballpark. A Yankees executive told a reporter in 1956, "You must remember that the Stadium is something more than just a ballpark. It's a national monument."

The Yankees dominated the spotlight throughout the decade, but other heroes and events occasionally claimed attention. Sugar Ray Robinson, Rocky Marciano,

Ezzard Charles, and Floyd Patterson battled foes in a boxing ring set up near second base. The New York football Giants won the NFL championship at the Stadium in 1956, then lost it two years later when the Baltimore Colts scored a touchdown in pro football's first sudden-death overtime period. Circuses and rodeos performed on the field during the decade. Throngs of Jehovah's Witnesses held meetings there, and huge assemblies attended sermons by Billy Graham and masses offered by Francis Cardinal Spellman.

Broadcaster Mel Allen referred to the Stadium as simply "the big ballpark." It was the most famous sports arena in the world, and a half century later it still is.

Yankee Stadium looked like this through the 1950s, arguably its most exciting decade ever. In this view, Bob Porterfield is pitching to Cleveland's Dale Mitchell. Mitchell would appear, with historic results, several years later in a Dodgers' uniform.

RIGHT: Bob Turley, seen here pitching in a 1955 game to Cleveland's Al Rosen, won 17 games for the Yanks that season, his first in pinstripes. In 1958 he added a curve to his rocketing fastball and became a dominant pitcher. He had 21 victories, an ERA of 2.97, and in the World Series against the Braves won the fifth game, saved the sixth, and won the seventh. He was named the Series MVP and captured the Cy Young Award. Turley said he ". . . mastered the art of pitching that season."

BELOW: In 1955, the Yankees finally came to their senses regarding black ballplayers and brought up catcher-outfielder Elston Howard. In the 1955 World Series, he hit the first pitch he saw for a home run. With Berra catching, Howard played in the outfield, but preferred catching. "I still like the catching job," he said. "I worry when I play outfield and that affects my hitting." When he became the Yankees' regular catcher in 1961 his batting average improved 103 points.

Stengel, a sixty-nine-year-old man who belonged to another time, noted at once that Howard, so able in other phases of baseball, was slow afoot. "They finally get me a nigger," he growled, in language not uncommon for the dugout and for many American working places, "and they give me one who can't run!" Those who knew Casey intimately, including not a few New York sportswriters sensitive to the nuances of racism, rejected the notion that Stengel was a bigot. They invariably pointed to the fact that Casey had played against blacks years before on the barnstorming circuit. They acknowledged that Casey frequently employed ugly words like "jigaboos" and "jungle bunnies." But they argued that Stengel had always treated Howard with respect. Whatever Casey's true feelings might have been, he often insisted that he'd be pleased to manage an all-black team made up of players like Robinson (who he happened to loathe), Mays, Newcombe, and Larry Doby.

Aside from Stengel's "Negro problem," he had other difficulties in 1955. The old platoonist had to juggle his lineup more than ever, almost from day to day. Injuries to many of his players forced him to rely on Mantle and Berra. Mickey led the league with 37 home runs and though he also led the world in bandages on his knees, this was one year he was relatively untroubled by the injury. Yogi won the Most Valuable Player Award for the third time. In Casey's mind, the durable, uncomplaining Berra was his perfect team player while Mickey, for all of his natural abilities, was a difficult fellow to manage. Stengel always hoped that Mickey would turn out to be his personal monument. But Mickey rejected any kind of father-son relationship, which probably prevented him from realizing his potential as the game's greatest player. In this case, the father (Casey) fumed at Mickey's behavior, while the son (Mickey) continued to kick water coolers and angrily toss bats.

Without a stable everyday lineup, Casey was still able to keep his club in the race. Cleveland was again the chief tormentor—but by the season's end the Yankees, with the help of eight straight victories in September, were in front of the Indians by three games.

As the Yankees came into the World Series against Brooklyn, they were favored to win. The fact that the Dodgers had literally walked off with the National League pennant by 13½ games still didn't seem persuasive with the predictors. After all, the Yankees had drubbed the Dodgers in five World Series since 1941. So why not once more!

Even when Stengel was forced to sit Mantle down in the first two games of the Series at Yankee Stadium after Mickey aggravated an old muscle injury, the Dodgers still failed to take advantage of this break. They lost both games, to Whitey Ford and Tommy Byrne, thus reinforcing the notion that they would never get over their Yankeephobia. But returning home to the Ebbets Field bandbox the Dodgers suddenly came alive, thanks mainly to the long-distance cannonading of Duke Snider, Roy Campanella, and Gil Hodges. They won all three games and led the Series, three games to two. Would this, after all, be the year the Dodgers, winless in every World Series they had ever played in, finally be victorious?

When Ford subdued the Dodgers on a four-hitter in the sixth game at jampacked Yankee Stadium, it looked like the Dodgers were still going to be denied their title. But on October 4, a gorgeous Tuesday for all Brooklynites, the long drought finally came to an end. Johnny Podres, a southpaw from Witherbee, New York, shut out the Yankees, 2–0, yielding eight scattered hits. Podres was fortunate that Mantle was in drydock again, much to Stengel's discomfiture, but he pitched the greatest game of his life.

It was a fortuitous strategic move by Dodgers' manager, Walter Alston, that sealed the verdict against the Yankees, who had not lost a seven-game Series since they were beaten by the Cardinals in 1926. In the sixth inning, with Podres nursing his 2–0 lead, Junior Gilliam was moved by Alston from left field to second base. Sandy Amoros, an unheralded little fellow from Havana, was asked to take over left field. When the first two Yankee batters, Martin and McDougald, reached base safely, a chill of impending doom began to settle over Dodger fans. Would the Yankees thwart the Dodgers yet again?

Podres threw carefully to Berra, the next batter. But being careful with Yogi didn't mean anything, for Yogi, as Podres knew, could make contact with darn near everything. The left-handed Berra then hit Podres's "careful" pitch in a long, opposite field drive down the left-field line. Amoros, who had been directed to play Yogi toward right field, didn't look as if he could catch up with the ball, which was precariously close to the barrier. But catch it he did, right in front of the stands. The key to this play was that

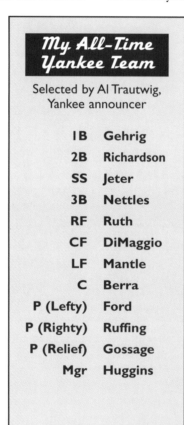

My All-Time Yankee Team

Selected by Al Trautwig, Yankee announcer

1B	Gehrig
2B	Richardson
SS	Jeter
3B	Nettles
RF	Ruth
CF	DiMaggio
LF	Mantle
C	Berra
P (Lefty)	Ford
P (Righty)	Ruffing
P (Relief)	Gossage
Mgr	Huggins

Sandy threw with his left hand and thus was able to snare the ball in his gloved right hand. Had Gilliam, a righty thrower, been in left field, it is unlikely the catch would have been made. Equally critical to the outcome of the game was that Amoros then unleashed a perfect throw to Pee Wee Reese at short, who then tossed it to Hodges at first base to double up the runner. The back of the Yankee rally had been broken.

"When I watched that fly ball," admitted Podres later, "I had the feeling it would never come down." But it did, in Amoros's outstretched glove, giving Podres a chance to complete his shutout. Euphoria reigned in Brooklyn and Stengel was remarkably subdued. "Those guys were just too much for us," he said. The old man was referring to Podres, and probably Amoros.

The next year Stengel was back again, looking for redemption. Age had not deprived him of his competitiveness. Another revered figure of the game, Connie Mack, died that year at ninety-four, after what seemed like a century in baseball. Why couldn't Casey keep going, just as Connie did?

Dwight Eisenhower, now in his second term as president, suffered a heart attack, and the prospect of his vice president, Richard M. Nixon, succeeding him caused a shudder in part of the American community. A new Prince Charming of politics, Senator John F. Kennedy of Massachusetts, wrote his popular book, *Profiles in Courage*, and some perceived him as a comer in the Democratic Party. Fidel Castro, a great lover of baseball who would become the bête noire of both Eisenhower and Kennedy, holed up in the rugged Sierra Maestra mountain range preparing to overthrow the Cuban dictator, Fulgencio Batista. Castro,

Sandy Amoros has just caught up with Yogi Berra's slicing fly ball in the seventh game of the 1955 World Series. In the foreground are Jim Gilliam, who was replaced by Amoros in left field the inning before, and Gil McDougald, who was doubled off first base. The double play crushed a Yankee rally and helped the Dodgers win their first world championship. Amoros was asked in the clubhouse how he made the play. He shook his head and said, "I don't know. I just run like hell."

A classic baseball tableau: Phil Rizzuto has made a diving stop, flipped the ball to Jerry Coleman, who is nimbly eluding a rolling block by Cleveland's Al Rosen and relaying the ball to first for a double play. Frank Umont is registering the out at second. The picture was taken in 1956.

it was erroneously reported, had been a pitcher of some talent in his native country. In the years to come, after Castro ascended to power in Cuba, some of that island's best baseball talent would leave their country and achieve star status in America.

It didn't take long for the merciless Yankees to get back on the winning track in 1956. And it was Casey's whipping boy, Mantle, who led the way with the most proficient season he ever put together. Following in the footsteps of Ty Cobb, Jimmie Foxx, Gehrig, and Ted Williams, all of whom had won the coveted Triple Crown in other years, Mickey won that award with his 52 homers, 130 runs batted in, and .353 batting average. It was the kind of performance that Casey had al-

ways envisioned for Mickey, yet he still would never let on to his disciple that he was satisfied. "He's still gotta grow up," Casey kept telling the amused New York press, even after Mickey put up such numbers.

The Yankees' victory, by nine games, naturally had other contributors. The pitching, led by Ford with 19 victories, right-hander Johnny Kucks, and newcomer Tom Sturdivant, was generally airtight. Bob Turley's fastball wasn't as overpowering as usual, so Don Larsen picked up the slack. But more about Mr. Larsen later.

Mantle wasn't the only Yankee to hit home runs that season. Yogi hit 30, matching his own highest total. Hank Bauer had 26 and Skowron banged 23.

Taking over for the departed Rizzuto at shortstop, the San Franciscan Gil McDougald hit .311 and wound up second in the Most Valuable Player balloting. Gil always played the game with great intensity, causing Casey to cherish him. He also carried himself with grace and dignity, supporting a Yankee tradition that had been violated on occasion by some teammates.

That year the Dodgers waged a dogfight with Milwaukee and Cincinnati to get into the World Series again with the Yankees. But there they were, a Brooklyn team defending its laurels. This time the Yankees were determined not to be caught short by fate or a last-minute substitution. With the Series tied up at two games each, they turned to a most unlikely hero, Larsen, to pitch the fifth game. What makes this choice so incredible was that in the second game Larsen had handed out passes like a crazed press

agent. He was under a hot shower and on top of a cold beer before two innings had gone by. "That's the last time I go to bed early," said the big right-hander, trying to analyze his failure.

Casey was fully aware of Larsen's conduct off the field, which sometimes rivaled legendary baseball boulevardiers like Bugs Raymond, Flint Rhem, and Rube Waddell. However, Stengel had experienced success handling this blithe spirit, even after Larsen had challenged a telephone pole with his convertible one early Florida morning in spring training that year. Indeed, Don was nominated to open the season and emerged with a win over Washington, just to prove that Stengel's forbearance was the proper medicine. By the end of the season Larsen had compiled an 11–5 mark, including four straight victories in the final month.

"This is the year Mantle should finally reach superstardom," Stengel said at the end of the 1956 exhibition season. On cue, Mantle produced his supreme season: 52 homers, 130 runs batted in, a .353 batting average, and a .705 slugging percentage. All the numbers led the majors and earned him the first of his three Most Valuable Player awards. He also exorcized the DiMaggio legacy. "I tried to do it, to live up to DiMaggio," he said. "It didn't work. I've quit trying now."

When Casey informed Larsen that he'd be starting in the fifth game of the Series, Larsen prepared for the mission by a nighttime visit to one of his favorite Manhattan haunts. He was accompanied by his buddy, Arthur Richman, a sportswriter who had grown up near Yankee Stadium. Richman had befriended Larsen almost from the moment that Don, a native of Indiana, had first set foot in the Big City. At midnight the two men hopped a cab for their return trip to the Bronx's Concourse Plaza Hotel. There Larsen wolfed down a pizza pie and studied the comics, his favorite reading matter, in his hotel room. Then he remarked to Richman that he hadn't gone to church that morning. To atone for this omission he pulled out a 20-dollar bill and handed it to Richman.

LEFT: After the Baltimore Orioles traded Don Larsen to the Yankees at the end of 1954, Jimmy Dykes, Larsen's erstwhile manager, said, "The only thing he fears is sleep." Larsen is seen here in the last of the ninth inning of his perfect game in the 1956 World Series. "My legs were rubbery, and my fingers didn't feel like they were on my hand," he said. "I said to myself, 'Please help me out somebody.'"

BELOW: Don Larsen is already in Yogi Berra's embrace, and is about to be engulfed by the rest of his teammates following his stunning perfect World Series game. Yankee co-owner Del Webb, alluding to Larsen's nonchalant approach to conditioning, said, "This will set spring training back ten years."

"Here, give this to your favorite church," he said.

"I don't go to church," Richman reminded Don, "I go to synagogue."

"Then tell your Mom to give it to your synagogue," replied Larsen.

The next morning, a Monday, Don awoke at eight and joined a long list of Series pitchers afflicted with a bad case of pregame jitters. He hadn't slept at all and when he got to the Stadium his stomach was still full of butterflies. As the day wore on, however, Don overcame his jitters. With 64,000 watching, Don proceeded to set down every batter that came to the plate. His mound rival, Sal Maglie, was almost as unyielding. It was just that Larsen was better. Using his newly acquired no-windup delivery, Larsen entered the seventh inning nursing a 2–0 lead over a Brooklyn club that practically featured an all-star lineup and had dominated National League baseball for almost a decade. At that stage of the game Don hadn't permitted a single enemy player to reach base. The Dodgers came close to getting a man on in the second inning, when Robinson smashed a line drive off Andy Carey's glove at third base. But McDougald quickly retrieved the ball and threw out Jackie. In the fifth inning Mantle made a backhanded catch of Hodges' long drive to center field. That was the extent of Larsen's permissiveness.

By the eighth inning the crowd was shouting encouragement to Larsen on each pitch. But on this afternoon Don didn't need to be implored. With two men out in the ninth inning, Dale Mitchell, a pinch hitter, took a called third strike. Many, including the annoyed Mitchell, were convinced that the pitch was at least a foot outside. But there was no angry outburst, for Larsen had accomplished his perfecto—the first in Series history, and the first perfect game in the big leagues since 1922. The mellifluous Brooklyn announcer, Vin Scully, proclaimed that "it was most assuredly the greatest game ever pitched in the history of baseball." The facts tended to support his judgment: 97 pitches thrown, 71 strikes, 26 balls, no hits, no walks, no hit batsmen, no errors, no runs, no sweat. In short, absolutely nothing. In his merry postmortem, Larsen acknowledged he'd had "a couple before the game, so it stands to reason that now I'm gonna have a couple the night after."

The following day the Yankees were befuddled by Clem Labine's 1–0 pitching for the Dodgers. Normally a relief pitcher, Labine limited the Yankees to seven hits in 10 innings, before Robinson singled home the winning run in the bottom of the tenth off Bob Turley. It was hard to know what to anticipate in the seventh game at Ebbets Field. But it turned out, sadly for Dodgers fans, to be a 9–0 laugher in favor of New York. Yogi led the way with two home runs, as the Dodgers made only three hits off Johnny Kucks. Once again big Don Newcombe failed to beat the Yankees in a postseason game. Not long after Brooklyn's latest disappointment, Jackie Robinson announced that he was retiring from the game at thirty-eight, weary in mind and body from his personal struggle.

For the seventeenth time the Yankees ruled the baseball universe. Equally relevant was that it was the last "subway Series" between the Dodgers and Yankees, for within a year the Dodgers and Giants were headed to California to open a whole new chapter of baseball history. The move earned Dodgers' owner, Walter O'Malley, the eternal wrath of all Brooklyn fans. In the mind of writer Pete Hamill, O'Malley was as much of a villain as Hitler and Stalin.

It is worth remarking that America was about to say goodbye to its age of innocence. The quintessential American, Dwight Eisenhower, hero of World War II, was on the verge of defeating the eloquent

My All-Time Yankee Team

Selected by Rick Cerrone, Yankee publicity director

1B	Gehrig
2B	Lazzeri
SS	Rizzuto
3B	Nettles
RF	Ruth
CF	DiMaggio
LF	Mantle
C	Berra
P (Lefty)	Ford
P (Righty)	Ruffing
P (Relief)	Rivera
Mgr	Stengel

Gil McDougald, in a 1957 photo, admiring the Yankee Stadium turf with head groundskeeper, Jim Thompson. McDougald was the spark in the Yankees' 1958 World Series comeback. With the Bombers down three games to one to the Milwaukee Braves, he doubled with the bases loaded and homered in the fifth game, hit the game-winning homer in the tenth inning of game six, and had two hits in the seventh game. He was an All-Star selection at three infield positions, and played all three in World Series games.

Democrat, Adlai Stevenson, for his second term in the White House; World Series tickets topped out at $10.50; Broadway shows, including *My Fair Lady*, offered good seats for eight dollars; and subway tokens were only 15 cents. Marilyn Monroe, the troubled sex symbol, made a tabloid heaven match with the Lincolnesque writer, Arthur Miller. And a fairy-tale prince took a Hollywood princess, Grace Kelly, for his wife.

But the turbulent sixties were on the way, with all the wrenching changes that would permanently alter the social and political landscape. The civil rights movement, with its marches and sit-ins, had erupted, as Southern governors stood grimly in the door trying to block progress. The birth control pill had become

reality. The charismatic John F. Kennedy would soon become president. Some politicians sought to put atomic shelters in everyone's backyard. The divisive, bloody Vietnam War was ready to move onto the front pages.

Not content to rest on their bat handles, the Yankees put together another of those postseason trades that so excite the New York press. They sent half a dozen players, including outfielder Irv Noren and pitcher Tom Morgan, to Kansas City, in return for third baseman Clete Boyer, the tiny southpaw Bobby Shantz (reputed to be the American League's best fielding pitcher), and right-hander Art Ditmar. The key to the deal was Boyer, who came from a family of ballplayers. His brother, Kenny, starred for many

Phil Rizzuto was unceremoniously released by the Yankees midway through the 1956 season. He was heartbroken and angry but held his tongue, and a year later the Yankees offered him a broadcasting job. He kept the "Holy Cow" job for the better part of the succeeding four decades. He's seen here chatting with former teammates Mickey Mantle, Hank Bauer, and Gil McDougald.

years with the Cardinals. Not much on hitting for average, Clete was an exceptional defensive player.

As the season began, Stengel pronounced that the race wasn't "gonna be a runaway"—and he was correct, for his team had to battle hard to get into first place after a rough start. In the past the Yankees had unfortunately been involved in two of the game's most tragic incidents on the field. In August 1920, the Yankees' submarine hurler Carl Mays hit Cleveland's shortstop, Ray Chapman, in the head with a ball at the Polo Grounds. Chapman collapsed at the plate and died the next morning. To this day Chapman remains the sole fatality in the game's history. In 1937 it was Yankees' pitcher Bump Hadley who threw a vagrant pitch into catcher Mickey Cochrane's temple at Yankee Stadium. On May 7, 1957, the Yankees again found themselves a participant in a tragic episode that nearly cost the sight of one of the game's most promising strikeout pitchers, left-hander Herb Score. McDougald, the second Yankee batter in a game at Cleveland's Municipal Stadium, slashed a ball back toward the mound that landed with a sickening thud in Score's unprotected right eye. At that instant Score remembered saying to himself, "Saint Jude, stay with me!" In a way, Score was lucky. He didn't lose his eye or his sight. But he was never the same million-dollar pitcher again. McDougald was never the same player again, either, although it can't be certain that his keen distress over Score's injury was the only reason for his decline.

As if that wasn't enough drama in the Yankee camp, barely a week later the Copacabana Affair exploded in the headlines. Several Yankees, including Billy Martin, were celebrating somebody's birthday at the Copa, when a drunken brawl ensued. It was never too clear exactly what happened or who was to blame. But one Yankee who was there, Berra—known for his straight talk—insisted, "Nobody did nuthin' to no-

body." Weiss, however, who always wanted his Yankees to behave like Boy Scouts, seized on the opportunity to get rid of Martin. Casey still loved his troublesome rebel, who could be charming when he wasn't drinking, but he was overruled. Martin was packed off to Kansas City, along with pitcher Ralph Terry, for the nearsighted relief pitcher, Ryne Duren, whose mere appearance caused batters to shudder.

Baseball brawls have long been overrated for their impact on teams. But in June a Pier Sixer between the Yankees and White Sox at Comiskey Park may have been the catalyst for a nine-game New York winning streak that hurtled the Yankees ahead of the embattled Chicago club.

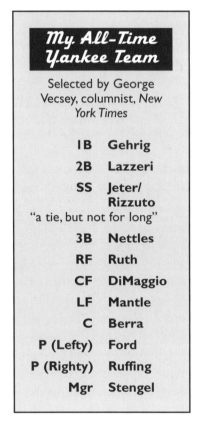

My All-Time Yankee Team

Selected by George Vecsey, columnist, *New York Times*

1B	Gehrig
2B	Lazzeri
SS	Jeter/ Rizzuto

"a tie, but not for long"

3B	Nettles
RF	Ruth
CF	DiMaggio
LF	Mantle
C	Berra
P (Lefty)	Ford
P (Righty)	Ruffing
Mgr	Stengel

With the Yankees winning their eighth flag in nine years, Casey was confident that Milwaukee wouldn't present too much of a problem in the World Series. After all, Mantle had had a year to remember, even if the thirty-nine-year-old Ted Williams had overshadowed Mickey with a .388 average and 38 home runs. Mickey's figures—34 homers, 94 RBIs and a .365 average—were fine. But by this time Mickey's ability to bang in runs was thwarted by pitchers who preferred to walk him. He drew 146 bases on balls in 1957, testimony to the anxiety that Mickey caused among enemy hurlers. Mike Garcia, the Indians hurler, was once asked by writer Donald Honig how he would pitch to Mantle in a close game. "You don't," was Garcia's curt response.

But Mantle's always brittle underpinnings continued to vex him. Skowron's back kept acting up as well. Stengel may have chosen to use them too much during the regular season because he always liked to pile up victories. By the time the Series rolled around, neither man was operating at full strength. As it turned out, Skowron played hardly at all in the seven-game Series, while Mantle was not a particularly potent force. Perhaps if the departed Billy Martin had still been on hand he would have rescued the Yankees, as he usually did in postseason play. But, more likely, it was the presence in a Milwaukee uniform of Lew Burdette, a right-hander often suspected of throwing an illegal spitball, that turned the tide against New York.

Burdette was overwhelming. He pitched three times in the Series, wrapping up the title for his team on two days rest in the final game at Yankee Stadium. Two of his wins were shutouts and he went the last 24 innings without yielding a run. His performance was remindful of the Giants' Christy Mathewson in 1905 and Cleveland's Stan Coveleski against the Dodgers in three complete game victories in 1920.

There was an antic subtext to the Yankees defeat. Upon arriving in Milwaukee, Casey sputtered that he regarded the whacky enthusiasm of Milwaukee's burghers as "bush league." Such disparagement didn't turn Burdette into a Yankee-killer overnight, even if, as a former Yankee farm hand, he may have been seeking revenge. But it did cause the Wisconsin natives to singe Casey's oversized ears with boos and hisses every time he stuck his nose out of the dugout. After it was all over, Casey turned into a perfectly charming gentleman. He ventured into the Braves' post-Series clubhouse celebration, stuck out his hand to manager Fred Haney and owner Lou Perini and told them, "you fellas done just splendid." For a man who loved to win, it must have hurt. But Casey said it with a grin.

If there was some feeling at this moment that Casey might decide to retire, there was no substance to such a belief. "He was never destroyed by defeat," Robert Creamer wrote. After all, Casey had been through it all in baseball and any man who had once liberated a sparrow from under his cap had to have a pretty sanguine view of life.

The Yankees rushed out of the starting gate in 1958 as if they wanted to commence the World Series in June. They were so far ahead that even a subpar performance in the last sixty games failed to make a dent in their lead over Al Lopez's White Sox. Ultimately, they won the flag by ten games. Reporters got the impression that Casey was burning to reverse Milwaukee's 1957 victory. He had the tools to do it, too, for he had a sizzling Bob Turley, who had had a 21–7

season, including six shutouts. Bullet Bob may have been the best Yankees right-hander since Allie Reynolds made his departure after the 1954 season. Ford was still winning ball games and throwing shutouts (he had seven), but insistent arm troubles curbed his work after early August. He did manage to get into the Series, but he wasn't the dominating postseason pitcher that he'd been previously.

Mantle led the league in homers with 42, though his average dipped to .304. Coming into his own, Ellie Howard hit .314, with 22 homers, while playing mostly in the outfield. Occasionally he filled in behind the plate, second banana to Yogi. Duren, the new relief star, became Casey's intimidator in the late innings.

During his Rookie of the Year season in 1957, Tony Kubek played all three outfield positions, shortstop, third base, and one game at second. "He can play lotsa positions," Casey Stengel said, "which is the way I like 'em." Kubek is also remembered now for his long career as a radio and television announcer.

Having won the National League pennant for the second straight year, Milwaukee was primed to repeat over the Yankees. They had bombers like Henry Aaron and Eddie Mathews, and the pitching was strictly prime time, with Warren Spahn and Burdette on hand. The Series that followed was as exciting as any that had been played in years, with the final result confounding everyone. Holding a comfortable three games to one lead, Milwaukee had only to win one more game to trim the Yankees for the second straight time. Up to that point, Spahn had won two games and Burdette won the other, though he was belted around a bit more than he had been in 1957.

But in the crucial fifth game Howard rescued the Yankees with a brilliant catch of Red Schoendienst's sizzling line drive that turned back a Milwaukee rally. Instead, the Yankees put together a big six-run inning off Burdette, of all people. That turned the tide, with the Yankees winning the last three games. Hank Bauer, who had hit only 12 homers all year, connected for four of them in the Series, proving that this man with a face like a "clenched fist" was one of the best

Among the Yankee legends must be counted Tom Greenwade, a scout who discovered and signed some of the club's most celebrated players. Sitting behind Greenwade are just a few of his prize finds: Hank Bauer, Elston Howard, Ralph Terry, Mickey Mantle, and Tom Sturdivant.

clutch hitters the team ever had. Not since Pittsburgh came back from a 3–1 deficit in the 1925 World Series had a team turned around a Series the way the Yankees had. In the final game, Skowron put the icing on the cake with a three-run homer that gave a victory to Turley, who was appearing in his third consecutive game.

It was Casey's seventh world championship, tying him with McCarthy. In addition, the Yankees had beaten every National League team at least once in World Series play.

After such a rousing performance in the Series in 1958 the Yankees were expected to win again. They would, pronounced the soothsayers, take five pennants in a row under Casey for the second time. Then, of course, they'd go on to beat whatever National League team was unfortunate enough to win the pennant. But baseballs sometimes take funny bounces,

even for such presumably omnipotent teams as the Yankees. And 1959, for a variety of reasons, proved that.

The club got off to a sluggish start. By late May, to the disbelief of millions, the team was ensconced in last place. In short order, the contentious New York press turned on its hometown team. In the good old days, the cry used to be "Break up the Yankees." But that's because they were so insufferably successful. Now the cry went out because they weren't successful at all. With a productive June, the Yankees managed to get back into the race. But in July, after a five-game battering by the Red Sox, it became apparent that this wasn't going to be a Yankee year.

By the season's conclusion, with Mantle having an off year (only 75 runs batted in) and a disastrous pitching slump for Turley, the Yankees came home with a third-place finish. They were 15 games out of the pic-

Mickey Mantle prior to the start of the opening game of the 1957 World Series. He followed up his banner season in 1956 with another MVP year in 1957, reducing his strikeouts from 99 to 75 and hitting .365, a figure topped only by Ted Williams's .388 mark. Red Sox hurler Frank Sullivan was asked how he pitched to Mantle, and he replied, "With tears in my eyes."

owner, felt that Casey was hurting the team. In fact, Topping made no secret that he wanted Ralph Houk, a tough, hot-tempered, World War II hero and an infrequently used reserve catcher, moved up to pilot the team, the sooner the better. It didn't happen sooner, for Casey was in no mood to yield to his detractors. He made up his mind to foil his critics. And that's what the game's most durable septuagenarian did in 1960.

There were dramatic changes in America and the world in the sixties, starting, of course, with the election in 1960 of John Fitzgerald Kennedy to the presidency. He defeated Vice President Richard Nixon by a razor-thin margin. In this case the word "razor" has assumed a double meaning, for Nixon, who debated on television with Kennedy, appeared unshaven and sweaty under the glare of the strong lighting. "He looked like somebody you wouldn't buy a used car from," wrote Harold Evans. Kennedy's opposite number in the Soviet Union was Leonid Brezhnev, a protégé of Nikita Khrushchev. More disquieting for Kennedy than America's relationship with the Soviets was the racial turmoil in the South, where black demands for equal rights were met by murderous resistance in Mississippi and elsewhere.

ture and only four games over .500, certainly the worst they had ever done under Casey. Yankee haters were ecstatic over this turn of events and the Stengel negativists also hummed a merry tune. It was widely rumored that the Old Man was snoring on the bench, that he was approaching senility, and that he had lost his brio and interest in the proceedings. Mantle made little secret of the fact that he didn't like Casey's constant barbs, although what that had to do with his failure to drive in runs was a puzzlement. Weiss remained a Casey supporter and refused to press him to get out of the way. But Dan Topping, ordinarily an absentee

Big changes were also taking place in the Yankees organization. Once again, the Yankees used the Kansas City roster as an appendage to their own franchise. In the winter of 1959 a trade was negotiated by Weiss that sent an over-the-hill Bauer, perfect gamer Larsen, Norm Siebern (who had had his troubles dodging the shadows in Yankee Stadium's left field), and Marv Throneberry to KC for Roger Maris and several others. The "others" didn't turn out to be important. But Maris did.

Roger, who wore his blond hair in a military-style crew cut, had been around for several years without causing any major excitement. He hailed from Fargo, North Dakota, a town that had about as many citizens as the Stage Deli in midtown Manhattan had customers on a crowded night. He had never before had to cope with anything like New York's intrusive media. In time, many in the Gotham press would regard Roger's introverted personality as sullenness. That was a disservice to a man who didn't care much about answering questions or currying favor with reporters. If he made anything clear, it was that he didn't like living and playing in a big city. A writer for *The New Yorker* magazine found him to be "about as garrulous as Calvin Coolidge."

However, Maris turned out to be a hustling outfielder with a rifle arm and a left-handed swing that was custom-made for Yankee Stadium's short right-field porch. When the Yankees dealt for this unprepossessing man to join Mantle in their outfield they had a good idea that he'd be helpful. But they never suspected that within a year he would turn the baseball community upside down with his assault on Babe Ruth's Sacrosanct Sixty home runs of 1927.

With Roger's help (even though he was on the disabled list for a while near the end of the season), the Yankees turned back the bid of a revamped Baltimore Orioles team. They took the pennant by eight games over the Orioles, solidifying their position with a 15-game winning streak in September. This was Stengel's tenth pennant, thus tying him with John McGraw.

Mantle hit 40 homers in 1960, one better than Maris. But Maris led the league in RBIs with 112 and played the outfield with great skill. Casey appeared to get along with his new player better than he had re-

This was the scene as press and publicity photographers prepared to take the 1959 team picture.

lated to Mantle; he spoke of him as "a good man . . . he can run, bunt and field . . . he's very good around the fences." For his efforts, Maris was anointed with the Most Valuable Player Award, beating out Mantle for the honor. There wasn't a single pitcher on the Yankees who won more than 15 games, which gave additional credibility to the selection of Maris.

Of course Stengel was mightily pleased with his team's victory. When he continued to make jokes about his age, he appeared to be responding to Topping's doubts. One of his lines—"Most people my age are dead at the present time"—probably will make it to *Bartlett's* one of these days. However, Casey couldn't laugh off the chest pains he suffered early in the season, which caused speculation that he had had a heart attack. It caused him to take a leave from the club for a couple of weeks, during which Houk, the heir apparent, took over the reins. Upon his return, Casey seemed spry and never stopped putting down reporters who asked him if he was in his last year as manager. He was convinced that this latest pennant triumph—and the World Series victory over Pittsburgh that he now

ABOVE: **"Do you know this man?" Casey Stengel asked, gesturing toward Hank Bauer. "He is a marine and the best hustler I ever had." This picture was taken before the third game of the 1958 World Series against the Milwaukee Braves, a Series that Bauer dominated. He hit safely in his seventeenth consecutive World Series game, and four of his 10 hits were home runs.**

RIGHT: **Fenway Park has been the most or least favored ballpark for Yankee players, depending on what side of the plate they hit from, or what arm they pitched with. This scene is from opening day in 1960. Boston's Tom Brewer is pitching to Roger Maris, and Ted Williams is in left field. Later that day Williams hit the forty-ninthth home run of his career.**

Roger Maris showed up for spring training in 1960 sporting a crew cut and white buck shoes. When a friend told him that he was not conforming to the Yankee image, Maris replied, "The hell with them. If they don't like the way I look they can send me back to Kansas City." Everyone, except the opposition, liked the look of Maris's quick and powerful swing.

anticipated—would be the proof of his competence. Surely it would keep him on the job, he thought. How could the Yankees fire this incomparable old gent if he won it all! The Pirates were not considered to be a distinguished team, although they featured several outstanding competitors, including their talented outfielder Roberto Clemente, and Bill Mazeroski, a second baseman who could field his position with the best of them. In most quarters, Casey's team was strongly favored to win; he agreed with this assessment, which may have contributed to his undoing.

Any way you look at it, the World Series of 1960 gets curiouser and curiouser. The Pirates won in seven tumultuous games but only after the Yankees had pummeled Pittsburgh pitching for a preposterous .338 average and record-breaking totals of 91 hits, 27 extra-base hits, and 55 runs. The Pirates had a team average of only .256, with four home runs and 27 runs. So what went on here? Manager Danny Murtaugh of the Pirates simply refused to allow his team to quit, not even when the Yankees had won three games by football scores of 16–3, 10–0, and 12–0.

Stengel selected a journeyman, Art Ditmar, to pitch the opening game. Ditmar didn't last through the first inning, as the Pirates held on to win, 6–4, despite the Yankees' 13 hits to Pittsburgh's eight. Maris and Ellie Howard hit home runs for the New Yorkers.

In the second game the Yankees thrashed the Pirates with a 19-hit attack. The next day Ford, exhibiting his old Series wizardry, shut out Pittsburgh to put the Yankees in front two games to one. At this stage Casey certainly envisioned still another Series triumph. But he failed to reckon with the fact that Pittsburgh led the universe in resiliency.

Luis Arroyo, seen here with fellow countryman Roberto Clemente prior to the third game of the 1960 World Series, won 15 games in relief in 1961, added 29 saves, and had a 2.19 ERA. He came in often to relieve Whitey Ford, who won 25 games that season, his career high. "Imagine finding a guy as good as him lying around dead somewhere," Casey Stengel said during Luis's fine season.

top of the eighth inning the Yankees led, 7–4, and Casey was convinced that his pitcher, Bobby Shantz, had things under control. He was so certain of this that in the top of the eighth, when his team got two men on base, with two out, and had a chance to blow the game wide open, he chose to let Shantz hit for himself. Permitting Shantz to bat was not exactly heresy, for Bobby was a good hitting pitcher. Casey might have figured that by sending up a pinch hitter for Shantz, the Pirates could have walked him, since first base was open. But that would have brought up Bobby Richardson, who had been enjoying a great Series. Up to that point, Richardson had driven in 12 runs, a Series mark. But whatever Casey was thinking, Shantz failed to produce. He flied out and stayed on the mound in the bottom of the eighth inning. The Pirates got their first man on against Shantz, bringing up Bill Virdon, a bespectacled outfielder who later became manager of the Yankees. Virdon hit what appeared to be a sure thing double-play grounder at shortstop Tony Kubek. But as Tony bent down to swallow up the innocent-appearing grass-cutter, a dismal pebble intruded. The ball took a wicked hop into Kubek's throat, putting two men

The fourth game at Pittsburgh went to the Pirates, 3–2, despite a home run by Skowron. When the Pirates won again the next day, 5–2, behind the little southpaw, Harvey Haddix, the odds makers didn't believe what was happening. But the Yankees still had a last gasp coming in the sixth game—and it turned game seven into one of the most implausible contests ever staged under the spotlight of the World Series. In that wind-up contest at Forbes Field, as a packed house of 36,000 looked on, the Yankees found themselves trailing after five innings. But the Yankees came up with four runs in the sixth to move ahead. By the

on base and forcing Tony to leave the game. Dick Groat then singled in a run, making the score, 7–5. At this stage Stengel looked to his bullpen. Jim Coates came in, replacing the distressed Shantz.

When Coates managed to get two quick outs, it again looked like Casey had made a winning move. But Clemente, always a dangerous competitor, bounced a tantalizing chopper toward first base. He beat it out, scoring a run, to make it 7–6. Catcher Hal Smith, hardly a candidate for Pittsburgh's Hall of Fame, then proceeded to bang one over the left-field wall to give the Pirates a 9–7 lead. With one final opportunity in the ninth to grab victory out of what seemed sure defeat, the Yankees rallied to tie the score, with the help of singles by Richardson, Dale Long, and Mantle. Now it came time for the Pirates to prove that this was the craziest of all World Series. With Ralph Terry on the mound for the Yankees, Bill Mazeroski came to bat. He didn't stay there very long. On Terry's second pitch to Mazeroski, it was all over. Bill hit a home run over the left-field wall, as Berra, playing in left, forlornly watched the ball sail over his head. "I can't believe it," mumbled Yogi, in the gloom of the Yankees' clubhouse. Oddly, Mazeroski's blow was the only time a Series had been terminated by a home run—and it also sealed the doom of an old baseball manager who had yearned for another ending.

A few days after Mazeroski's dramatic walk-off homer, the Yankees invited New York's writers to an elaborate press conference at the Savoy Hilton Hotel. There, amid a waterfall of drinks, canapés, and speculation, Dan Topping and Del Webb broke the news that Casey's career as Yankees' manager was kaput. In his shrewd and quirky way Casey had been an enterprising pilot, and brilliant enough to court the writers with his mangled syntax and endless anecdotes. But many of the players chafed under Stengel's needling and criticism.

In dismissing Stengel, Topping emphasized that when the Yankees originally signed Casey some 12 years before, they had been regarded as asinine. Now, Topping added, the Yankees were being assailed for getting rid of him. Topping concluded that Casey's advanced baseball age of seventy was sufficient cause to say goodbye to him.

There was some truth to what Topping said. But Casey, refusing to bow out diplomatically, was as unyielding as ever. He was blunt about his beheading. "I was fired," he asserted. "I'll never make the mistake of

My All-Time Yankee Team

Selected by Marty Appel, former Yankee publicity director

1B	Gehrig
2B	Lazzeri
SS	Rizzuto
3B	Rolfe
RF	Ruth
CF	DiMaggio
LF	Mantle
C	Berra
P (Lefty)	Ford
P (Righty)	Ruffing
Mgr	McCarthy

being seventy again." So Casey drifted away from the Yankees, not exactly kicking and screaming, but getting in the last word, like he usually did.

In two years Stengel was hired to manage the New York Mets, the new National League team in town, a club cobbled together with retreads, culls, has-beens, and over-the-hillers. Carrying with him the memory of his 10 pennants with the Yankees, Casey spent many dreary days sleeping in the Mets dugout and, no doubt, dreaming of his glory days at Yankee Stadium.

The Yankees weren't through making changes. Their dour, humorless front office man, George Weiss, now sixty-five, was dismissed. He had been with the organization since 1932, and although he was tardy in coming to terms with the integration of the game, as general manager he had been instrumental in building successful minor league teams. The Yankees treated him more kindly than they had dealt with Stengel, giving him a five-year contract as an "adviser."

The man who had been waiting patiently in the wings to succeed Casey was Houk, a sensible, no-nonsense sort of fellow. Houk was a popular choice with the players, for they regarded him as a welcome relief from the nattering of Stengel. In the late war Houk had been through his share of bombardment. However, he was scarcely prepared for the season-long bombardment that was about to explode from the bats of Yankee sluggers, including Mantle, Maris, Johnny Blanchard, Berra, Howard, and Skowron. Aiding and abetting in the final home run totals was the expanded American League schedule of 162 games in a 10-team loop.

When the season began, even the most prescient of observers would not have predicted that Ruth's home run record was going to be at risk. But as the season progressed and the powerful bats of Mantle and Maris heated up, it was clear that their competition had become an echo of the earlier battles between the Babe and Lou. As the home runs kept coming, the interest of the fans was piqued.

Though Roger and Mickey were roommates, they were temperamentally as different as chalk and cheese. Mantle wanted to find out if there was a "broken heart for every light on Broadway" (as a Manhattan columnist once sobbed in an essay). He drank heavily and never went to bed early. It was hardly a state secret that he often showed up for games unable to walk a straight line. Maris, on the other hand, was something of a straight arrow. If he went to the race track, he was a two-dollar bettor. He was a family man, taciturn and introverted.

What turned out to be a thrilling, season-long duel between Mickcy and Roger actually started in slow motion, for Maris didn't connect for his first home run until April 26, in the eleventh game of the year. For a while Roger even complained that his eyes

were bothering him. When he had them checked out the doctors prescribed eyedrops. There is little evidence that the drops produced any immediate miracles, for Roger's fourth homer of the year arrived only by game 29 at Yankee Stadium (the first that he hit on his home grounds). By that time, Mickey already had 10 homers.

Then Maris's smooth, left-handed swing suddenly fell into a groove. In his next 38 games, covering five weeks, Roger hit 24 homers, overtaking Mantle. By this time the clamoring members of the New York press began to close in on Roger. The questions came thick and fast and mostly had to do with the Babe's record. Did he want to become another Ruth? the questioners asked Roger. More often than not, Roger brushed off such queries.

"I'm not Ruth," said Roger, bluntly. "And I never wanted to be."

Casey Stengel was fired shortly after the 1960 World Series. His less voluble successor was longtime back-up catcher Ralph Houk, seen here with Yankees' co-owner Del Webb during a 1961 spring training game.

Although she posed graciously with Roger Maris innumerable times during the 1961 season, Babe Ruth's widow, Claire, hoped the Babe's record would stand.

But as Roger's home runs kept coming, so did the questions. Some reporters, married to the past, even challenged the validity of his siege on the Babe's mark. Such putdowns put more of a load on Roger than his day-to-day assault on the Babe.

Mickey and Maris ran neck and neck through the All-Star Game, with Mickey again applying pressure. By July 19, Roger had 35 home runs, while Mickey had 33. Roger's fortieth came on July 25 against the White Sox, his fiftieth was delivered on August 22, in his 125th game. When the Babe had cracked 60, in 1927, he didn't reach that figure until September 4.

By early September, Mantle was still applying heat to Maris. When Roger hit his fifty-third on September 2, Mickey had 51 in the bank. It was a horse

race all the way. The pressure on Roger, some self-inflicted, some press-inflicted, had become so acute that his short-cropped hair started to fall out in clumps. The baseball world appeared to be divided into detractors who didn't want to see him break the Babe's record (this contingent included Claire Ruth, Ruth's widow, who publicly admitted she didn't want Roger to succeed), and those who appreciated Roger's effort and were pulling for him to do it. At this point Roger did get one break: Mickey came up with a sore forearm and an abscessed hip, thus minimizing his own attempt to catch up with Maris.

With 20 games to go Roger needed four homers to tie the Babe and five to pass him. When the 154th game of the year arrived Roger was two short of the

As Roger Maris began to threaten Ruth's home run mark in 1961, Yankee Stadium crowds transferred the boos they had bestowed on Mickey Mantle for a decade to Maris. "They are a lousy bunch of front-runners," he said. "Hit a home run and they love you. But make an out and they start booing." Such straightforward statements only provoked more booing.

record; his team was only one win away from the American League pennant, a small matter that had been overlooked by many who were obsessed with the home run marathon.

Maris tried to keep things in proper perspective. "If I can win this game with a bunt," he said to Manager Houk, "would you mind if I bunted?" Houk, a firm admirer of Maris, responded that he would be proud of him if he chose to do that. Maris hit his fifty-ninth home run that day, helping the Yankees to clinch the flag.

The sixtieth and Babe-tying homer came in game 159 against Jack Fisher of Baltimore, at Yankee Stadium. In the final game of the 1961 season, with 23,000 fans looking on (with the pennant already won, most of those present were there to see Roger take a last-ditch crack at the record), Maris flied out in his first time at bat. Then, in the fourth inning, he poked the record-slashing blast off Boston's right-hander Tracy Stallard into section 33 in the lower right-field stands, an area known fondly as Ruthville.

The crowd let out a roar of acclamation as Roger made his triumphant tour around the bases. A young fan, swept away by the moment, trespassed on the field in order to congratulate the conquering hero. When Maris touched home plate, a phalanx of teammates clustered around him, pounding his broad back. A few days before, when Roger had hit number 60, he had been reluctant to wave to the fans from the dugout steps. Now he smiled broadly, an unemotional man who was, at last, savoring his role in history. He waved his cap, took several curtain calls, then retreated to the bench.

Of the 61 home runs he had hit, 30 were pounded in Yankee Stadium. In another curious connection with Ruth, Maris had hit 30 homers with men on base,

Pursuing the hallowed record, Roger Maris coped with unrelenting stress, both on the field and off. He told a writer, "I was unconsciously heading into problems and pressures that I had never known existed." This is home run number 41, hit against Camilo Pascual of the Twins in August.

As Maris and Mantle both pursued the Babe's homer record, press, radio, and TV interviewers demanded more and more of their time. But none did so more collegially than Red Barber, whose rapport with the players is evidenced in this photo, taken late in the season by Lou Requena, another favorite of the Yankees.

exactly what the Babe had done in 1927. Ten of Roger's blasts came with two men on base. However, he had none with the bases loaded. An unfair and begrudging curiosity was that Commissioner Ford Frick, who had been Ruth's pal and a ghostwriter for the Babe, suggested that since Maris had not accomplished his record in a Ruthian 154 games there should be a pesky asterisk next to his name in the record book. (In fact, the record book no longer includes such a demeaning mark.)

Maris's successful if painful foray into the Babe's hallowed territory almost overshadowed the critical foreign and domestic events that took place in 1961. At home, "freedom riders," pressing for equal rights for black Americans, met with violent and hostile resistance in the South while America and Cuba went to

the brink of atomic war after the ill-conceived invasion of the Bay of Pigs. Only the last-second common sense of President Kennedy and the Soviet Union's Nikita Khrushchev managed to tamp down this frightening post-World War II confrontation.

"In such a climate of doubt," wrote author Harvey Rosenfeld, "people tend to reach back into a past that is fixed and immutable." Thus Rosenfeld tried to account for the hoopla surrounding Maris and those who clung to the shirttails of the Babe.

The World Series of 1961 was anticlimactic after the turmoil over Maris. But many of those writers who had bludgeoned poor Roger now ceased their caterwauling. Some began to praise his courage and dedication.

In the Series, which the Yankees won in five

Roger Maris connecting with a pitch from Red Sox pitcher Tracy Stallard for his sixty-first home run of the season. "I have nothing to be ashamed of," Stallard said. "He hit sixty others, didn't he?" Mickey Mantle watched the game from a hospital bed. "I got goose-bumps when he hit it," Mantle said. "If they had high fives in those days the guys in the dugout would have all busted their hands."

games over Cincinnati, Maris's bat cooled off considerably. He hit only .105, with two hits, but his one home run, in the ninth inning of the third game, settled the issue, 3–2. It could have been the turning point of the Series. Mantle played hurt, appearing in only two games and producing only one single. But what held up, as usual, was the tricky left arm of Whitey Ford, the Chairman of the Board. He tacked on 14 innings of shutout pitching against the Reds, giving him 32 consecutive scoreless innings of World Series pitching. This obliterated the former Series mark set by Ruth in 1916 and 1918, when he was still a pitcher for the Red Sox. "Maybe now I'll go after some of Babe's batting records," joked the cocky Ford, after passing Ruth's mark. It was, as Don Honig has pointed out, a very bad year for the Babe.

The victory in the Series led to a suspicion that Houk was every bit the genius that Casey had been. As a first-year manager, Houk joined Bucky Harris of Washington and Eddie Dyer of the Cardinals as the only pilots ever to win it all in their inaugural seasons. Houk had quickly earned the respect of his players, even if many felt that anyone could manage this team and win. When he repeated with the Yankees the next year, with the club finishing five games in front of Minnesota, Houk could make the claim that he could

win, like Casey, but was much less trouble for management.

Houk could do it even though Mantle played in only 123 games, hitting 30 homers—24 less than the previous season. Maris went from the heights down to 33 homers, giving support to naysayers who had suggested he was a false hero. What helped more than these two sluggers was the development of Tom Tresh at shortstop, who took over after Kubek went into the army. The sparkling year that Richardson put together at second base, as he led the American League with 209 hits, was also a prime factor in the Yankees' success. Bobby may have looked and acted like an Eagle Scout, but he could show his grit when it counted. On a team of beer drinkers, he supported the cause of milk long before Madison Avenue introduced its ad campaign on behalf of the wholesome beverage.

On the mound Ralph Terry won 23 games and although Ford won "only" 17, he was still regarded as one of the game's best southpaws. The right-hander, Jim Bouton, who later won renown for his hilarious, best-selling diary, *Ball Four;* won seven games in his first season with the club. He would have only a short career with New York, winning 21 games in 1963, but his quirky intelligence made a mark on the game. For years the Yankees refused to invite Bouton back for Old-Timer's games because of his chef d'oeuvre, which didn't exactly portray Mantle and other Yankees as heroic figures. In time, however, the front office relented and the witty "Bulldog" Bouton was welcomed into the tent.

So it was not surprising when the Yankees confronted their longtime rivals, the Giants, in the 1962 World Series. In the days of McGraw and Durocher, the Yankees had engaged the Giants when they were rulers of the Polo Grounds. Now the Giants hailed from San Francisco, where Willie Mays held forth. Oddly, Mays, who had been such a beloved wunderkind in New York, was not as popular in San Francisco. A San Francisco columnist said of Willie: "They cheer Khrushchev here and boo Willie Mays."

The cross-country World Series proved to be exciting, but almost never ending. It took 13 days to complete the affair. There was a one-day postponement in New York and three straight days of dismal weather in San Francisco. The delays may have muf-

My All-Time Yankee Team

Selected by Lee Lowenfish, baseball historian

1B	Gehrig
2B	Lazzeri
SS	Rizzuto
3B	Nettles
RF	Mantle
CF	DiMaggio
LF	Ruth
C	Berra
P (Lefty)	Gomez
P (Righty)	Hunter
Mgr	McCarthy

fled the bats of Mantle, Mays, and Maris (the latter did hit one homer, preventing the power boys from being shut out in that department). But it took unheralded Chuck Hiller, the second baseman of the Giants, to provide the fireworks. In the fourth game, which the Giants won, Hiller hit the first bases-loaded homer whacked by a National Leaguer in a Series game.

Ford won the first game, 6–2, though his Series streak of scoreless innings was halted. Neither team could put together two victories in a row, bringing the classic down to game seven in San Francisco. Terry, with one victory and one defeat in the Series, was nominated by Houk to pitch the Yankees to the championship. Jack Sanford, a right-hander, was picked by former Giants' shortstop, manager Al Dark, to oppose Terry.

The Yankees eked out a 1–0 lead in the fifth inning, when Bill Skowron scored on a double play. This slim margin was tenderly nursed by Terry until the last of the ninth inning, when Giants' pinch hitter Matty Alou bunted safely to lead off the inning. Terry followed that hit with strikeouts of Felipe Alou, Matty's brother, and Hiller. That left it up to Mays, as 44,000 screaming locals implored him to hit one out of the park. Willie didn't do that, but he did crack a double into the right-field corner, sending Alou to third base. Maris made a quick recovery of the ball and his precise throw to Richardson at second base forced Alou to hold up at third. If Alou had risked scoring on Mays's hit, he would surely have been out at the plate.

Thus it remained for Willie "Stretch" McCovey to face Terry with the game and the Series on the bases. Earlier in the Series McCovey had nailed Terry for a long homer. One didn't have to be a mind reader to appreciate that Terry must have been haunted by that, as well as the famous Mazeroski Series homer he had yielded a couple of years before. Houk knew this, too. So he walked to the mound to inquire if Terry would prefer to give the left-handed McCovey an intentional pass (first base was open), and instead pitch to the right-handed Orlando Cepeda. It was a Hobson's Choice—but Terry didn't bite at the option. He chose to pitch to McCovey. Within seconds, McCovey's bat had unleashed a sizzling line drive toward right field. But Richardson snared it at eye level and the Series was over. Had McCovey's smash been a foot or so higher he, and not Terry, would have been the hero, and the Giants would have been world champs, instead of the Yankees.

After the game the disappointed Mays insisted Richardson had been playing out of position. "He was playing on the outfield grass in short right field," Willie said. "If he'd been where a second baseman should be, it would have gone through for a hit."

Maybe Richardson knew something that Willie didn't.

Terry was humble in the boisterous Yankees locker room. "You don't get many chances—second chances—to prove yourself in baseball," he said. "I'm just grateful I did."

Mickey Mantle

Mickey Mantle carried the most perfect little boy baseball name this side of his chief competitor, Willie Mays. But during his too-short life of sixty-four years he also carried warts and flaws that were generally not exposed to his worshipping public and were never inscribed on bubble gum cards or Wheaties boxes.

However, for all of Mickey's carousing and mindless excesses, he remained an idol to millions of his generation. "For reasons that no statistics or dry recitation of facts can possibly capture, he was the most compelling hero of our lifetime," said announcer Bob Costas, in his touching eulogy for Mickey on August 15, 1995. "He was our symbol of baseball at a time when the game meant something to us that perhaps it no longer does. . . . he exuded dynamism and excitement, but at the same time touched your heart. We knew there was something poignant about Mickey before we knew what poignant meant. You didn't just root for him, you felt for him."

If such affection was misplaced—and some insist it was—there is no doubt that Mickey connected with millions in a way that few professional athletes ever have. He inspired fantasies and dreams among his fans that could not be diminished by his self-destructive impulses.

Was Mantle deserving of being considered the greatest ballplayer of an era that was limned by Elvis Presley, Howdy Doody, the coming of McDonald's, the rages of James Dean and Marlon Brando, and the morality play led by Martin Luther King, Jr.?

Yes, says Allen Barra, the *Wall Street Journal* columnist. "What Mickey did accomplish ranks him among the handful of greatest players of all time. His record needs no apologies for what might have been."

If you want records, of course, Mickey had them. Despite all of his injuries and physical misfortunes plus the harsh fact that he was rarely free of pain, Mickey played more games in a Yankees uniform than any other man. From 1951 to 1968 he appeared in 2401 games—more than the Babe, Gehrig, DiMaggio, or Berra ever played. At the end he was a ruined performer, both in body and spirit. In his last years his batting average dipped below .300 and the home run production withered.

But it is best to remember him from the rousing days of the mid-fifties, when he could do more things better and more often than any other player. Was there ever a better switch-hitter or World Series player? Was there ever anyone who could reach base more, on bases on balls? Was there anyone who could run bases faster? (He was not a prolific base stealer because the Yankees didn't need such measures.) Oddly, Mickey never made as many as 200 hits in a season

A young Marv Albert interviewing Mickey Mantle during the 1962 season. The Mick was not always the easiest man to interview, and appears eager to get this one over with.

(188 was his highest total in 1956), but his walks more than compensated for that omission.

In his early years, when Mickey was such a disappointment to his cranky manager Stengel, Mickey never understood the intensity of the feelings that his fans had for him. But when his career was ebbing he finally seemed to appreciate this reaction. On a day in September 1965 that was given over to honor him at Yankee Stadium, Mickey listened to fans yell and scream and holler his name. Yes, he knew that some of these people were the same fans who had once booed him in their frustration and perversity. But when it came time for Mickey to say his little piece, and to thank these same fans, he delivered words that were reminiscent of Gehrig's farewell 24 years before.

"A lot has been written about the pain that I play with," said Mickey. "But when one of your fans says, 'Hi, Mick, how ya' doin', how's the leg?' it makes it all

worth it." Then as he surveyed the homemade banners and listened to the roar of the thousands in the stands, he gulped and wiped his forehead. "I just wish I had fifteen more years to play here," he concluded.

For 11 straight years Mickey was an All-Star. He won three Most Valuable Player awards before reaching the age of thirty-one. He may have been capable of hitting a ball farther than any other player (before Mark McGwire) and that includes Ruth, Jimmie Foxx, and Hank Greenberg. Had he not been haunted and tormented by the early deaths of all the men in his family (his father was thirty-nine when he died), there is no telling how differently Mickey might have behaved, or how much better he might have performed. At the end of his life, Mickey said, with a touch of bitter humor, that if he had known he was going to live as long as he did, he might have taken better care of himself.

1963-1972

THE TIMES THEY WERE A-CHANGIN'. BUT DESPITE THE STORM OF SO-
CIAL TRANSFORMATIONS, BASEBALL AND THE YANKEES WENT ON.
CIVIL RIGHTS MARCHERS WALKED FROM SELMA TO MONTGOMERY, ONLY
TO BE BEATEN AND HOSED. GOVERNOR GEORGE WALLACE OF ALABAMA, CYNI-
CAL AND PUGNACIOUS, VOWED "SEGREGATION FOREVER," AS HE STOOD
SNARLING IN A SCHOOLHOUSE DOOR. THE CUBAN MISSILE CRISIS CAME AND
WENT AND THE WORLD DIDN'T END IN AN ATOMIC FIRESTORM, AS MANY

thought it would. The seductively charming President Kennedy was assassinated in Dallas by an obsessed former marine. And other people kept getting assassinated—Malcolm X, Bobby Kennedy, the president's brother, Martin Luther King, Jr. Idealistic young people traveled to the South on behalf of black rights and were murdered.

It all seemed unreal. An America full of dropouts, freakouts, counterculturists, combat veterans protesting a Vietnam War that had numbed their senses. Friends argued with one another, as they kept watching the killing fields on television. Students at Kent State in Ohio were shot down by the National Guard, the Watts district in California burned down, and Detroit and Newark had riots.

President Lyndon Johnson, haggard and frustrated by his own guns-and-butter policies, announced he would not again seek the presidency, and Nixon, in the eighth of his nine lives, weirdly talked football to angry youths in the capital.

In 1963, still powerful, although some sensed their decline, the Yankees won their fourth straight pennant, with Houk making it three in a row under his jurisdiction. His team won 104 games, leading the Chicago White Sox, under the long-suffering Al Lopez, by 10½ games. The Yankees got little out of Mantle, who hobbled through the year with a broken bone in his foot. Mickey played in only 65 games and delivered 15 home runs. At one stage of the season the

OVERLEAF: **This quartet, Clete Boyer, Tony Kubek, Bobby Richardson, and Joe Pepitone, played together from 1963 to 1965. "I've been around this organization since 1947," Ralph Houk said, "and I say this is the toughest infield to hit a ball by."**

Yankees won ten out of 11 games *without* him in the lineup. Mantle's brother-in-arms, Maris, who was also hurt much of the time, banged 23 homers, thus reducing himself to mere mortal. In Yogi's last year as an active player, Elston Howard did all of the catching and turned out to be the league's Most Valuable Player. Skowron, once so dependable at first base, had been traded off to the Dodgers, to be replaced by Joe Pepitone. In his first full season, Pepitone fielded the position adroitly most of the time and hit 27 home runs. Compared to other laconic Italian Americans such as DiMaggio, Crosetti, and Lazzeri, Pepitone could talk a blue streak. Kubek, back from the service, lost two weeks in midseason to injuries.

What really pulled the Yankees through was their pitching staff, still headed by the clever Ford, who put together a 24–7 season, at the age of thirty-four. If Whitey was old as pitchers go, he didn't show it. Cincinnati's pitcher, Jim Brosnan, who also wrote insightful books about the game, once said of Whitey that, "he is like a machine that just clicks, whirs and spins into action for each pitch." On a club that invariably came up with great southpaws—Pennock in the Roaring Twenties, and Goofy Gomez, who took up where Pennock left off—Ford, a relatively small, compact athlete, had shown unexpected durability. After Ford, the Yankees had Bouton, who won 21 games in his sophomore year, including six shutouts. Terry finished with 17 victories, while losing 15. Another smallish lefty, Al Downing, who was half of the Yankees' first impressive all-black battery, won 13 games with a supercharged fastball.

As they faced the Los Angeles Dodgers in the 1963 World Series, the Yankees were strong favorites

Former U.S. Postmaster General, James Farley, who once aspired to be a ballplayer, was a regular Yankee Stadium attendee during the 1960s. Yankees' Manager Ralph Houk and Mickey Mantle flank him here on opening day in 1963.

dale, as intimidating a duo as one could imagine. They even held out together. In 1963 they won 44 games between them, with Koufax contributing 25 of the victories. They struck out a total of 557 batters, over 300 of them chalked up to Sandy. Why anyone would have expected Sandy and Don suddenly to melt in the face of a Yankee team that had had its share of depleting injuries was a puzzle. In fact, they didn't.

In the first game of the Series at Yankee Stadium Koufax fanned 15 Yankees (a new record), including the first five to come to bat. Over 70,000 rubbed their eyes in amazement at the performance of the "Jewish kid," (as Stengel had referred to Koufax). So overwhelming was Koufax's stint that Jim Hearn, the former Giants' right-hander, who was sitting in the press box, felt that the game had been "boring." Without a doubt it had been boring—and frustrating—for the Yankees, who couldn't see much of what Sandy was throwing.

Sandy was boring again in the fourth game, when he beat Ford for the second time, despite a late Mantle home run. That made it four straight for the Dodgers. Not since the Yankees had been drubbed four in a row by McGraw's Giants in 1922 (although one game was tied) had the team suffered such ignominy. Six times in Yankees history they had swept foes in four straight. Now they knew how it felt to have the tables turned on them.

"That was the worst beating I've ever seen this team take," Mantle said, in a subdued locker room after the debacle was over. As a team the Yankees had batted .171, an anemic output unprecedented in Series play.

Following their defeat, the Yankees made a major change (no pun intended). They switched Major Ralph Houk from his manager's perch into the front office,

to win. Their reputation had preceded them, even with the odds makers, who were usually less sentimental about such matters. After all, the Yankees had barely squeaked through to a Series triumph over the Giants in 1962, and Ford, the preeminent clutch pitcher, had fallen to 1–3 in his most recent Series efforts after going 9–4 in earlier contests. Like the Yankees, the Dodgers made it to the Series mainly because of their superior pitching. They were led by southpaw Sandy Koufax and right-hander Don Drys-

where he became general manager. Houk always seemed better equipped, physically and emotionally, to be with the troops on the field. Even more stunning was management's choice as successor to Houk—none other than Lawrence P. "Yogi" Berra. The choice was, to understate it, serendipitous. Nobody contested that the fans delighted in the promotion, since Yogi had always been their darling. Whether he was equipped to manage was another matter.

The move was generally hailed as a public relations tour de force, and as a gambit to deflect some of the media attention from the new team in town, the Mets. Stengel, the old monologuist, continued to get plenty of newspaper space, simply because he never stopped talking. He even talked about Berra. When he was asked what he thought of Yogi's potential as a manager, Casey winked and said, "He was always interested in winning and accumulating money."

It turned out that Yogi had a hard time winning acceptance as a final authority. Many of his players who had been his teammates still were fond of him, but they had reservations about taking orders from him. Yogi knew as much about the game as any of them but he lacked the bluffness and friendliness of Houk. He was never too sure how to handle his men. Whether that was the reason that the team performed sluggishly in the first part of the season is open to question. More likely the troubles the Yankees had could be attributed to injuries and the onset of age. Mantle's wobbly legs brought him pain much of the time, although he still managed to hit 35 homers and knock in 111 runs. That, of course, was better than Maris's 26 homers and 71 RBIs. In addition, Maris never really became accustomed to the New York press, even after he had survived the trial by fire in 1961.

By the time August arrived the Yankees were battling to stay alive in the pennant race, with Baltimore and Chicago both in front of them. By this time, too, the front office had convinced itself that it had made a mistake in presenting Yogi with the pilot's job. In over his head, they said privately. Then an incident took place on the team bus, following four straight defeats at the hands of the White Sox. With the bus stuck in traffic outside of O'Hare Field, Phil Linz, a utility infielder, grabbed his harmonica and proceeded to play

The sure-handed Clete Boyer. "I can throw to first base with my eyes closed," he said, "and from any position, sitting, kneeling, or standing." During much of the decade, Boyer had the misfortune to be compared with Brooks Robinson, as well as his older brother, Ken.

a few riffs of "Mary Had a Little Lamb." Yogi felt this was a frivolous response to the team's 10 losses in 15 games, so he demanded that Linz immediately cease his impromptu concert. When Linz continued, Yogi, rarely known to lose his temper, imprudently suggested where Phil could shove his harmonica. This elicited howls of laughter from other occupants of the bus. But Linz finally halted his playing.

Was this incident really a catalyst for a Yankee revival? Anyway, revive the Yankees did, and the harmonica myth achieved more than a smidgen of acceptance. The Yankees fought their way through 31 wins in their last 40 games, including a 22–6 mark in the dog days of September. As Chicago and Baltimore faded, the Yankees managed to trim the White Sox by one game for the pennant, as they won their fifth straight championship. It is likely, however, that Messrs. Topping, Webb, and Houk had decided to relieve Yogi of his post, even before the team rallied to win, though they weren't about to do the unthinkable and replace him before the World Series with the St. Louis Cardinals got under way.

Under Johnny Keane, a steady, patient man who had spent a lifetime in the minor leagues before making it as Cardinals' manager, the Cards team had survived a brutal pennant chase. They won it by a game on the last day of the season, taking advantage of the almost inexplicable collapse of the Philadelphia Phillies. Ahead by 6½ games, with only 12 to play, the Phillies lost 10 games in a row, blowing the pennant. Keane's team included a number of outstanding black players, including pitcher Bob Gibson, a splendid all-around athlete, Lou Brock, Curt Flood, and Bill White, the first baseman who years later became president of the National League. David Halberstam, in his book, *October 1964*, relates how some of these men had relationships with white Cardinals off the field, which was highly unusual but reflected changes taking place not only in American society but in baseball's tight little world of exclusion. On a more ironic note, the brilliant Gibson, who channeled his anger into an unleashed desire to win, turned out to be the ultimate clutch pitcher. He defied the dismal stereotype that black players were incapable of coping with game pressures.

Bobby Richardson was the MVP of the 1960 World Series, and led the league with 209 hits in 1962. He still holds the record for consecutive games played in the World Series with 30. In 1966, at age thirty-one, he retired to spend more time with his family. "Del Webb never did understand that money wasn't involved in my decision," he said.

The Series evolved into a memorable week of exciting games. The Yankees led two games to one, with Mantle reaching back in the third game to hit a tremendous ninth-inning game-winning blast off the knuckle ball relief pitcher Barney Schultz. There was great joy in the Yankee clubhouse after Mantle's big hit. Whitey Ford "sold" a fake ball to Mickey for $1,000, assuring him that it was the home run ball he'd just hit. However, the authentic ball had been caught by a gentleman who came to present the prize to Mickey. Only then was Whitey's hoax apparent. It was the last horselaugh that the Yankees experienced in the Series.

The Cardinals tied it up in game four, with the help of a grand slam by Kenny Boyer, Clete's older

Mel Stottlemyre was promoted to the Yankees in August 1964. A year later he won 20 games and recorded a 2.63 ERA. Whitey Ford retired in 1967, and in 1968 Stottlemyre won 21 games. No one could replace Ford, "the Chairman of the Board," but Stottlemyre was named "Chief of Staff."

brother. The next day the Cards moved into the Series lead behind Gibson, who fanned 13 straining Yankees. Tim McCarver, Gibson's catching partner, stung a three-run homer. But it wasn't over yet, as Yogi Berra himself might have put it. For, in game six, Maris and Mantle hit farewell back-to-back blasts, supplemented by Joe Pepitone's bases-loaded homer, to give the Yankees another tie in the Series. With the seventh game looming, Manager Johnny Keane of St. Louis nominated Gibson to face the Yankees with only two days of rest. Rookie Mel Stottlemyre, later to become one of the most astute pitching coaches in the game (with the Yankees), was given the ball by manager Berra. He had won the second game, but this time he wasn't quite up to the task.

The Cards mounted a six-run lead by the fifth inning and Stottlemyre had to leave the game. But by the late innings the indomitable Gibson was exhausted. Mantle hit his eighteenth Series homer, which was his last (he had already passed the Babe's Series mark of 16), and when Linz and Clete Boyer added home runs in the ninth, Gibson appeared to be on the ropes. But he drew on his residual strength to stagger through to a 7–5 victory, giving St. Louis the world championship.

When Keane was asked after the game if he had ever considered removing Gibson for a fresh relief pitcher, he shook his head. "I had a commitment to this man's heart," he said, a statement that must have given Gibson great satisfaction. Gibson was the Most Valuable Player of the Series, with McCarver finishing close behind him.

The Series had been dramatic from the opening pitch. But that was nothing compared with what transpired after the final out. In the strangest reward on record for winning an American League flag on his first try, Yogi was dismissed as manager right after the Series. He had rallied his team from the doldrums in a race that seemed lost, and then almost won a tough World Series. But now he was out of his job. Yogi was not prepared for such an indelicate exit. He was convinced he'd done a competent job; management obviously disagreed. However, the fact that the Soviet Union's Khrushchev lost his post the same day might have eased the pain for Yogi. After all, Mr. K. lost a country; Yogi only lost a team, while retaining the hearts of his countrymen.

Adding to this weird scenario, the man picked to replace Yogi was Johnny Keane. By midseason the Cards had, more or less, decided to unseat Keane. But when he won everything they chose to keep him. But Keane had other ideas. Dismayed by the rumors swirling around his head and angered by a vote of no confidence, Keane beat the bosses to the punch and quit. He then signed with the Yankees.

If such a managerial duet had been featured in a Marx Brothers movie people would have roared with laughter. But this was real life. Keane, unfortunately for him, didn't appreciate that the Yankees' camp which he had chosen to join was growing enfeebled. The dynasty years were about to come to an abrupt, inglorious end. Keane had always been better working with young players, who responded to his stern orders. But now he found that he was with an aging team that couldn't respond, even if they wanted to. Meanwhile, Yogi, shaken by the raw deal he thought

Mel Stottlemyre holds an unusual record for a pitcher: On July 20, 1965, he became the only hurler to hit an inside the park grand slam home run. The Boston Red Sox were the victims.

The Yankees played the Detroit Tigers on opening day in 1966, and lost 2–1. The team went on to finish in last place for the first time since 1912. St. Matthew, an unlikely source for a baseball quote, was quite right when he said, "But many that are first shall be last."

he got, signed on with the Mets as a coach under eminence grise Stengel.

In August 1964 the Columbia Broadcasting Company (CBS), entertaining high hopes that the Yankees would continue their dominance of the sport, bought the club for a record $11.2 million. They must have thought that Ruth, Gehrig, and DiMaggio were still cavorting in Yankee uniforms. Within a year CBS realized that something had gone wrong. It started with the trade of Ralph Terry to Cleveland, then it continued with the startling decline of Jim Bouton, who was now writing better than he pitched. In 1965, Jim was 4–15, his worst year ever. But he was in good company. Mantle, hurt and aging, batted .255, with 19 homers. He managed to drive in the winning run in only six games. Maris was hurt a good deal of the time, too, while shortstop Kubek, reliable for so long, had such a poor year that he made up his mind to retire. A dynasty had turned into a dud almost overnight. Keane, whose religiosity was resented by some of the Yankees, could do nothing to turn the tide.

At season's end the Yankees had a record of 77–85, which dropped them to sixth place, miles behind Minnesota's pennant winners.

The decline of the Yankees occurred at a time when America's psyche was roiled by rancor and divisiveness over the Vietnam War. The protests over United States involvement in that far-off land were now in an incubating stage. This is not to suggest that Yankee players were distracted by the rending of the country's fabric. Most of them, like ballplayers of earlier generations, paid scant attention to world affairs or political issues. But it is a fact that coincidental with the tumultuous times across America, the once-proud Yankee machine disintegrated.

Few may have seen it coming or predicted it. But when the bad times flooded Yankee Stadium there were cheers that erupted from the country's Yankee

My All-Time Yankee Team

Selected by Bill Madden, columnist, *Daily News*

1B	Gehrig
2B	Lazzeri
SS	Jeter
3B	Rolfe
RF	Ruth
CF	DiMaggio
LF	Mantle
C	Berra
P (Lefty)	Gomez
P (Righty)	Ruffing
Mgr	McCarthy

haters. For many years baseball had been faced with its "Yankee problem," if, indeed, it was a problem. Wherever they went the Yankees were booed and hissed as a bloodless corporate entity that smashed the hometown boys to smithereeens. This was true, even as the Yankees had become a national symbol of athletic excellence. Baseball attendance zoomed when the haughty Yankees roared into town. But now that the Yankees weren't roaring there was less reason for disgruntled Auslanders to pay their way in to chastise them.

Unknowingly, poor Keane had been "handed the captaincy of a baseball Titanic," as Donald Honig tartly put it. In 1966, his club finished dead last, the first time since 1912 that such misfortune had descended on them. They were the victims of aging players, a failing farm system, gnawing injuries, and perhaps the inevitable law of averages, even though to that point the law of averages had been nullified by continued Yankee brilliance. Whitey, Mickey, Ellie Howard, and the rest were no longer the fabled Yankees of old. In fact, Whitey gave it up in 1967, after a career that made him the greatest Sidewalks of New York Yankee since Gehrig. Because of this state of affairs, Keane was out of a job in 1966, after the Yankees lost 16 out of their first 20 games. Less than a year later, Keane died of a heart attack at the age of fifty-five. Major Houk was hustled back into the managerial post but there was scarcely anything he could do about the team's skid.

By now CBS, befuddled by a business that it shouldn't have been involved in, thought it had a solution in the person of a colorful character named Mike Burke, who was named president of the club. Burke, with a haircut that made him look like he belonged to King Arthur's Round Table, had a romantic curriculum vitae, including stints as a Penn halfback, World War II special agent (with all manner of derring-do that that implied) and circus impresario. But it was never clear what all of that had to do with baseball, a peculiar institution that had put more experienced men than Mike to shame. Ironically, Burke's credentials qualified him more in the area of marketing than in the selection of baseball talent. So who could have anticipated that he would commit an egregious public relations blunder?

As the disastrous 1966 campaign drew to its conclusion, Burke imprudently cashiered Red Barber, one of the game's most distinguished broadcasters, who had been an adornment in the Brooklyn Dodgers' booth for many years before he signed on with New York.

The unloading of the Old Redhead was enough to make people forget that Burke was capable of making deft moves off the playing field. He arranged to get Robert Merrill, the Metropolitan Opera star, to sing the National Anthem at Yankee games, which suited Merrill so much that he's been doing it ever since. He also enticed Marianne Moore, the tiny, baseball-loving poet, to throw out the first ball at an opening game at Yankee Stadium. While Burke demonstrated that he appreciated culture, he had no adequate explanation for what he did to Barber. Just what had Red done to expedite his departure?

He simply had made the mistake of saying on the air that there was a pitifully small crowd in the Stadium to watch a game against the White Sox near the end of the season.

"Judge Landis once said to me, 'report everything you see,'" explained Barber. What Barber saw that drizzly, foggy day at the Stadium were rows of empty seats. So he leaned into the TV mike and said, "I don't know what the paid attendance is today, but whatever it is it's the smallest crowd in the history of Yankee Stadium and the smallest crowd is the story, not the ball game."

Nelson Fox, the White Sox's second baseman, said, "On two legs Mickey Mantle would have been the greatest player who ever lived." To save wear on Mantle's damaged legs, the Yankees stationed him at first base in 1967, where he remained until he retired a year later. This photo was taken in 1967 during a game with the Orioles. Mark Belanger is the Baltimore base runner.

Mickey Mantle announced his retirement in March 1969 after a few spring training games convinced him he could no longer ". . . hit when I need to." During his 18 years with the Yankees, the team won 12 pennants and seven world championships. He still holds World Series records for most home runs, runs batted in, runs, and walks.

Barber had said it, he had reported it. Later, when he was on the radio side, Barber announced the exact number of paying fans that day: 413. A few days later Burke rewarded Barber for his candor by dismissing him. A few years before that, Mel Allen, the ebullient, popular "Voice of the Yankees," had been fired from his job in the booth. Now it was Barber. To this day the mystery of Allen's dismissal has never been explained to anybody's satisfaction. Even when Mel died in 1996 the newspaper obituaries failed to point out why the Yankees had gotten rid of him.

Never content in New York and displeased with having been asterisked by baseball's mahouts over his 61 homers in 1961, Maris was shipped to the St. Louis

Bobby Murcer was briefly touted as the next Mickey Mantle, and it was a burdensome expectation. He established his own identity in 1971 with a .331 average and an All-Star Game appearance, and the next year he belted 33 homers for the Yanks.

Cardinals for third baseman Charlie Smith after the 1966 season. In his final campaign with the Yankees, Roger played with a broken left hand that never healed well. As a result, he told the Yankees front office he wanted to call it quits. "I thought they could have respected me a little bit," said Maris, "and let me retire."

After playing in five World Series with the Yankees, Maris played in two more with the Cardinals. Roger's relationship with the fans and press in St. Louis appeared to be more comfortable.

Bobby Richardson also retired at the end of the 1966 season, at the age of thirty-one. He returned to his native South Carolina and coached the baseball team at the University of South Carolina in Columbia. When he attempted a political career, flashing his conservative credentials, he failed in his run for Congress.

Mantle played through his valedictory season in 1968, with his average dwindling to .237. His career, marked by more ups and downs than a scenic railway, remains one of the more fascinating "might have beens" in Yankee annals. At the end he had 536 homers, many of them tapemeasure connections. His celebrants will continue to argue that he was better than the Giants' Willie Mays and the Dodgers' Duke Snider, the other members of the center-field triumvirate that lifted baseball to a level of excellence in New York that may never be equaled.

Others who tried to succeed Mantle had a difficult path to follow. Pepitone, always an unreconstructed fellow, was a pale shadow of Mickey. Bobby Murcer, like Mickey an Oklahoman, had arrived with the Yankees as a highly touted infielder. In fact, he became a solid southpaw-hitting center-fielder for New York. But trying to follow in Mickey's footsteps was never an enviable task. After his baseball career was over in 1983, following two separate tours of duty with the Yankees, Bobby became a popular broadcaster of Yankee games. Another outfielder, Roy White, was dependable and a favorite with the fans, but it is unlikely he would ever have won a regular perch in the days of Yankee dominance.

Of all the new faces that emerged in the late sixties, a time of dreariness and loss, the best of the lot was the hard-nosed youngster Thurman Munson. He came out of Kent State in Ohio, which was the scene in 1970 of four student killings by the National Guard during antiwar protests. Munson soon established himself behind the plate as a worthy successor to a long line of catching eminences, including Wally Schang (from the early twenties), Bill Dickey, Yogi, and Howard. Munson was a tough presence on the diamond and soon became the team's leader.

In the years in the wilderness Houk compiled the following record: ninth place in 1967, fifth in 1968, fifth in the East in 1969, second in 1970, and fourth place finishes in the East in 1971, 1972, and 1973. The subpar performance of the Yankees diminished attendance and also the zeal with which fans followed the team's lackluster fortunes. Baltimore and Oakland were too much for the Yankees in the first years of the seventies and Houk could do little to rally his forces.

While the club remained in disrepair, Burke, who had long felt that the Bronx was not a suitable venue for the Yankees, began looking at New Jersey as a possible site for the team. He was fully aware of the history and mystique surrounding the Stadium, but, prodded by his masters at CBS, he was sending out a message that the club might not remain in the Bronx forever. This was a quarter of a century ago, but the venue game about the Stadium still goes on. It has long been a political issue in New York and every mayor of the town has had to confront it and deal with it. One decision that Burke did make was to renovate the Stadium after the 1973 season, with the aim of getting the ballpark ready to play by 1976. In the meanwhile, the Yankees would become tenants of the National League's Mets at Shea Stadium. This called up ghosts of the past,

Thurman Munson played in 26 games for the Yankees in 1969, became the team's regular catcher a year later, and on the strength of his .302 batting average and solid plays behind the plate was named Rookie of the Year. In 1976, he won the MVP Award, becoming the first Yankee player to win both trophies.

when the Yankees had been the lowly tenants of McGraw at the Polo Grounds.

After 1973 it was clear that CBS had reaped the results of its baseball ignorance. If CBS had wanted the Yankees to be their plaything, it hadn't worked out that way. Instead, the Yankees were a headache for nearly a decade and the man who had inherited the headache was Houk. At the close of the 1973 season Houk resigned, which was the first indication that something earthshaking was about to occur in the Bronx. The intermediary in this evolving situation was Gabe Paul, a knowledgeable baseball man, then the

matic. He had also coached Purdue's football backfield. Like the famed Broadway song and dance man George M. Cohan, he was born on the Fourth of July.

Upon his arrival in New York, Steinbrenner insisted that he wouldn't be involved much in the day-to-day details of running the Yankees. But he did say that New York fans deserved a winner and he would do everything he could to accomplish that. Steinbrenner's self-knowledge may have been limited, for, in short order, he turned out to be the consummate hands-on executive, whether he was plotting trades for players or demanding lettuce for his tuna fish sandwiches. He showed an interest and concern in almost everything, from the soap in the player's washroom to the tonsorial habits of his charges.

vice president and general manager of the Cleveland Indians. Paul contacted Burke and asked him if he'd like to meet a dynamic man named George Steinbrenner. Burke said he'd never heard of the fellow but would be pleased to make his acquaintance.

Steinbrenner, a wealthy Cleveland shipbuilder, worked out a deal to buy the Yankees, bringing in a number of limited partners to cement the purchase for an estimated $10 million. CBS probably lost a few million in order to rid themselves of their Yankee "problem." It didn't take long for the New York public to learn a few things about the new man in town. Steinbrenner, it turned out, had been a student of Shakespeare at Williams College in Massachusetts, which may have accounted for his sense of the dra-

ABOVE LEFT: Eddie Layton has been playing the organ at Yankee Stadium since 1966, and has not missed a Yankee home game since then. He watches most of the team's road games aboard the 26' tugboat that he operates out of Tarrytown harbor on the Hudson River. "The only thing I hate more than rough seas," he said, "is extra-inning ball games. Or rain delays."

ABOVE RIGHT: From 1939 to 1964 Mel Allen was the spirited voice of the Yankees, revered by Yankee fans and reviled with equal passion by Yankee haters. His tenure encompassed 19 pennants, and he became a preeminent symbol of Yankee supremacy. <u>Variety</u> wrote that he possessed one of the "twenty-five most recognizable voices" in the world. He described more World Series games and All-Star contests than any contemporary. "How about that" indeed!

In the ensuing years of Steinbrenner's suzerainty, he was characterized variously as generous, venal, scheming, forgiving, unforgiving, brilliant, impulsive, manipulative, cruel, engaging, and thoughtful. Such a range of chameleon-like qualities made him an ideal subject for tabloid headlines. His controversial personality, often intemperate and boorish, may have contributed to increased attendance at Yankee Stadium as the years rolled by. But columnists were always quick to point out that no fan had ever paid his way into a ballpark to watch an owner chomp on a hot dog in his executive suite. However, there was one thing that nobody doubted about Steinbrenner: He wanted to preside over winners and, in the process, he wanted to make money. Some of his moves over the years—for example, the rehabilitation of players such as Darryl Strawberry and Dwight Gooden—bordered on the altruistic, and he was duly applauded in the press when he did it. At the same time, he could be authoritarian and excessively demanding of his subalterns.

In short, Steinbrenner was human and rarely dull. That he had an enormous need for newsprint, which seemed as vital to him as the oxygen he breathed, added to his complexity. The first order of business for him was to hire a new field manager. His surprising choice was in stark contrast to his own persona. It was the mild-mannered Bill Virdon, a former Gold Glove outfielder with the Cardinals and Pirates, who had started his professional baseball life with the Yankees. Virdon had managed the Pirates to a division title in 1972 but lost his job after a run-in with two of his players. Virdon was actually Steinbrenner's second choice behind the volatile Dick Williams, the Oakland manager. Williams had "a my way or the highway attitude," which might have been ideal for Steinbrenner, but Oakland refused to release him. So Steinbrenner settled for Virdon, who was as talkative as Harpo Marx and a good deal less imaginative.

Before Thurman Munson ascended to the post of Yankees captain in 1976 to become the first player in that position since the revered Gehrig dropped out of the lineup in 1939, he confirmed that he had never thought much about it. In fact, Yankee managers after Joe McCarthy had decided to leave the captaincy open (remember, the job has little more than symbolic and ritualistic value) because of the enormous respect they had for the late Iron Horse.

Then, one day in 1976, Billy Martin, at the time managing the Yankees, called Thurman aside and told him that Mr. Steinbrenner wanted the team "to have sort of an official team leader . . . and we agreed that you're the best choice for the job." Munson accepted the assignment with a shrug, for he could be as prickly as Arizona cactus.

"Yeah, I was honored," Munson said, "but the history of the assignment was lost on me, and I didn't appreciate it as much as I might have."

In time, however, Munson made it his business to learn a few things about Yankee history, causing his pride in the captaincy role to grow. "I was touched by the honor," declared the gruff Munson, who was a man who generally said what he thought, even if it was impolitic.

A former Yankee outfielder, Gene Woodling, had scouted Munson when Thurman was at Kent State in Ohio. Thurman had just completed his senior year at the school and he was already causing tongues to wag among the baseball cognoscenti. Woodling's endorsement of Munson was summed up in two imperative words: "Get him!" And the Yankees did.

The Yankees assigned Munson to their Binghamton, New York, Double-A club in the Eastern League. His pay was $500 a month and his first manager was Cloyd Boyer, the older brother of Ken and Clete. Boyer became Thurman's first connection with Yankee royalty.

Munson was up with the parent club by 1969, where in one year's time he established himself as the rightful heir to such preeminent Yankee backstops as

Dickey, Berra, and Howard. Casey Stengel had once said, in all of his wisdom, that "without catchers you get passed balls." Well, as Thurman developed into one of the best defensive receivers in the game, the Yankees didn't have to worry about passed balls. Munson became as good, if not better, than his contemporary rival Carlton Fisk of Boston and later Chicago, and he rated right up there with Mickey Cochrane, Gabby Hartnett, and Roy Campanella, who were around before Munson made it to the majors.

Munson was quick to absorb the word of Houk, who told him that his presence behind the plate could win as many games for New York as his bat. In his first season Munson cracked the .300 level by two points

Thurman Munson became the fifth Yankee captain in 1976. During each of the years 1975–1977 he hit over .300 and drove in more than 100 runs. He hit .576 in the 1976 World Series and had six straight hits to tie a record. "I like the good batting average," he said, "but what I do every day behind the plate is a lot more important."

and though he showed little home run power that season he became the kind of take charge guy that Steinbrenner always found appealing. He was voted American League Rookie of the Year, growing into stardom almost overnight.

By the World Series of 1976 he was considered by many to be the equal of Cincinnati's Johnny Bench, who may have been the best catcher of his time. When Reds' manager Sparky Anderson was asked—after his team trounced the Yankees in the 1976 World Series—if Thurman (who batted .529 in that Series) was as good as Bench, he was disdainful of the query. "Don't embarrass anyone by comparing him to Bench," he said. Munson happened to have heard Anderson's remark. He refused to argue the point, but others would have rebutted, for many of them knew what a tough competitor Munson was.

In his peak years Munson was one of the best clutch hitters in the American League. He made his league's All-Star team seven times and was especially productive in postseason games, with a batting average of .357 in the American League playoffs and World Series.

Injuries never kept him out of the lineup. But by 1979 his body had taken a bad beating, which necessitated his switch to the outfield. "He spent most of the 1979 season in pain," wrote Marty Appel, his biographer.

"Smart lad, to slip betimes away, From fields where glory does not stay, And early though the laurel grows, It withers quicker than the rose," were the words written by England's A. E. Housman. Those phrases applied so poignantly to Munson, whose young life was snuffed out suddenly on August 2, 1979. While flying his own $1.3 million twin-engine Cessna Citation plane at the Akron–Canton (Ohio) airport, Munson, at the controls, was unable to clear an embankment. The plane crashed in flames and two friends who had been on the aircraft with Munson were unable to pry him out of the fiery wreckage.

Not since Gehrig's untimely death in 1941 had the Yankees suffered such a loss. The country's newspapers mournfully related the details of Thurman's passing, at thirty-two, on their front pages.

My All-Time Yankee Team

Selected by Stan Isaacs, former columnist, *Newsday*

I covered the Yankees during the Mantle-Berra-Ford glory days and succumbed to the demands of professionalism by burying my anti-Yankee feelings for more than a decade. Now I'm free at last to express my true feelings.

My favorite Yankee club was the 1966 team that finished tenth in the American League East. Horace Clarke, where are you now!

However, despite this visceral reaction, I still have some Yankee favorites.

1B **Felipe Alou,** one of two Alous on the 1973 team that finished fourth of six in the East.

2B **Phil Linz,** the harmonica man who later became a Met.

SS **Tony Kubek,** a stand-up guy to the press.

3B **Red Rolfe,** who actually wrote a guest World Series column for the *Daily Worker* in the days when people weren't searching for Communists under every bed.

RF **Tommy Henrich,** one of the few approachable Yanks in the McCarthy era.

CF **Bernie Williams** because somebody from the current nicely-nicely Yanks ought to be recognized.

LF **Hector Lopez,** "What a pair of hands."

C **Arndt Jorgens,** over Buddy Rosar.

P (Lefty) **Whitey Ford,** the sly wit.

P (Righty) **David Cone,** a classy fellow who never should have left the Mets.

Mgr **Casey Stengel,** for whom the post office should issue a stamp. But Joe Torre deserves a spot next to Casey.

1973–1982

IN 1974 STEINBRENNER DECIDED TO BREAK OPEN THE VAULT IN ORDER TO RESTORE THE WINNING TRADITION AT YANKEE STADIUM. HE HAD BEEN A FERVENT ADMIRER OF THE TALENT OF JAMES "CATFISH" HUNTER, THE CY YOUNG AWARD RIGHT-HANDER OF THE OAKLAND ATHLETICS, FOR SOME TIME. WHEN CATFISH BECAME A FREE AGENT IN THE NEW, UNINHIBITED FREE ENTERPRISE ZONE OF BASEBALL, STEINBRENNER RELENTLESSLY PURSUED HIM. ■ THERE WERE OTHER TEAMS, TOO, THAT GAZED LONGINGLY AT THE CATFISH

but Steinbrenner's persuasiveness and seemingly unlimited bankroll won over Hunter to the Yankee cause. A complicated deal was concocted for Catfish's services, featuring enough ambiguous language to keep a battery of lawyers lucubrating for months. In the final analysis the contract was worth over $3 million to Hunter. Even more important was the clear signal Steinbrenner was sending up that he meant business.

In his first year with New York, Hunter won 23 games, which wasn't enough to bring the Yankees home in front. But it was a harbinger of good things to come in the Bronx. The wheeler-dealing Steinbrenner also brought Bobby Bonds, the San Franciscos outfielder, to the Stadium for Bobby Murcer. Bonds, father of the can't miss future Hall of Famer Barry Bonds, could run and hit with power. His presence in the lineup brought still another spark to New York. The activist Steinbrenner now brought another activist into his front office when he hired Gabe Paul, a shrewd baseball man, to whisper into his ear.

With Virdon gone as manager in midseason of 1975, Steinbrenner embarked on his first rollicking adventure with the undisciplined Billy Martin. The Yankee owner had long looked upon Billy as a "win-

OVERLEAF: **In 1974, Yankee Stadium was closed for renovations for two years. It reopened for the 1976 season with a new design that featured more conveniences but less majesty. Someone pointed out that the scoreboard alone cost more to construct than the entire ballpark did in 1923.**

RIGHT: **In 1973, George Steinbrenner and an investment group bought the Yankees from CBS for $10 million, less than the media conglomerate had paid nine years earlier. During a press conference after the purchase, Steinbrenner said, "I won't be active in the day-to-day operations of the club at all. I'll stick to shipbuilding."**

ner." Now he made up his mind that Martin, with his instinct for the foe's jugular, would make an ideal manager of the Yankees. Billy had just been jettisoned as Texas's pilot, causing Steinbrenner immediately to order Paul out to Colorado, where Martin was trout fishing. Paul's task was to talk Billy into managing the Yankees. In this instance, Steinbrenner caught his own big fish. As a Yankee player, Martin had been the consummate hustler. Steinbrenner envisioned that Billy

ABOVE LEFT: Another hoodwink engineered by the Yankees over the Red Sox brought "Sparky" Lyle to the Yankees in 1972. In his first year in New York he won nine games, saved 35, and had an ERA of 1.91. In 1977 he became the first relief pitcher to win the Cy Young Award, but a year later was dealt to the Texas Rangers. As Graig Nettles put it, "He went from Cy Young to sayonara."

ABOVE RIGHT: Free agent Jim "Catfish" Hunter joined the Yankees in 1975 and won 23 games. The next season he won 17 games and the New Yorkers made it to the World Series for the first time in 12 years. George Steinbrenner said, "He exemplified class and dignity and taught us how to win."

RIGHT: Rich "Goose" Gossage in full flight. His flailing windup unleashed a blistering fastball that few hitters dared dig in against. He retired Carl Yastrzemski in the last of the ninth to seal the Yankees' playoff game win against the Red Sox in 1978. "I wasn't going to get beaten by anything but my best," he said. "I just wound up and threw it as hard as I could. I couldn't tell you where."

Robert Merrill has become a fixture singing "The Star-Spangled Banner." He did so to help dedicate the renovated Yankee Stadium on April 15, 1976.

could make others hustle, with his inimitable brand of combativeness and energy.

By the time Billy became Yankee manager he was already one of those larger-than-life figures that the press found so enchanting. "He always thought of himself as a cowboy from the Old West," a friend told author David Falkner, who wrote a biography of the embattled Billy. "Even in New York he dressed that way, with boots, jeans, jacket, the whole thing. He considered himself the underdog, the old-fashioned gunslinger, who'd come into town to take on the big guy." In creating his own persona, Martin became something of a working-class hero, playing a role with his old team that he might have dreamed about when he was a pugnacious youngster growing up in modest circumstances in West Berkeley, California.

Glad to be out of their tenancy at Shea Stadium, the Yankees, in 1976, responded to Martin's leadership in his first full season at the helm. After 12 years of

pennant drought the Yankees had a winner, although they needed more than Billy's combustible nature to produce the flag. Steinbrenner/Paul brought out-fielder Oscar Gamble from Cleveland, corralled the fleet-footed Mickey Rivers from California, and wangled the highly regarded minor league second base-man, Willie Randolph, from the Pittsburgh system. Right-hander Ed Figueroa and the free spirit Dock Ellis joined the Yankees pitching staff from California in still another transaction. These men all made significant contributions to the Yankee cause in 1976.

As one might suspect, it was a tumultuous year for both Martin and his boss. Even if Steinbrenner had promised Martin he wouldn't interfere with any of Billy's moves there probably wasn't a day in Steinbrenner's life when he wasn't trying to call the shots. Their entente worked that year, for Steinbrenner craved a winner—and that's what Martin gave him. The season was topped off by a tension-filled five-game playoff with Kansas City, as first baseman Chris Chambliss delivered the coup de grace in the ninth inning of the fifth game at Yankee Stadium, with a first-pitch home run off Mark Littell. Starved for victory, the capacity crowd went wild as Chamblis gamboled around the bases, fending off hysterical admirers who almost blocked his way.

"People had forgotten what it meant to root for the Yankees," cracked the ebullient Martin, as he got his team ready to face the Cincinnati Reds in the 1976 World Series. The Reds were a powerful, well-balanced club that refused to join in the general celebration for the Yankees and "Casey's Boy," Martin. Manager Sparky Anderson's Big Red Machine was one of the most formidable teams in history, featuring such headline icons as Joe Morgan, Johnny Bench, Tony Perez, Pete Rose, and George Foster. Bill James, the baseball Euclid, pronounced "the 1975–76 Reds as having one of the most diverse, broad-based offenses" anyone ever had seen. It turned out that James was not exaggerating. Martin and his men could do nothing to prevent the Reds from sweeping four straight games. Bench was a one-man wrecking crew. He drove in six runs and hit .533. The Yankees could muster only eight runs in four games, even though the never-say-die Munson banged out nine hits for the Yankees, including six in his last six times at bat. Needless to say, such scant production brought little joy to Martin's heart. It hardly caused him to cut down on his imbibing.

Though the crowds were large at Yankee Stadium in this comeback year, with over two million flocking there, Steinbrenner was not satisfied. He felt that his club had been embarrassed by Cincinnati and he wanted to retaliate. So, once again, he went to his wallet. He signed the free agent Don Gullett, the Reds' ace left-hander, who had beaten the Yankees in the first Series game. But ultimately Gullett turned out to

be injury-prone and of little value to his new team. Instead, it fell to Ron Guidry, a wiry fellow from southwestern Louisiana, to quickly join the long line of illustrious New York southpaws.

In the winter of 1976, Steinbrenner conducted his pursuit of the garrulous, thirty-one-year-old Reggie Jackson, who hit prodigious home runs and struck out with equal panache. Steinbrenner courted Reggie up and down the length of Manhattan Island. Pundits believed that Jackson had already made up his mind to join the Yankees and thus did not need to be proselytized. Nevertheless, Steinbrenner introduced Reggie to every posh restaurant in sight and Reggie was espe-

Chris Chambliss has just connected for one of the most fabled home runs in the history of the Yankees, a ninth-inning shot against the Kansas City Royals that won the 1976 pennant for the New Yorkers. He began circling the bases, but was quickly swarmed over by celebrating Yankee fans. "I was worried about getting trampled," he said. "I wasn't even worried about touching bases anymore."

LEFT: Slender southpaw Ron Guidry, nicknamed "Gator" and "Louisiana Lightning," captured the Cy Young Award in 1978 after posting a 25–3 record, including 13 wins in a row, a 1.74 ERA, and 9 shutouts. A local newspaperman wrote, "From the first moment he brought his remarkable left arm and his great heart to the Stadium, he has done honor to his uniform. He has brought the past to the present."

BELOW: As accomplished at bat as he was in the field, Graig Nettles hit 37 homers and drove in 107 runs in 1977, the best numbers ever produced by a Yankee third baseman. During the 1970s only two American League hitters drove in more runs than he did. But he is best remembered for his brilliant fielding, especially in the third game of the 1978 World Series when he left the Dodgers and their fans awestruck.

RIGHT: An immovable object behind the plate, Munson was an unrelenting competitor. He growled at enemy hitters and challenged his teammates to excel. His death in a private plane crash in 1979 devastated the team. After Munson's funeral, Lou Piniella said, "I still can't believe I'm not going to walk into the locker room and see him standing there."

ABOVE LEFT: The body language of Reggie Jackson and Billy Martin betrays their mutual wariness. In a June 1977 game at Fenway Park they had to be separated in the dugout after Martin took Jackson out of the game for what he considered listless play on Reggie's part. "You showed me up," Jackson screamed. "You showed me up. How could you do it to me on television?"

ABOVE RIGHT: Billy Martin was unrepentant after his run-in with Reggie Jackson at Fenway Park. "He jogged toward the ball," Martin said, "fielded it on about the fiftieth hop, took his sweet time throwing it in, and made a weak throw in the general direction of the pitcher's mound."

cially pleased when headwaiters and bystanders recognized him. A complicated and articulate man, Reggie was one of baseball's most celebrated narcissists. He may have had an ego higher than Abe Lincoln's stovepipe hat, but he also had the talent to back it up. A caustic intimate of Jackson once said of him that his main goal in life was to die in his own arms.

When Reggie finally succumbed to Steinbrenner's blandishments he was awarded a five-year contract that measured out at $3 million a year. That was pretty decent pay; Reggie had sniffed the air of entertainment commerce and had played his cards well. His symbiotic relationship with Steinbrenner meant that it was inevitable that he would wind up in the Bronx. The Yankees' owner certainly hadn't signed on Reggie to pacify the troops. He must have realized that Reggie would further roil the waters in the Yankee club-

house, already far from tranquil under the stormy leadership of Martin and with such egos as Munson and Graig Nettles, the wise cracking third baseman.

Even before he climbed into his Yankee pinstripes, Jackson predicted that it wouldn't be long before a candy bar would be named for him in New York. He had probably heard that Babe Ruth had the popular chocolate confection, Baby Ruth, named after him. That was historically inaccurate for the chewy Baby Ruth had actually been named for President Grover Cleveland's daughter and not for the Bambino.

But Reggie's braggadocio did not stop there. Early in the season *Sport* magazine ran an article in which Reggie was quoted in his ineffable style. "I am the straw that stirs the drink," he said, rather poetically. Not leaving well enough alone, Reggie added that Munson, still the acknowledged team leader, could only stir it "bad." Whatever possessed Reggie to issue such a pronouncement defies comprehension. When Munson read the words, his neck turned red. Their relationship, always prickly, worsened.

The press had now taken to calling the Yankees the "Bronx Zoo." The chief lion tamer in the cage was the chronically angry Martin, who had not wanted Reggie to come to the Yankees in the first place. It was only a matter of time before Martin would explode. "Baseball is a long novel whose story grows in complexity and richness over the course of months," Pulitzer Prize author David Maraniss has written. He must have had the Yankees of 1977 in mind.

With the Red Sox playing the Yankees at Fenway Park in midseason—as a national TV audience watched—Martin suddenly confronted Reggie in the dugout. He was accusing Reggie of loafing on a fly ball hit in his area. For a moment it appeared as if the two men would entangle themselves in a brawl. But cooler heads managed to intercede. Coaches Berra and Howard pulled them apart in an act of practical diplomacy that prevented any skulls from being broken.

Having witnessed the confrontation on TV, Steinbrenner, in a fury, wanted to fire Martin on the spot. But Jackson, of all people, rode to Billy's side. It wasn't an act of magnanimity for him to be an advocate for Billy. Rather it was that Jackson appreciated what a firm hold Martin had on Yankee fandom and he didn't care to be blamed for such an auto-da-fé.

This had turned out to be a hectic, strange summer in New York. It was almost as if the vibrant old village had lost its equilibrium. An itinerant mountain

Reggie Jackson clouting the third of his home runs, hit on three successive pitches, in the sixth game of the 1977 World Series. "God, it was a great moment," he said. "It was called the greatest game a hitter ever had in a World Series," Jackson said. "I can live with that."

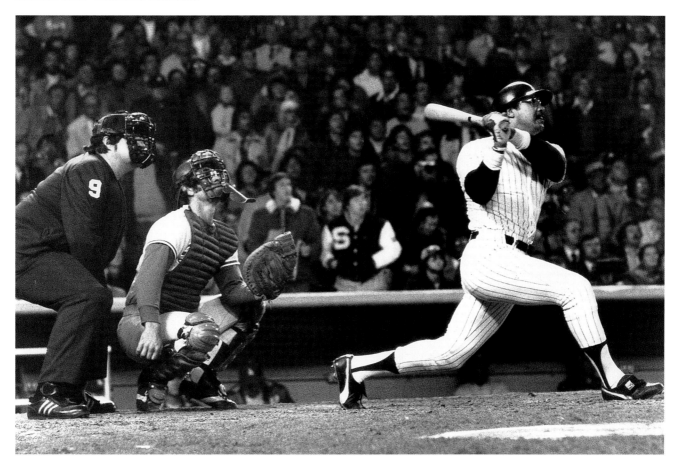

climber from Queens fearlessly scaled the World Trade Center; Puerto Rican nationalists exploded bombs in several Manhattan office buildings; a psychopathic serial killer with a revolver and a tabloid-manufactured name of Son of Sam became a roving Hitchcock movie; a Consolidated Edison blowout ignited a looting binge; and at one point the sweltering streets were exposed to a near-record temperature of 104 degrees. On the national stage three unique personalities—Leopold Stokowski, Groucho Marx, and Elvis Presley—died.

All the while, Reggie, Billy, and the others in the Yankees' dysfunctional family battled to the wire against Kansas City for the American League flag. If there was proof needed that the Yankees were more than a vaudeville act, their performance confirmed that fact. Led by Reggie's 32 homers and 110 runs batted in, plus his 129 strikeouts in 525 at bats—which was consistent with the future Hall of Famer's lifetime total of 2,597 strikeouts (twice the number of Babe Ruth's whiffs)—the Yankees survived one of the most tempest-filled campaigns in baseball history.

After winning the Eastern Division title, the Yankees had to face Kansas City again. And again the playoff was decided in the ninth inning of the fifth game as the Yankees scored three runs to win, 5–3. Reggie had some help from a new shortstop, Bucky Dent, who had been obtained in a trade with the White Sox in exchange for Oscar Gamble. A strong right-hander, Mike Torrez, was also acquired from Oakland. However, it was the slender Cajun, Guidry—who won 16 games, and led the league with an earned run average of 2.82—who made the largest contribution on the mound.

With their victory, the Yankees now revived their World Series rivalry with the Dodgers, whose lineup embraced four players who hit thirty or more home runs—Steve Garvey, Dusty Baker, Ron Cey, and Reggie Smith. In his first year as manager at Los Angeles, Tommy Lasorda, the most verbal man to pilot a big league team since Stengel, had a pitching staff led by southpaw Tommy John and right-hander Don Sutton.

The Yankees thirsted for a Series triumph, which they hadn't enjoyed since 1962. They would get it, but only after one of the most astonishing one-man shows in the history of the fall classic. Naturally it was Reggie who provided the drama and sinew. As the Yankees took a 3–2 edge in the Series, Reggie warmed up to his task with homers in the Saturday and Sunday games at Los Angeles. The scene then shifted to Yankee Stadium. On Tuesday, October 18, 56,000 people jammed The House That Ruth Built, unprepared for what they were about to witness.

In the second inning Reggie walked and scored ahead of a homer by Chambliss. In the fourth inning Reggie came to bat with his old "friend" Munson on base and the Dodgers in front, 3–2. He proceeded to hit the first pitch from knuckleballer Burt Hooton on a line into the right-field seats. The blow knocked Hooton out of the box, and put the Yankees ahead, 4–3.

With one Yankee on base in the fifth inning, Reggie promptly banged Elias Sosa's first pitch into the Ruthville enclave in right field. As the Yankees were now ahead, 7–3, Martin might have replaced Reggie in the outfield as a late-inning defensive move. Martin had committed this heresy before, risking the ire of Jackson. But Paul Blair was not called on at this point to fill in for Reggie. After all, when is the star performer jettisoned before the last act comes to a climax?

This time Reggie faced Charlie Hough and his knuckleball, a pitch not unlike Hooton's. Again, on the first pitch, Reggie smashed Hough's delivery over 450 feet to dead center field, an area that remained

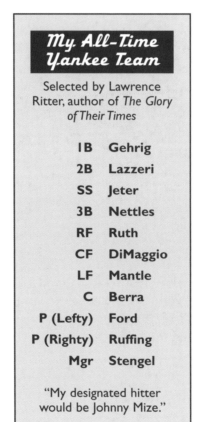

My All-Time Yankee Team

Selected by Lawrence Ritter, author of *The Glory of Their Times*

1B	Gehrig
2B	Lazzeri
SS	Jeter
3B	Nettles
RF	Ruth
CF	DiMaggio
LF	Mantle
C	Berra
P (Lefty)	Ford
P (Righty)	Ruffing
Mgr	Stengel

"My designated hitter would be Johnny Mize."

unoccupied by fans in order to give batters a background free of white shirts. The crowd, almost en masse, leaped to its feet with a collective roar, even though some were probably not aware that Reggie's three home runs had been hit each time on the first pitch. Only Babe Ruth had hit three home runs in a Series game; he had done it twice, in 1926 and 1928. But the Babe never did it on three appearances in a row and on three pitches.

As Jackson rounded first base on his third blow, first sacker Steve Garvey of the Dodgers, fully appreciative of a feat he'd never seen before—and probably would never see again—quietly clapped into his glove. "I thought it was worth my applause," he told reporters.

In his last nine times at bat in a Series he had dominated, Reggie hit five home runs out of a total of six hits, scored seven times, and proved to any doubters who may have been left that he was much more than an inflated ego. The press and Steinbrenner at once adopted the nickname of "Mr. October" to describe him. "It was the happiest moment of my career," Reggie said. Now he felt vindicated and at peace with himself. After all the turmoil and fractiousness, Jackson sat on top of the sports world and there was Steinbrenner grinning in the background. How could anyone possibly criticize Steinbrenner for his tactics in chasing after Reggie?

Just how long would such euphoria last in the Yankee camp? What could Reggie do for an encore in 1978? Amazingly, in the first game of the 1978 season Reggie picked up right where he left off in the final game of the 1977 Series.

Roger Maris, who had exiled himself from the Bronx for 12 years, returned to the Stadium for the opener against the White Sox. He helped to raise the

The annual Old-Timer's Day celebrations are a cherished Yankee Stadium tradition that invariably attract capacity crowds. Joe DiMaggio, gray-haired but with uniform number 5 in crisp condition, stands for the national anthem before the festivities in 1978.

It wasn't a tape measure shot, but Bucky Dent's home run that barely cleared Fenway Park's Green Monster was lengthy enough to crush Red Sox hopes in the 1978 playoff game. "I didn't know it cleared the wall until I was past first base," Dent said. Boston pitcher Mike Torrez, who surrendered the homer, started for the dugout, certain that Dent's high fly would be a routine out. "I looked over my shoulder on the way to the dugout and couldn't believe it," he said.

team's first world championship flag in 15 years. Thousands of "Reggie" candy bars were distributed to the fans before the game. Then, on the first pitch he saw in the new season, Reggie connected for a three-run homer. As he trotted out to his right-field position in the second inning, Reggie's delirious fans threw their "Reggie" bars onto the field. It took five minutes to clean up the debris, but it was another sweet moment for Jackson.

Never content to stay pat with his roster, Steinbrenner picked up the fastballing relief pitcher, Rich "Goose" Gossage. He already had Sparky Lyle, the 1977 Cy Young Award winner, in the bull pen. But he always believed that a team could never have enough pitching, especially the kind that Gossage could pro-

vide. If that meant hurting Lyle's feelings, so be it. When Gabe Paul resigned in January, Steinbrenner brought in Al Rosen, the former Cleveland third baseman, to replace him as team president. Like Martin, Rosen was adept with his fists, having been a fine boxer in his younger years. But unlike Martin, he was not paranoid and didn't go around picking fights. He knew he had plenty to cope with in Billy but felt he could handle the challenge. Meanwhile, the relationship between Reggie and Billy, which for a few moments had warmed up after Reggie's Academy Award performance in the Series, soured again. Reggie had an outspoken distaste for Billy's effort to recast him as a designated hitter. As Reggie brooded, Billy drank and became more sullen than ever.

By mid-July the club was stuck in a slot 14 games behind the Red Sox, who looked like a cinch to win the flag. About the only thing working properly for the Yankees was Ron Guidry's left arm. Guidry was enjoying the kind of season that every pitcher dreams about. He wound up with a 25–3 mark. But what was transpiring on the field had to take a back seat to the never-ending Mack Sennett comedy that ran like a dismal virus through the organization. Billy fought with Rosen, Reggie seethed over Billy, Steinbrenner hassled with Billy, even as he kept reminding him that he was his boss. It was a season of discontent if ever there was one.

It didn't seem possible that there would be any more firestorms in the Yankee tent. But on the night of July 17 Martin did it again, with the help of Reggie. With the Yankees tied with Kansas City in the last of the tenth inning at the Stadium, Munson reached first base with nobody out. Reggie had failed to hit in his first four appearances and now it was his turn to bat. Billy signaled to him that he wanted him to lay down a bunt, thus moving the potential winning run to second base—normal procedure in baseball. But not for Reggie Jackson. He had not been called on to bunt all season and regarded the instruction as an insult to his imperial presence.

The first pitch was too high for Reggie to bunt. But when Reggie moved into his bunt posture, Kansas City's infielders were alerted to Martin's intentions. Billy immediately switched his plan and removed the bunt sign. Aware of Billy's altered strategy, Reggie still insisted on trying to bunt. He fouled off three attempts, probably more because of his anger than anything else, and was declared out for his efforts. In the dugout Billy was hardly able to suppress his rage. He was the Yankee manager, nobody ignored his orders. If the insubordinate player was Jackson, that made it even worse. But when Reggie returned to the bench and removed his

My All-Time Yankee Team

Selected by Al Silverman, former editor, *Sport* magazine

1B	Gehrig
2B	Lazzeri
SS	Jeter
3B	Rolfe
RF	Ruth
CF	DiMaggio
LF	Mantle
C	Berra
P (Lefty)	Ford
P (Righty)	Bump
	Hadley
Mgr	McCarthy

glasses, Billy did not take up the implicit challenge to fight. Adding insult to injury, the Yankees lost the game.

As a result of his blatant disregard of Martin's orders, Reggie was suspended for five days by Steinbrenner and Rosen. But that didn't end the matter. Close to nervous exhaustion, Billy kept stoking the fire. When Reggie returned to action, Billy called him a liar. He went on to remind people that Steinbrenner had once been "convicted." A less diplomatic remark couldn't have been uttered by anybody working for Steinbrenner, for the Watergate-related conviction remained a dark episode in Steinbrenner's biography.

Martin's remarks made lively reading in New York's newspapers, as Billy must have known they would. But he had also proven his self-destructiveness. Within hours he submitted his resignation to his employers, beating them to the punch. Rosen at once suggested that Hall of Fame right-hander Bob Lemon, his former Cleveland teammate, take over the Yankee portfolio. Lemon, who had been dismissed as White Sox manager earlier in the year, had a personality in sharp contrast to the embattled Martin. He was taciturn and easygoing, and when he had a drink or two he didn't become bellicose, which was Martin's besetting sin. His experience finishing second to the Yankees all those years when he was a player should have given him insight into the New York club's toughness. As Lemon took over the reins Martin sounded a bittersweet valedictory. "The team has a shot at the pennant and I hope they win," he said.

But it was hardly a valedictory. For five days later, as the Yankees staged Old-Timers Day at Yankee Stadium, Steinbrenner unleashed a surprise that almost defied belief. Bob Sheppard announced to the capacity crowd over the public address system that Martin— yes, Billy Martin—would be returning as Yankee manager in two years. What caused this plot switch had more to do with the howls of protests from loyal Martin fans than with any resuscitated love affair between Billy and George. It was rumored that Martin had apologized to Steinbrenner. More likely Billy's return evolved because George was tired of being assailed in the press. Had he concocted this stunning scenario to placate the legions of Billy boosters?

When the season resumed under Lemon, the Yankee clubhouse had become a beach of tranquillity. What's more, the team started to win and never stopped. Harmony may be an overused word in baseball circles, but in their last 68 games the Yankees won 48. In a head-to-head confrontation with the Red Sox in early September, the Yankees obliterated the Boston club in Fenway Park. The Yankees took four games in a row, all by lopsided scores, as the unruffled Lemon made moves that stamped him as a wise man. Manager Don Zimmer of the Red Sox (who would in the 1990s become a soothing presence in the Yankee dugout alongside Manager Joe Torre) couldn't explain what had happened to his team. Led by their fine outfielder, Carl Yastrzemski, the Sox were a good club. But they had crumbled before the Yankee onslaught. Even so, the Red Sox would have one more opportunity to prove that they could compete with New York. When the Yankees stumbled at season's end, a one-game playoff for the American League flag was scheduled for October 2 at Fenway Park, presumably giving the home field advantage to Boston.

If precedent meant anything, Cleveland had defeated the Red Sox in 1948, also at Fenway, in a one-game showdown for the pennant. Things looked good on October 2 for the Red Sox as they held a 2–0 lead behind Mike Torrez. For once the Curse of the

Bambino seemed to be relegated to the ashcan. Then, the superstition-haunted Red Sox fans again lived to see their recurring nightmare played out. In the seventh inning, the normally light-hitting shortstop of the Yankees, Bucky Dent (.243 in 1978), inched a drive over the infamous Green Monster wall in left field, with two men on to put the Yankees ahead. Dent later admitted he didn't think the ball was going over. But go over it did. With only four other home runs that year, Dent became an overnight Yankee idol. His dark-haired good looks helped him as much with the female clientele, as his serendipitous "bloop" home run.

Tommy John, his arm reconstructed, won 21 games for the Yankees in 1979, and a year later, at age thirty-seven, won 22. Before the operation that repaired his throwing arm, John asked the surgeon to implant Koufax's fastball. "The only problem was," John said later, "he gave me Mrs. Koufax's fastball."

Dave Righetti was named Rookie of the Year in 1981, and on July 4, 1983, he pitched a no-hitter against the Boston Red Sox at Yankee Stadium. He ended the game with a flourish, striking out a .365 hitter named Wade Boggs with a high fastball. "For an instant everything seemed to stop," Righetti said. "Then I just wanted to cry."

The Red Sox tried valiantly in the last of the ninth inning to redeem the season. But Lou Piniella's artful pantomime in right field on a ball that he lost in the late fall sun saved the Yankees. Pretending he was about to catch the ball, a fly hit by second baseman Jerry Remy, Piniella prevented a runner from moving up a base. A long fly followed, which would have tied the score. As it turned out, Yastrzemski popped out on a Goose Gossage pitch to end the game, 5–4, in favor of New York. It couldn't have gotten any closer than that. But that didn't mitigate the pervasive gloom over New England.

For the third straight year the Yankees faced Kansas City in the playoff. Naturally, again it was Mr.

October who led the way. He had a three-run homer in the first game, then added another circuit blow in a later game, as the Yankees took the series, 3–1. Jackson's output was six runs batted in and a .462 average, blunting any criticism of the Great Man that might have come from some quarters.

In the World Series against the Los Angeles Dodgers that followed the victory over Kansas City the Yankees again fell into their habit of battling from behind. This time they dropped the first two games to the Dodgers and had their backs to the wall. In the second of those defeats Reggie staged a memorable confrontation with the young Dodgers' right-hander, Bob Welch. In the ninth inning, with Los Angeles ahead, 4–3, the Yankees had two men on base with two out. Now accepted as one of the premier postseason hitters of any era, Reggie worked the count to 3–2, after fouling off several blazing pitches. With the runners moving on the bases, Reggie swung lustily at the next pitch and struck out. This was heartstopping stuff for millions of fans, who were glued to their sets by the duel. Forgotten was the fact that Ron Cey of the Dodgers had knocked across all four runs for Los Angeles.

Returning to Yankee Stadium, the Yankees suddenly were unbeatable. They took three in a row on their home grounds, aided immeasurably by third baseman Graig Nettles, who put on a defensive show at his position that would have put Hall of Famer Pie Traynor of Pittsburgh to shame.

In the fourth game Reggie again became the center of attention, but not by hitting a homer or striking out. This time, with Los Angeles ahead, 3–1, in the sixth inning, Munson was on second and Reggie on first, with one out. Lou Piniella hit an easy double-play ground ball to shortstop Bill Russell, who stepped on second and threw to first. However, Russell's toss hit Reggie on the hip and dribbled into right field, permitting Munson to score. The Dodgers screamed to high heaven that infidel Reggie had deliberately allowed himself to be hit by the throw. But the argument with the umpires went nowhere, and that was the end of the Dodgers. Ultimately, they dropped that game in the tenth inning on Piniella's single. The next day the Yankees smashed the Dodgers' hopes with a 12–2 victory.

Back in Los Angeles nothing was very different. The Dodgers had complained that New York's boisterous fans and their darn Stadium were to blame for their misfortunes. But in game six it was the Yankees again on top, 7–2, as Jackson squared accounts with Welch with a two-run blast. The Yankees batted .306

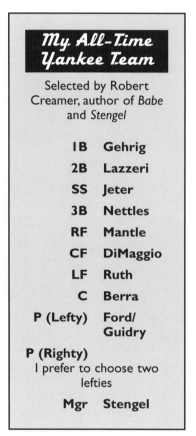

My All-Time Yankee Team

Selected by Robert Creamer, author of *Babe* and *Stengel*

1B	Gehrig
2B	Lazzeri
SS	Jeter
3B	Nettles
RF	Mantle
CF	DiMaggio
LF	Ruth
C	Berra
P (Lefty)	Ford/Guidry
P (Righty)	I prefer to choose two lefties
Mgr	Stengel

in the Series, a record for six games. This marked the Yankees' twenty-second championship, and nobody could protest that they had been front-runners. "They play best under pressure," George Brett of Kansas City observed, and not very happily. He knew what he was talking about.

These pleasant events seemed to presage another productive year in 1979, with the Yankees chasing a fourth straight pennant. The word "dynasty" always came easy to writers and other observers when they discussed the Yankees. The New Yorkers had been there before, many times, and the feeling was that they would do it again. Reinforcing this feeling was the fact that Steinbrenner had gone into the money market again. He obtained southpaw Tommy John, who had had a successful surgical procedure on his elbow, and he also plucked the colorful Cuban veteran Luis Tiant out of Boston's pitching ranks.

But, strangely, an atmosphere of doom settled over the club almost from the beginning of the season. On April 19, some dozen games into the campaign, an unscheduled round of fisticuffs took place between indispensable bull pen ace Gossage and fill-in player Cliff Johnson after an exchange of quips. When the dust settled, Gossage had badly hurt his thumb. He spent three months on the bench as a result. As far as Johnson was concerned that ended his career as a Yankee; in June he was shuffled along to Cleveland.

With Goose on the agony list and Lyle, the other relief ace, gone to Texas, the Yankees were in sad shape. Baltimore took advantage of a badly wounded Yankee team and marched to the flag, under manager Earl Weaver, a firm believer in three-run homers. The thirty-six-year-old Tommy John put together an excellent season of 21–9, but by mid-June the Yankees had sunk to fourth place and that meant the end of the road for Bob Lemon. Steinbrenner didn't think that Lemon had control of his personnel, overlooking the impact on Lemon of the recent death of his son in an auto accident.

Hoping to rejuvenate his troops, Steinbrenner gave a pink slip to Lemon and replaced him with his eternal designated manager, Billy Martin. Billy may have been a battler but there was precious little that he could do with a team in a catatonic state. What's more, on August 2, Munson crashed his plane in Ohio and was killed. It was not an event that could recharge the Yankees, who were numbed by the sudden death of their catcher. A day later they lost to Baltimore, 1–0, at Yankee Stadium, as a mournful crowd came to say farewell to Thurman. In the charred remains of Munson's jet were the cinders of a wrecked season. Oddly, as the season ended, the front office announced that over 2½ million fans had attended Yankee home games, a new record.

Even after such a lugubrious season for Yankee supporters, the grim scenario was not yet completed. After the World Series (won by the Willie Stargell-led Pirates over Baltimore in seven games), Martin again found himself in the wrong place at the wrong time. He punched a person described as "a marshmallow salesman" in a Bloomington, Minnesota, hotel bar, a not uncommon place for his peccadilloes. Billy insisted he'd been goaded into the fight, although he couldn't recall what was said or who said it. The salesman ended up on the floor with hurt feelings and a gashed lip. And Billy ended up a few days later with a dismissal from the enraged Steinbrenner. It marked still another departure for Billy from a team that he sobbed meant more than life to him.

This time Steinbrenner went to Dick Howser, the third-base coach under Martin and a former infielder and college coach, to replace Billy. To some it seemed like a fortuitous choice, for Howser was not given to

Don Mattingly and Dave Winfield flank Pete Sheehy, the Yankees' seemingly eternal equipment manager, who served from 1927 to 1985. The clubhouse was later named after Sheehy, and a plaque in his honor is affixed to the dugout wall.

Monument Park, one of the most popular attractions at Yankee Stadium, dates back to 1932 when a tablet was placed near the bleachers wall in honor of former manager Miller Huggins, who had died suddenly in 1929. Another monument was added in 1941 in memory of Lou Gehrig, and a third in 1949 for Babe Ruth. Many visitors to Yankee Stadium imagined that their heroes were buried beneath the marble memorials.

The three monuments were in play, although nearly 460 feet from home plate. Once during the late 1950s an opposing batter drove a ball over Mickey Mantle's head. The ball bounced against and then behind the monuments, causing Casey Stengel to jump to the top dugout step and shout,

"Ruth, Gehrig, Huggins! Somebody throw the ball!"

During the years preceding the Stadium's remodeling in 1975, spectators were permitted to exit the ballpark via the outfield warning track. On their way out most fans gazed reverently at the three monuments. When the renovation was complete the monuments and plaques were tucked into a section between the new outfield fence and the old bleachers wall.

More memorials have been added over the years, as well as a display of retired Yankee uniform numbers. Tours of Yankee Stadium and Monument Park, conducted by the knowledgeable Tony Morante, are now a year-round diversion. Long lines of the faithful, including bus loads of children, wait patiently every day to enter the hallowed grounds.

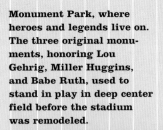

Monument Park, where heroes and legends live on. The three original monuments, honoring Lou Gehrig, Miller Huggins, and Babe Ruth, used to stand in play in deep center field before the stadium was remodeled.

unseemly outbursts or loud second-guesses of his men.

For most of 1980 Howser had things under control. His team mounted a substantial lead over Baltimore by August. Then the club went into a dive, losing a half-dozen games to the Orioles as they watched their lead disintegrate. Fortunately, the Yankees revived in September and beat out the Orioles by three games. Howser never cracked under such pressure, and as his team entered the playoff against Kansas City one more time, it appeared that the Yankees, winners of 103 games, would advance in the postseason. Reggie, with 41 home runs and 111 runs batted in, may have had his best season, and he was looking forward to buttressing his reputation as Mr. October.

In the first game against Kansas City, the Yankees tallied two quick homers, one by Piniella and another by Rick Cerone, who had become a fine replacement for Munson. But after that, it was all downhill. George Brett, unwilling to accept still another defeat at the hands of the New Yorkers, busted loose. He hit a decisive three-run homer in the third game at Yankee Stadium to make certain the Yankees wouldn't get up again. And Reggie proved that he was human after all. There were no home runs in his big bat, although he did connect for three hits, one a double, in the three straight losses to the Royals.

However, a key moment for the Yankees came in the second game when third-base coach Mike Ferraro waved Willie Randolph home from first base on a long drive by Bob Watson. If Randolph had made it the score would have been tied in the eighth inning. Instead, Brett made a perfect relay to catch Willie at home. That was really the end of the Yankees—and Steinbrenner was unrelentingly harsh in his second-guess of Ferraro's judgment. When Howser was supportive of his coach's decision, Steinbrenner, bitter over the three-game trouncing, let the press know about his feelings. "It's embarrassing as hell to me," he barked. This placed Howser in a rather unenviable position. He chose to resign, even though it looked to most people like a forced resignation. Gene Michael, once the Yankees shortstop and now the general man-

ager of the club, was appointed by Steinbrenner to succeed Howser. Dick went off into the sunset quietly, which was his style.

With the low-key Michael—known as "Stick" to his associates—at the helm, 1981 began as if it would be a year of renewal for the Yankees. The team had signed Dave Winfield, who, like Reggie before him, had become the focus of Steinbrenner's desire. Winfield was a college-bred (University of Minnesota) all-around athlete who stood six inches over six feet, weighed about 225 pounds, and had spent eight seasons in relative obscurity pounding balls for the San Diego Padres. Steinbrenner's pursuit of Winfield made the Padres outfielder the biggest fish in the free agent market. A longtime Yankee scout, Birdie Tebbetts, once a top-notch catcher and manager, had reported to Steinbrenner that, with a good ball club, Winfield's batting average was bound to go up at least 30 points. A complicated contract was drawn up to lure Winfield. After it was put through the computer it appeared that the big, handsome fellow was going to make about $23 million spread over ten years.

But perhaps even more costly to both the Yankees and baseball was a strike called by the Baseball Players Association on June 12. The players and owners had been battling for years over rising player salaries, as well as the issue of what compensation clubs should get when they lost stars to free agency. The reserve clause had previously given the owners the upper hand over the players. But the situation was changing, with the help of a veteran steel workers' organizer, Marvin Miller, who had been hired in 1966 by the players to represent them in hard-nosed bargaining with the owners. Both sides remained adamant in the summer of 1981 and the strike got under way.

Sadly, the stoppage of big league play came at a time when the old game had become increasingly attractive to millions of new fans. Attendance and TV ratings were booming, despite baseball's unenlightened leadership and anemic marketing efforts. The faceless officials off the field had always taken this wonderful durable game for granted, believing that the sport's romance, charm, and aesthetic beauty could overcome their own public relations limitations.

Those who professed to speak for baseball assumed that nothing could harm their game, not even their own malfeasance and cupidity. They accepted the permanence of the pastime, just as they had always assumed that the Yankees hegemony would go on forever. But now the angered fans were unwilling to root either for the owners or their janissaries.

"The fans weren't ever very philosophical about it," said Dave Winfield. "They were just pissed."

By the time the strike was finally settled almost two months later, 706 games had been wiped off the ledger. Since something had to be done to repair the fractured season, not to mention the grievances of the fans, one of the game's Einsteins came up with a "split season" solution. The standings as of June 12 were frozen. That became the first half of the season. Division leaders at that stage of the campaign were pronounced first-half winners. Second-half winners would then meet the first-half leaders in a best three out of five mini-playoff, to be concluded with a regular playoff between division champions. For the most part, the plan was regarded with scorn, since teams with the best overall record didn't make it into the postseason games. Having finished two games over Baltimore in the first half, the Yankees won the right to play in the first round of the playoffs. The fact that their cumulative record would not have gotten them into the postseason contests didn't matter.

Though it became certain that the Yankees would be involved in postseason combat, Steinbrenner wasn't happy with the way Michael was running the club. It wasn't clear what Stick had done—or hadn't done—to displease his boss. But several weeks after the strike was over, Michael was jettisoned. Steinbrenner reached out again to the familiar: he rehired Bob Lemon for the last month of the season. The placid Lemon handled matters in his usual "don't disturb the animals" manner. The team won only 11 games in 25 under his leadership. But there they were, facing Milwaukee in the mini-playoff.

After jumping off to a two-game lead over Milwaukee, mainly thanks to superb relief pitching from Gossage and Ron Davis, the Yankees returned to Yankee Stadium to finish off the job. But Milwaukee wasn't subscribing to such a scenario. The Yankees proceeded to lose two straight at home, with one more game to be played at Yankee Stadium. After the two defeats Steinbrenner was nearly apoplectic as he fumed in the Yankees locker room, accusing his players of every crime except barratry. One player in particular, Rick Cerone, was singled out for abuse by the owner and Rick didn't take kindly to it. Cerone had made a base-running blunder in one of the Yankee losses. He wasn't perfect. But who is? Cerone rebutted Steinbrenner with some scatological comments. And matters stood that way until the next day, when the Yankees won, with the help of home runs by Reggie, Oscar Gamble, and, you guessed it, Rick Cerone!

This set up an American League title series against Oakland, now managed by none other than Billy Martin, who had installed his special brand of Billy Ball with the Athletics. If anything, Martin was more aggressive and strident than ever before, perhaps baseball's best manager from the first pitch to the last. "But," wrote author David Falkner, "it was the last pitch to the first the next day that got him into trouble . . . his life away from the field was as rudderless as ever."

However, Martin's tactics against the Yankees produced no positive results. His club dropped three straight games to the Yankees, as Nettles went crazy at bat with nine RBIs, and his usual alacrity at third base. In a postseries party, the hero, Nettles, got into a scrape with Reggie, and it took three big men, Bob Watson, Winfield, and Gossage, to pull the two of

My All-Time Yankee Team

Selected by Jack Lang, secretary of the Baseball Writers Association, 1965–1990

1B	Gehrig
2B	Lazzeri
SS	Rizzuto
3B	Nettles
RF	Ruth
CF	DiMaggio
LF	Mantle
C	Berra
P (Lefty)	Ford
P (Righty)	Ruffing
Mgr	Stengel

them apart. So much for togetherness. Here was a team on the way to a World Series against Los Angeles and they were fighting among themselves. You read about such behavior in meretricious sports novels. But this was real life—and it was really happening.

When the Yankees drubbed Los Angeles in the first two games of the Series, both at Yankee Stadium, everybody shrugged at the brotherly battles. But when the games moved out to Los Angeles, the bottom seemed to drop out of the universe for New York. First, the Mexican pitching sensation, Fernando Valenzuela, put them away. When the Dodgers added the next two games, the Yankees were down 3–2. Following these three defeats, Steinbrenner, in a blind rage, became involved in a mysterious incident in an elevator. He claimed that he had been waylaid by a couple of bellicose Dodger fans and had broken his hand as he defended his honor. His distemper didn't improve when the Dodgers, on a roll, wrapped up the Series in game six, helped along by home runs by Steve Yeager and Pedro Guerrero.

Making a strange contribution to Yankee history was relief pitcher George Frazier, who got "credit" for losing three games in the Series. Only the infamous Claude Williams had also lost three games in the World Series—and he accomplished that feat when he was one of the alleged fixers on the 1919 Black Sox team that lost to Cincinnati.

Outside of the dejected Steinbrenner, nobody was more disappointed with the outcome of the World Series than Winfield. The expensive slugger just didn't slug very much in the Series. He followed a 1–13 performance against Oakland with only one hit in 22 times at bat against the Dodgers. There had once been a more mellow time when a Series slump such as Winfield suffered could have elicited the ecumenical prayers of an entire borough. Gil Hodges' 0–21 in the World Series of 1952 against the Yankees won that kind of sympathetic reaction from Brooklynites. (Other formidable players such as Ted Williams, Stan Musial, and Barry Bonds have also fared badly in post-season play without bringing down the wrath of their home town fans.)

But Steinbrenner was not in the mood to send up prayers for Dave. Instead, he issued an "apology" to the people of New York for his team's performance in the Series. After the apology Winfield stopped by the boss's office before going home for the off-season. Dave noted that Steinbrenner had his chin in his hands. He told the Yankees' owner that he appreciated getting the chance to play in New York and added that finishing second wasn't good enough for him either. "I owe you one," said Dave.

One Yankee who didn't choose to act as equably as Winfield was Reggie. Although Steinbrenner probably had Winfield in mind when he issued his apology, Reggie was furious with the statement. He said that he didn't have anything to apologize for. In fact, he had held his own, with four hits in 12 at bats, including one home run.

The next year Jackson was gone from the Yankee tent. He had chosen to sign a five-year deal with the California Angels, who still believed there were plenty of hits left in his bat. After five seasons with the Yankees, during which he had become a lightning rod for headlines, as well as garnishing his claim to join the Hall of Fame, Reggie was sorely missed by Yankee fans.

Sadly, too, Steinbrenner's treacly words would prove to be something of a watershed in Yankee history, for over the next 14 years the club lost its winning habit. These turned out also to be the years of the so-called Reagan Revolution. Though there was no discernible connection between the Yankees' downfall and Mr. Reagan's politics, baseball found it had a formidable cheerleader in the nation's chief executive. An affable, tall storytelling ideologue, Reagan had started his professional life (before he went to Hollywood) as a baseball broadcaster in the midwest. There he reported Chicago Cubs games "live," working from a telegraph relay 300 miles away, and relying on "his quick wits and painterly imagination," as author Garry Wills has written. Of all American presidents Reagan was perhaps the most informed about baseball, even edging out his fellow Republican George W. Bush. If he had still been doing ball games in the 1980s Reagan would surely have come up with appropriate adjectives to describe the span of arid years that confronted the Yankees.

In the spring of 1982, the Yankees welcomed back their prodigal son, Reggie, who was now in a California uniform. When he arrived at Yankee Stadium as a foe Reggie was batting less than .200. But he immediately proceeded to hit a towering home run that ignited the audience. Here were 35,000 Yankee fans screaming out their mantra of "Reggie, Reggie!" even as they castigated Steinbrenner with their vile imprecations. Steinbrenner's failure to re-sign Reggie obviously had not gone down well with Yankee supporters.

So the dismal year went. The team skidded downhill, almost from the start, and Steinbrenner kept shifting managers around, going from Lemon, back to Michael, and then to Clyde King, a former pitcher. None of these men could help much and at the end the Yankees posted a mediocre record of 78–83 as they finished 16 games out of first place. Winfield, now nastily derided as "Mr. May" by Steinbrenner (in an obvious contrapuntal reference to Jackson's "Mr. October"), had a productive year in spite of everything. He hit 37 homers, an especially handsome output for a righthanded batter in Yankee Stadium.

Dave Winfield

By his own admission, Dave Winfield was no Reggie Jackson, in character and temperament. Neither was he a shrinking violet. Author E. B. White once said that "New York could bestow on any person who desires such queer prizes the gift of loneliness and the gift of privacy." But neither man sought anonymity when he decided to play the outfield for the Yankees.

Dave always maintained a good sense of humor about his role in New York. "Maybe I'm just the lime on the lip of the glass," he said. But Steinbrenner always wanted much more out of him—pennants and World Series victories, for instance. And that only came once in Dave's eight years on the Yankee payroll.

Despite the lack of victories, Winfield was an extraordinary athlete who never stopped hustling. He was essentially a power hitter in his early years with the San Diego team, and with the Yankees he hit 24 or more home runs in each of his seven full seasons.

In 1984, in an effort to prove to himself that he could hit for a higher average if he cut down on his home run stroke, Winfield ended the year second only to his teammate, Don Mattingly. There were only 19 homers off his bat that year. But he succeeded in making his point. However, in battling down to the wire with Mattingly, he experienced only disappointment and aggravation. In his first full season with New York, Mattingly was having a splendid year full of base-hits. (He ended up with 207 hits to Dave's 93.) By midseason Winfield was in front of all American Leaguers, including Mattingly. But Winfield declined in the second half, giving Mattingly an opportunity to catch up to him for the title. Their stirring competition was the only thing that remained for Yankee fans to follow from day to day, for the team was so far back that even the most optimistic person was inclined to ignore the standings.

Going into the final game of the season Winfield still led Mattingly by 1.57 points. The Yanks were at home against Detroit, the division champs, and a good crowd was on hand to watch the last lap of the batting crown duel. Most of them also came out to cheer for Don, much to the discomfort of Winfield. Every time Mattingly stepped to the plate he was applauded. Dave's angry jousts with Steinbrenner had cost him heavily in the arena of public opinion. Now, when he was deserving of support, he was hearing little more than catcalls and hisses.

Mattingly rose to the occasion in that last contest, pumping out four hits to Dave's one. Thus he edged Winfield out in the final averages, .343 to .340. It was only when Dave came up for his last time at bat—and grounded out—that he heard some appreciative noise for his season-long efforts. But by that time Mattingly had sewed up his batting crown.

To say that Dave was distressed was to put it

After eight seasons in San Diego, Dave Winfield joined the Yankees in 1981. He hit .340 in 1984, and during the season Yankees' Manager Yogi Berra said, "Nobody did as much for us this year as Winfield." George Steinbrenner, with whom Winfield would later clash, said, "I still say Dave Winfield is one of the greatest athletes in the game today."

mildly. But his disaffection had nothing to do with Mattingly. He sincerely believed that his performance had helped to encourage people to continue to come through the Stadium's turnstiles, but he had been undercut by the hostility between Steinbrenner and himself. "When it was all over," said Dave, "I showered, congratulated Donnie, and left the clubhouse, knowing that if I talked to the press I would say something I'd regret. Opting for silence was the most gracious thing I could do."

What little solace Winfield would derive from his season were the remarks made about him by his manager, Yogi Berra, who had been rehired after a twenty-year absence. "He was my most valuable player," Yogi said.

Winfield began his life in 1951, in St. Paul, Minnesota. Although St. Paul was mostly a white commu-

nity Dave grew up in a predominantly black neighborhood. As a youngster Dave played American Legion ball and participated in state and city tournaments. He became an all-around athlete while attending the University of Minnesota. Dick Siebert, a former major league first baseman, was Winfield's coach at Minnesota. He was "a gruff guy who ran his team like a tyrant," remembers Dave—but Siebert managed to overlook Winfield's slugging aptitude. Dave was a successful pitcher for his team until he developed some soreness in his right arm. At that point, Winfield shifted his attention to the outfield.

Although he never paid much attention to basketball, Winfield went out for the Minnesota team and in short order became a star. The basketball team was good enough one year to advance to the NIT. But what made Winfield even prouder was his election by

his teammates to the captaincy of the baseball team. At this point, Winfield's intuition told him that he'd be better served by professional baseball than the National Basketball Association.

By his senior year he was picked by San Diego in the first round of the major league draft. Curiously, though he had never played a single down of high school or college football, he was chosen by the Minnesota Vikings in the sixteenth round of the National Football League draft. For good measure, the Atlanta Hawks in the NBA made him a fifth-round choice in their draft. But Winfield's mind had been made up—he would play baseball.

By June 1973 Winfield was playing for a weak San Diego team, under its cardplaying manager, Don Zimmer. "Zimmer was a lead-by-example guy," said Winfield. "He took one look at the hitch in my batting stance—my starter mechanism—but let me alone, despite what the coaches wanted to do with me. He worked, instead, on my confidence." (It was this trait of Zimmer's that would become an integral part of the Yankees' bench strategy 25 years later, under manager Joe Torre.) The Padres finished last, despite Winfield's presence, and although Winfield became an in-creasingly impressive player, the San Diego team was rarely a factor in the pennant race.

When he finally arrived with the Yankees, Winfield received considerably more notice than he had in San Diego. He was a dependable slugger with New York and a six-time Gold Glove winner. But he was never able to lead the Yankees to the kind of postseason that Yankee fans had come to consider as their birthright. In addition, it was the disagreeable relationship with Steinbrenner that came to dominate the outfielder's career in the Bronx. This rancor centered mainly on one element: Steinbrenner's realization, only too late, that Winfield's cost of living escalator in his contract would yield him some $23 million, as opposed to the $16 million that the owner had expected to pay. It was never easy for Winfield after that. Although the big fellow kept batting in runs and hustling, he was never as popular a figure as Reggie or Mattingly. Mattingly never won with the Yankees but he became one of the most beloved Yankees in history. Nobody blamed Mattingly for Yankee failures. Winfield even managed, inadvertently, to bean a seagull with a throw one day in Toronto. That was the story of his life with the Yankees.

1983–1992

FOR A GOOD PART OF HIS CAREER GEORGE BRETT OF KANSAS CITY HAD AFFLICTED THE COMFORTABLE (THE YANKEES), WHILE ALSO BEING AFFLICTED BY THEM. BUT HE REACHED HIS OWN SUMMIT OF FRUSTRATION AGAINST THE YANKEES ON JULY 24, 1983, AT YANKEE STADIUM, IN WHAT HAS COME TO BE KNOWN AS "THE PINE TAR INCIDENT." BRETT HAD JUST HIT WHAT HE THOUGHT WAS A TWO-RUN, NINTH INNING HOMER THAT PUT HIS TEAM IN THE LEAD, WHEN THAT RAPSCALLION BILLY MARTIN PROTESTED TO THE

umpires that Brett's bat was illegal. In solemn conclave the umpires then agreed that the blow was null and void because the pine tar that Brett had rubbed on his bat went too far up the handle.

Brett reacted by throwing a tantrum that has had few equals in baseball tantrumdom. "He was a man possessed," wrote Professor Michael Seidel of Columbia University. "His face was bright red and he was jumping up and down and pumping like Rumpelstiltskin, gesticulating wildly as if his air supply had been shut off."

Four days later the American League president, Lee MacPhail, a former Yankees' general manager, reversed the umpire's ruling, saying that Brett had not "violated the spirit of the rules." The game was declared suspended, with the score, 5–4, in favor of Kansas City. Three weeks later, after two court decisions went in favor of Brett, the game was completed in ten minutes. Martin, as enraged by this time as Brett had been, watched three of his batters quickly make outs in the ninth, before a muted gathering of less than 2,000 fans. The Pine Tar Game became comic history, overshadowing a Yankee year that saw the team finish seven games out of first place. The highlight of the year was southpaw Dave Righetti's no-hitter on July 4 against the Red Sox at the Stadium. It was the first such performance for New York since Larsen's perfecto in 1956. In future years Righetti would become an enormously effective bull pen operative, one of the Yankees' all-time greats in a lackluster period.

It may have been "morning again in America," as President Reagan, his head cocked to the side, cheerily told his countrymen, but the fog didn't lift for the Yankees in the eighties. Nor did it lift for some American troops. A Marine unit headquartered in a Lebanon office building was attacked by a suicide bomber, killing 241 men. Not long after that the tiny island of Grenada in the Caribbean, whose leaders were suspected of Marxist inclinations, was invaded by American Marines. The "incursion" was meant to restore order, but there was some suspicion that it was an overblown reaction to an anarchic local situation.

Meanwhile, back at the Yankee ranch, Yogi Berra couldn't do better than third place with his team, even as Mattingly squeaked out the American League batting crown. Don was the first Yankee to win the title since Mantle had won it in 1956. What's more, Mattingly was so impressive in the field that he was adjudged the "best glove" that the Yankees had ever had at first base. The next season Mattingly added the Most Valuable Player Award to his list of accomplishments, the first Yankee since Munson won it in 1976.

The 1985 season was unsettling and disappointing for the Yankees. Just 16 days into the season, Yogi was handed his release as manager by Steinbrenner. At the time the team was 6–10 and several key players were hurt. The jettisoning of Yogi was quite unexpected, considering that during spring training Steinbrenner had advised Berra that he wouldn't be fired even if the team got off to a poor start. This set the stage for Yogi to refuse to appear in Yankee Stadium for almost fifteen years. Yogi felt especially bruised because Steinbrenner did not deliver the bad news to him face-to-face. Some Yankee players, including Don Baylor and Mattingly, reacted angrily to the firing, kicking anything in sight upon hearing the story of Yogi's dismissal. According to the sports pundits, the

Don Mattingly first played for the Yankees in 1982, a year after they appeared in the World Series, and retired in 1995, a year before the New Yorkers played in their next classic. During the intervening years Mattingly compiled a .307 lifetime average, 2153 hits, nine Gold Glove awards, and a Most Valuable Player trophy. "Donnie Baseball" was a consummate professional, a throwback to past eras. "I love playing the game," he said. "That's what I'm here for."

incident represented Steinbrenner at his impulsive worst.

Replacing Yogi was the eternal jack-in-the-box, Martin, back for his fourth semester as Yankee leader. But the team did not respond to Martin's alchemy. By August the Yankees were 9½ games out of first. However, Martin managed to rally his troops for an eleven-straight victory surge in September that brought the Yankees close. Still, no cigar. Frustrated by a loss to Toronto, Billy, ever uncontrolled ("a mouse studying to be a rat," was how columnist Red Smith described him), got into two more squabbles late in the season. In one of them, against Ed Whitson, a disgruntled Yankee pitcher, Martin had his arm broken and ribs cracked. The result was that, once

again, Martin lost his job. Lou Piniella was asked to replace him.

Piniella kept his team in the race in 1986, thanks to the usual competence of Mattingly, who seemed to hit more doubles than singles (he surpassed both Earl Combs and Gehrig in this department, as he pounded out 238 hits). Rickey Henderson, the enigmatic lead-off man, led the league in runs scored and stolen bases (ultimately, he would become the all-time leader in stolen bases, as he played on into his forties).

What was lacking in the Yankee mix was decent pitching. The starting rotation had Ron Guidry (he was hardly the hurler he'd been just two years before) and no one else of distinction. Righetti was a tower of late-inning strength in the bull pen, but he couldn't bring the Yankees home in first. They ended up in second, 5 1/2 games behind the Red Sox. Boston went on to lose a nailbiter seven-game World Series to that *other* New York team—the Mets.

Steinbrenner was never certain of Piniella's talent for managing. He was constantly egged on by the opinionated broadcaster Howard Cosell, who whispered (all right, shouted) in his ear about Lou's pre-

sumed deficiencies. When the Yankees zoomed ahead of the field before the All-Star break in 1987 Steinbrenner began to think that Cosell was wrong about Piniella. But when the team took a nosedive in the second half of the season, ending up fourth, nine games out of first place, Steinbrenner could contain himself no longer. Personally fond of Lou, but impatient with defeat, (the Yankees had not won a world

Yankee second baseman Willie Randolph played beside Don Mattingly for six years, sharing the same work ethic and quiet pride in accomplishment. "I'm not very outspoken or flamboyant," he said. "I understand my job." He was selected to the All-Star team six times, and played more games at second base than any player in their history. He began his job as third-base coach in 1994.

title since 1978, adding to Steinbrenner's sense of urgency about the matter), Steinbrenner kicked Piniella upstairs into the role of general manager. Once again, he brought back his stormy talisman, Martin.

It turned out to be a strange and chaotic year, even as Billy's Boys won nine of the first ten games of the season. It was the kind of lift that Steinbrenner wanted, not only for his team but for the box office. Could this be the year the Yankees would rebound? Had Billy really been reformed and chastened?

The answer turned out to be an emphatic no. In early May, after a particularly tough loss in Texas, Billy sullenly retreated to a nearby topless bar. He wasn't there to read his newspaper, either. After a few drinks, who should appear but his old buddy, Mickey Mantle, who happened to be staying at the same hotel. Mickey was going to play in a golf tournament the next day. Billy could keep up with anybody in the booze department; this night was no exception. In the men's room Billy got into a scuffle with a customer, who may or may not have challenged his manhood. The two ended up brawling in the parking lot, with Billy receiving the brunt of the damage—at last count as many as eighty stitches in his face and body. It was a dismal episode, made to order for the New York tabloids, which for years had dutifully reported on Billy's off-the-diamond pugilism.

If the Yankees hadn't been performing well at the time, Billy would have been out of his job immediately. But Steinbrenner waited until June to ax his disciple. By then the club had started to lose badly, dropping seven out of eight games. To make matters worse, Billy kicked dirt on an umpire one day—and he had no excuse, he hadn't even been drinking. Steinbrenner studied a report handed over to him by Clyde King, his trusted emissary, who had been following Billy around. King was convinced the season could be saved if Martin was given his pink slip. So Steinbren-

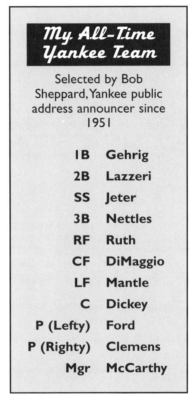

My All-Time Yankee Team

Selected by Bob Sheppard, Yankee public address announcer since 1951

1B	Gehrig
2B	Lazzeri
SS	Jeter
3B	Nettles
RF	Ruth
CF	DiMaggio
LF	Mantle
C	Dickey
P (Lefty)	Ford
P (Righty)	Clemens
Mgr	McCarthy

ner pulled the plug, Martin was gone, and Piniella was back in the dugout.

Piniella was smart enough to realize that even a three-year contract wouldn't provide much security for him if the team faltered. Until the final week of the year the Yankees were competitive. Ironically, it was Boston, which usually succumbed to them, that knocked the Yankees out of the race in the last days of the campaign.

Considering that Winfield and Mattingly had respectable seasons (Dave had 25 homers and 107 RBIs, while Don slumped a bit to .311, with 18 homers), the Yankees had managed to stay in the race until the end. But they were hurt badly by the injury to John Candelaria, a southpaw, who compiled a 13–7 record until forced out in August.

The most curious setback that the team experienced was the performance of Jack Clark, a free agent who had come to the team in the off-season. Clark had been a dynamic slugger in the National League. But with New York he hit a feeble .242 as he struck out 141 times. Reggie used to strike out a lot, too, but he also banged out important home runs. After his one bad season with the Yankees, Clark was gone. But he didn't walk softly into the night; he argued that if the Yankees had kept Martin the club would have won. There were precious few who agreed with Jack's assessment.

When the year ended with the Yankees in fifth place, Piniella, as anticipated, was fired. This time the incessant game of musical chairs put Dallas Green into the manager's job. Green, a ruggedly handsome man, regarded himself as a baseball version of John Wayne. Using his drill sergeant persona, Green hammered out a world title with the Phillies in 1980. In 1989, with New York, his snarling protestations that his team "stunk" didn't pay off. He openly castigated Steinbrenner, was hurt additionally by the season-long

Rickey Henderson doing what he did best—stealing a base and disrupting the opposition. In 1986, he hit 28 homers and drove in 74 runs, batting leadoff. He stole 87 bases, breaking a Yankees' record he'd set the year before. His manager Yogi Berra said, "He can run anytime he wants. I'm giving him the green light." Early in 2001, his fourth decade in the majors, he drew his 2063rd walk, topping Babe Ruth's record. "Passing Babe Ruth in any category is meaningful," he said.

absence of Winfield and shortstop Rafael Santana, and by August joined the long gray line of ex-Yankee managers. When he was removed, the Yankees had lost nine more games than they had won. The hero of 1978, Bucky Dent—at the time managing in Columbus—was recruited to replace the harsh Green.

Dent couldn't produce any late-season miracles, although the Yankees did put together a nine-game winning streak in September. At this stage Steinbrenner's relationship with many of the folks who came to the Stadium had reached an all-time low. The team's failures, the never-ending shuffling of managers, the disappearance of so many standbys—Henderson, Guidry, Tommy John—and the general aura of discontent around the club had caused many Yankee adherents to voice their displeasure with the owner. It was common practice for vile epithets to be flung at Steinbrenner. The cry of "George must go!" was one

of the milder slogans to come from the mouths of dissident fans. There was no doubt that Steinbrenner, an intensely competitive but sentimental man, was hurt by these attacks.

On a more tragic note, the year ended with the sudden death of sixty-one-year-old Billy Martin on Christmas Day in Binghamton, New York. Riding in his Ford pickup truck without his seat belt on, Billy was killed when the car skidded on a patch of ice and plunged into a drainage ditch. His neck was broken and he died instantly. A friend who was also in the car survived. Had Martin been drinking before the accident? Yes.

Martin's funeral, at New York's St. Patrick's Cathedral, was attended by many notables, some of whom knew Billy slightly, and others who knew him only as a tempestuous figure involved in the turbulence around the Yankees. In their eulogies, the newspapers proclaimed that Martin was the best baseball manager of his generation.

The Yankee psychodrama persisted into 1990. Much of the Bronx film noir still had to do with the owner himself. Steinbrenner was severely chastised by commissioner Fay Vincent for his alleged role in a matter involving Winfield. Vincent ruled that Steinbrenner had "an undisclosed working relationship" with Howard Spira, a self-confessed gambler, who was facing federal extortion charges. Spira supposedly received $40,000 for feeding Steinbrenner negative information about Winfield. For such conduct, Vincent ordered that Steinbrenner cease running the Yankee franchise, with his role reduced to that of limited partner. Steinbrenner was to have no involvement in the day-to-day operation of the club. Out of baseball for what evolved into a two-year period, Steinbrenner had become, in the words of historian Ken Burns, "the most hated man in baseball since Andrew Freeman, the Tammany politician who owned the New York Giants 75 years earlier."

It wasn't long before Winfield was traded off to the California Angels, after playing in twenty games for the Yankees at the start of the 1990 season. Dave hit two final home runs for New York, then banged 28 for California, while batting in 109 runs. The turmoil in New York infected every part of the team's operation. Dent was replaced in June by Stump Merrill, a minor league manager straight out of central casting. Under Dent things had gone poorly; at one stage the Yankees dropped 13 out of 14 games. Stump carried on with a mediocre lineup that seemed to change every morning. The club finished with a 67–95 record, the worst in the American League and the third worst mark in the team's history. The team's batting average was the lowest in the league. The starting pitching rotation embraced names that few could remember. The top winner on the staff was a fellow named Lee Guetterman, who had 11 victories, all in relief. The colorful boca grand, Deion Sanders, the football player, batted .158. It was clear that he much preferred the gridiron game. By season's end he was back with the Atlanta Falcons.

With Steinbrenner sulking in absentia, the club was in the hands of general manager Gene Michael. Merrill remained in place as pilot in 1991, giving him another opportunity to lift the team in the standings. But the club stayed in a state of disrepair. Only three years before, in 1988, the club had drawn a record high of 2,633,701 to Yankee Stadium, but now the grand old baseball palace had become more a place of memory than achievement. "The fans were driven away," mourned writer Roger Angell in *The New Yorker*. When things become so patently absurd, baseball men often play other tunes. In this instance, Michael began to pick on the tonsorial habits of his players. Mattingly, the team's captain and a man so devoted to the game that he was nicknamed "Donnie Baseball," had always worn his hair slightly long in the rear, a concession to the counterculture of the sixties. Now he was commanded to clip off those unreconstructed hairs. When he refused, saying he was not a sloppy person, Mattingly was benched

Frank Messer and Bobby Murcer formed a popular broadcasting team during the 1980s. Murcer can still be heard on Yankee telecasts.

Before he served as the president of the National League, Bill White handled broadcasting duties for the Yankees for more than 15 years. He's seen here interviewing Roger Maris at an Old-Timer's Day celebration. Roger is considerably more at ease in this interview than he was during the unceasing inquisitions in 1961.

by Merrill. He sat out for three days, then reluctantly had his hair trimmed. More attention was paid to the fact that Mattingly auctioned off his hair droppings for $3,000 (which he gave to charity) than to the dismal record of the team on the field.

There were some brief, shining moments during the season, including the sporadic home run hitting of Kevin Maas, a youngster with movie star looks, who connected for over twenty home runs in each of his first two seasons. Mel Hall, an outfielder, didn't perform too badly, either, after coming over from Cleveland. Steve Howe, the one-time Los Angeles relief pitcher who had been battling drug addiction, did some commendable work after he joined the team in early spring. But by the season's conclusion the club was ensconced in fifth place, 20 games out of first.

Almost from the day he was hired Merrill had never had the respect of his players. Making matters worse were the stories that appeared in the press quoting players who were openly derisive of him. Though he had a year to run on his contract, Merrill was fired right after the season ended. His successor in 1992 was the thirty-five-year-old Nathaniel "Bucky" Showalter, a man far removed from Merrill in temperament and character. Not since Ohioan Roger Peckinpaugh signed on to manage the Yankees back in 1914 at the age of 23 had the New Yorkers hired such a young person for the job. A diligent product of the Yankees' minor league system, Showalter was a prisoner of the work ethic. He was also a dugout doppelganger of the hyperconscientious Calvin Ripken, Jr.,

the man who broke Gehrig's consecutive game mark. Some believed that Bucky went to bed dreaming of late-inning lineup switches. He was known for scouting umpires in order to give his players a greater awareness of how they called balls and strikes. And enemy pitchers were studied much the way the archcriminal Moriarty analyzed his antagonist, Sherlock Holmes.

Immediate results were still not apparent under Showalter, although the feeling was that things had begun to percolate in the Yankee tent. Expensive free agent Danny Tartabull, for whom over $25 million was ladled out, had nine RBIs in one game against Baltimore. The rest of the time his batting average failed to rise much over .260. Mike Stanley, a catcher with power, signed on also, and became a popular figure in the Bronx. He could play catcher or first base. Although he was no Munson, Stanley provided the best support behind the plate that the Yankees had had for some time. The pitching was just short of awful and there wasn't much that Showalter could do about that.

The news emerging from the commissioner's office in late July announced that Steinbrenner would be permitted to start running the team again the following March. That, of course, would have scant bearing on the pennant race. For the fourth consecutive year the Yankees ended up below .500. But even before the profligate boss could get back into full harness, the Yankess swung some deals that were reminiscent of the earlier big buck transactions that netted folks like Reggie, Catfish, and Winfield.

1993–2001

A DEAL THAT WOULD HAVE THE MOST LONG-RANGE IMPACT ON THE FOR-
TUNES OF THE YANKEES WAS MADE IN NOVEMBER 1992. OUTFIELDER
ROBERTO KELLY, ONCE TICKETED FOR STARDOM IN THE STADIUM,
WAS MOVED TO CINCINNATI FOR ANOTHER OUTFIELDER, PAUL O'NEILL. AT
THE TIME MANY OBSERVERS THOUGHT THAT THE REDS GOT THE BETTER OF
THE TRADE. THEY POINTED TO O'NEILL'S DUBIOUS NUMBERS IN THE RHINE-
LAND—A LIFETIME MARK OF .259, WITH HOME RUNS NEVER REACHING 30

in any season. But Michael had observed rightly, as it turned out, that O'Neill's strong southpaw swing was perfect for the low right-field porch in Yankee Stadium. Also, it was apparent that O'Neill played each game with all-consuming intensity, a trait that soon would make him a favorite of the fans as well as the Yankee owner.

At this stage Michael wasn't through wheeling and dealing. He was willing to take a risk on lefty Jim Abbott, who was born without a right hand and had pitched remarkably for the United States Olympic team in 1988. In two seasons with California, Abbott, a product of the University of Michigan, had a losing record. But Michael had taken notice of how effectively Abbott had worked to minimize his handicap.

An even more important signing followed on the footsteps of the Abbott move. The well-respected southpaw Jimmy Key, with a 116–81 lifetime mark, left Toronto, where he'd been a mainstay, to join the Yankees. It had long been a Yankee tradition to grow capable left-handers (think Pennock, Gomez, Lopat, Ford, Guidry). With the addition of Key, an intelligent pitcher, once again they had come up with a true southpaw stopper.

Last, the Yankees dipped into the market again and came up with the veteran Red Sox star, Wade Boggs. For years infielder Boggs had been a veritable hit machine for Boston, much like Tony Gwynn, his opposite number in San Diego. Steinbrenner was happy to invest $11 million dollars over three years for Boggs's bat, overlooking his poor 1992 year, when

OVERLEAF: **Yankee Stadium on a sunny, summer afternoon.**

Boggs posted an uncharacteristic career low of .259. The Yankees made the offer, even as they were aware of Bogg's back difficulties. They chose to be more impressed by his lifetime mark of .338 and his near-compulsive work habits. Wade's well-publicized eating idiosyncrasy, consisting of chicken at every meal, could easily be supported by his new riches.

As he mixed these new ingredients, Showalter at long last had emerged with a serious contender. The Blue Jays were New York's hottest rival in 1993 and the pennant was strictly up for grabs going into September. During that last month, Abbott's no-hitter (the first by a New York hurler since Dave Righetti's job in 1983) over the Indians appeared to spark the club. When Abbott left the mound after inducing Carlos Baerga to ground out for the no-hitter clincher in the ninth inning, the Stadium crowd of 27,000 erupted. The fans were showing their appreciation for a truly gutty performer.

However, Abbott's moment didn't produce any Yankee miracles. During the rest of September the Yankees went into a slump, assuring that Toronto would sew up the pennant. At 88–74 the Yankees finished second. However, the fans, once so blasé about Yankee victories, were impressed with their team's first winning record since 1988.

Attention was now focused on 1994. At last, the Yankees did not disappoint. They marched along at a fast pace as O'Neill lived up to expectations with an enormous season at the plate. Key, meanwhile, was practically unbeatable on the mound. Showalter was proving to be a first-rate manager, although his somber mien suggested that he was engaged in heart

Paul O'Neill joined the Yankees in 1993 and was the first of several key acquisitions that produced a world championship three years later. Early in the 2001 season he recorded his 2000th hit in a game against the Twins in Minnesota. The host fans gave him a standing ovation. "It surprised me a lot," he said. "I'm not used to getting a standing ovation when I hit a single to right field, but it was appreciated."

surgery rather than a little boy's game. With the team at 70–43 and on the way to its first division crown since 1981, a calamity occurred. On August 12, faced by intransigent owners, the players chose to go out on strike. Determined to control ever-rocketing salaries, baseball's entrepreneurs refused to give in, and the season, which had looked so promising, went down the drain. With no agreement in sight, the two adversarial sides were also forced to cancel the World Series, the game's long-honored (90 years) premier event. Millions of fans felt that their trust and love had been violated. As it turned out, the strike couldn't be resolved during the winter. The acrimony carried over into the start of the 1995 season, with almost everybody in the country, including President Bill Clinton, volunteering to try to bring the players and owners together.

By the time the season resumed late in April, with the Yankees missing 18 games, the game had paid a heavy price for its labor war. Baseball has always sold its romance, the continuity of its record books, its nostalgia, and the feeling that it is an integral part of each fan's summer. Needless to say, many people were angry about the vacuum left in their lives, and when the season started up again people stayed away in droves. Yankee attendance plummeted some twenty percent; other teams suffered even more than that.

After they had shown some promise in the curtailed 1994 season, the Yankees finally fought their way back into the postseason in 1995. But it didn't come easy. There was a period in which it looked like another forlorn year. In June the Yankees actually hovered around the basement for a spell. Then, thanks mainly to a newcomer, the veteran right-hander, David Cone, who came to New York in July in a trade with Toronto, the team revived. Once a top performer for the Mets, Cone won nine games for the Yankees, while losing only twice. His performance offset the loss of Key, who went down with rotator cuff surgery. In keeping with their past history, the Yankees also added the promising southpaw Andy Pettitte, who won 12 games.

The positive changes in the pitching staff, Boggs batting .324, and 22 wins in their final 28 games brought the Yankees into the postseason mix for the first time in 14 years. However, they never would have

made it without the newly installed wild card, which many fans didn't support.

At thirty-four, Mattingly at last, had made it into the postseason. It turned out to be his valedictory to the game. He had been bothered by injuries and also a yen to go back to Indiana, where he could spend precious time with his family. Donnie had always given every ounce of devotion to his team and Steinbrenner spoke out openly in appreciation of Mattingly's efforts.

Mattingly's celebrated first base predecessor of another era, Gehrig, who had owned what everyone assumed was an invulnerable record of 2,130 consecutive games, was eclipsed in 1995 by Baltimore's Cal Ripken, Jr. Like Iron Horse Lou, Ripken never succumbed to a runaway ego.

In August, Mantle died of cancer at sixty-three. He had not treated his muscular body properly over the years. What amazed many was that he had performed as well as he did despite his neglect. But liquor and late hours had taken an inevitable toll. Mantle's own words provided his suitable epitaph. "If I would have known that I was going to live this long," he said,

ABOVE: **Wade Boggs played for 15 seasons before winning a world championship ring. After the last out of the 1996 World Series he celebrated by climbing up on a policeman's horse. "That was something for me because I'm afraid of horses," he said. He played for the Yankees through five seasons, but was in a Tampa Bay uniform when he collected his 3000th career hit in 1999.**

RIGHT: **The usually composed Buck Showalter was thrown out of this game and returned the favor by thumbing out the umpire. Showalter managed the Yankees from 1992 to 1995, winning 313 games and losing 268, and was on track for postseason play late in 1994 when a strike ended the season prematurely.**

"I would have taken better care of myself." In his last weeks, Mantle received a liver transplant, setting off the final controversy of his life. But the dispute over organ donations ebbed when it became clear that Mantle's operation had succeeded in focusing attention on the subject.

As they advanced into 1995's postseason, the Yankees confronted Seattle in the first round. At this stage Showalter had won points with Yankee fans for his diligence. But it turned out to be his misfortune, ironically, that he led his team to two victorious games at Yankee Stadium as capacity crowds roared their happiness. When the Mariners stormed back to win the next three games at the Seattle Kingdome, the wails of anguish could be heard wherever Yankee fans gathered.

These five games were gripping and close and the players performed with a July Fourth zeal. However, it was the Yankees' sad fate to be playing against a team as hungry and talented as they were. What the confrontation *did* do remarkably well was inject juice into the bloodsteam of the New Yorkers as the fans immersed themselves once again into "Yankee baseball."

Not even the immense contribution of Mattingly had stemmed the Mariner tide. Donnie had batted .417, with six runs batted in. The second game went 15 innings, and took over five hours, before Jim Leyritz cracked a two-run homer off Tim Belcher. At

Late in the 1996 season, after four months out of action because of shoulder surgery, David Cone started a game against the Oakland A's and pitched seven no-hit innings before being relieved after 85 pitches. The gritty performance boosted the Yankees' pennant drive. Two seasons later, at age thirty-five, he won 20 games, leading the Bombers to their greatest season.

that moment Yankee fans were convinced that this had sealed ultimate victory for New York. But if the fans were counting on momentum—that overworked sports phrase—it didn't work out that way.

In the fifth game the Yankees had gone one run ahead in the top of the 11th inning but big Jim McDowell couldn't hold the lead. In the end it was a burst of speed from the young legs of Seattle's Ken Griffey, Jr., in the bottom of the 11th, that carried the Mariners to victory in the deciding game.

Frustrated by defeat, Steinbrenner maintained that he wanted to retain Showalter as his manager in 1996. But when the owner asked Showalter to fire several of his coaches, Bucky turned down the request. That meant that he would have to go. After almost twenty years in the organization, Showalter tearfully decided to leave. "New York somehow obliterates you," author Willie Morris wrote, "especially the outlander." However, his impressive reconstruction work with New York enabled Showalter quickly to land a post as manager of the new expansion club in Arizona.

In the fall of 1995, Bob Watson, a former Yankee player who had started out as a National Leaguer, was named general manager of the Yankees. He became the second African American to rise to that position in the major leagues. The ethnic parameters of the team had radically changed since the days of George Weiss.

With Showalter gone, a new manager had to be hired. It turned out to be the fifty-six-year-old Joe Torre, a Brooklyn native and nine-time All-Star as well as a former manager of the Braves, Mets, and Cardinals. Despite his slowness afoot, Torre had

In 1996, his second year in the majors, Andy Pettitte won 21 games, lost only eight, and finished second in the Cy Young Award balloting. Early in 2001, he won his 89th game. At that point only two pitchers, Greg Maddux and Pedro Martinez, had won more games than Pettitte since 1996, each with 90 victories.

Dwight Gooden celebrating his no-hitter against Seattle in 1996. When asked how it felt to notch the first no-hitter of his often brilliant and sometimes checkered career, he said, "I was just looking at the fans, acknowledging them, thanking them for their support. What a great feeling." Shortly thereafter, following David Cone's shoulder surgery, Gooden moved into the rotation, won 11 of 18 games, and kept the Yankees on track for the flag.

demonstrated what an effective hitter he was when he captured the National League batting crown in 1971. The choice of Torre was greeted with some skepticism by the press, for he had never won any championships in his previous managerial tours of duty. "Clueless Joe," barked the tabloids. It had been Art Richman, the special assistant to Steinbrenner who had shared quarters with Torre when they were both employed by the Mets, who had put the bug in the owner's ear about Torre. From a list of Davey Johnson, Tony LaRussa, Sparky Anderson, and Torre, Richman had strongly recommended Torre. At first, Steinbrenner rejected the nominee, then he reversed his field, turning Richman into a prophet. Torre, a man with a tough exterior, turned out to be avuncular and a manager of equable disposition. Under his guidance the Yankees soon turned out to be the team to beat in 1996.

Meanwhile, Steinbrenner made other strategic moves that turned out to be advantageous for the Yankees. He signed the former wunderkind of the Mets,

Dwight Gooden, who had appeared to have thrown away his career to drug abuse. But the one-time fire-balling right-hander confounded the diamond world on May 14 against Seattle at the Stadium by pitching a no-hitter in his seventh start for New York. In all of his brilliant years with the Mets, Gooden had never been the architect of a no-hit game. (Curiously, no Mets pitcher to this date has ever thrown a no-hitter.)

At the finish of his no-hit effort Gooden was more emotional than he'd ever been before. He leaped in the air, pumping his fists in triumph. He talked feelingly about his father, Dan, who was waiting to undergo open-heart surgery in Florida. "With all that I've gone through," said Gooden, whose life had had more ups and downs than a man on a pogo stick, "this is the greatest feeling."

It was a magical moment in a year that often resembled a municipal soap opera. Continuing to exhibit a side of himself that had usually been obscured from public view, Steinbrenner dipped into the reclamation market again and signed another ill-starred former Met, Darryl Strawberry, once a teammate of Gooden. Strawberry seemed to have self-destructed as a drug user, but as he evolved into a part-time Yankee player, one imagined that he might finally have taken control of his unhappy life. He hit one game-winning home run in July and followed that with three straight homers to crush the White Sox in early August. A roar of approval from over 33,000 fans exploded around Strawberry's ears as he circled the bases on his third blow. "I'm not finished yet," Darryl said to an astounded group of reporters after the game. At the age of 34, was it conceivable that Strawberry was about to put his jigsaw puzzle of a life back together?

Sunday, August 25, with the Yankees apparently on the way to their first flag in fifteen years, was set aside to honor Mantle, dead for little more than a year. In an emotional ceremony, a Mantle monument was unveiled in the Stadium's Monument Park in center field. Comedian Billy Crystal, who worshipped Mickey when he was a little boy, recalled how he had delivered his Bar Mitzvah speech in an Oklahoma drawl. "I limped for no reason," added Crystal. But he really knew why, for Mickey had his own inimitable limp.

The melodrama went on when David Cone, recuperating from surgery to remove an aneurysm and

RIGHT: Center-fielder Bernie Williams has shouldered the weighty legacy of DiMaggio and Mantle gracefully. In 1996, his sixth year in pinstripes, he blossomed, hitting .305, with 29 home runs and 102 runs batted in. From 1997 to 2000 he won four consecutive Gold Glove awards and four All-Star selections.

BELOW: Darryl Strawberry launching the 300th home run of his career on July 28, 1996. It was hit in the bottom of the ninth with one on, and won the game 3–2. While celebrating the Yankees' 1996 World Series victory he told a reporter, "This is definitely one of those days that I never expected to be part of." The tantalizing "what if" question haunted him through most of his career, and in the following years.

Pennants & Pinstripes *The New York Yankees 1903–2002*

have a vein grafted into his right shoulder, returned to the firing line on September 2. In a bravura performance, he pitched seven no-hit innings against Oakland, at Oakland. After 85 pitches, Torre, who had become as prudent as Alan Greenspan, removed Cone from the game. Baseball people had always known how competitive Cone was. Now they could add desire and heart to his attributes.

By September the Yankees had a 12 game lead over Baltimore. But as the Orioles kept hitting homers by the bushel, the New York margin was whittled down to 2½ games. In the process of winning 33 previous pennants the Yankees had never lost out after holding a lead of more than six games. In 1933 they had led by six games the first week in June, only to finish six games behind the Washington Senators, led by Joe Cronin. In 1935 they had a 5½ game lead by June 20, then succumbed to Mickey Cochrane's Detroit Tigers. In 1987 they had galloped to a five-game advantage in July, but they ended up in fourth place. Could the Yankees become one of eight teams in history to blow a lead of 12 games?

However, even as Yankee fans uncomfortably sniffed impending disaster, Torre's men began to win close games again. They sewed it up on September 25 with a battering of Minnesota, 19–2. With their 92–70 record, they advanced into the playoff system.

For several seasons the doe-eyed, soft-spoken Bernie Williams, from the tiny town of Vega Alta in Puerto Rico, had been promising to live up to his celebrated predecessors in center field, Combs, DiMaggio, and Mantle. He may not have had quite the velvety sureness of DiMaggio, but he had become the equal of others in his league on swallowing up fly balls. In addition, he was a clutch hitter in the middle of the lineup, much in the mold of shortstop Derek Jeter, who had emerged as a patient hitter who watched over the strike zone like a mother hen. Only 22, Jeter had been a first-round draft pick out of Kalamazoo, Michigan, Central High School in 1992. Tino Martinez, acquired from Seattle, became a Yankee favorite in short order, which was a singular accomplishment, considering that he had succeeded the ever-popular Mattingly.

Late in the year, Cecil "Big Daddy" Fielder arrived from Detroit in another of Watson's moves to strengthen the team. Fielder had the dimensions of a 1930s outfielder named "Fatty" Fothergill, but Fothergill never hit as many long balls as Big Daddy did. Pettitte had become a winner on the mound and he was backed up in the bullpen by John Wetteland, working under his sweat-stained cap, and Panama's Mariano Rivera, a slight man with an overpowering fastball. Joe Girardi, everyone's manager of the future, was helped behind the plate by Jim Leyritz. Although Paul O'Neill was pestered by injuries he was still a competent guardian of right field. He had Tim Raines, once the premier basestealer in the National League, to help him out, or to appear as the designated hitter.

What made this Yankee group so appealing, even to those who had once been appalled at the mere thought of rooting for them, was that they were seemingly an egoless, resourceful bunch of men, marked by an ethnic diversity that typified the city that they represented. They were young and old (in baseball terms), veterans and reclamation projects, all handled by Torre with patience and sureness. There may have been no Mantles, Babes, Lous, or DiMags here. Instead, in a sport that was essentially created out of individual sweat, they had made it a team effort.

To open the three-tiered playoff system, the Yankees faced Texas. Despite trailing in each game, the New Yorkers licked the Rangers, 3–1, even though Juan Gonzalez, one of the bright new performers in the game, exploded for five home runs against Yankee pitching.

As the last hurdle before the World Series, the Yankees confronted Baltimore, which had won the right to play the Yankees by defeating Cleveland. Before the first game with the Orioles on October 9, a

RIGHT: **Tino Martinez took over at first base in 1996, succeeding the retired Don Mattingly, and drove in 117 runs, the most by a Yankee first baseman since Mattingly's total of 145 in 1985. In 1997, he clouted 44 homers, the most by a Yankee first sacker since Lou Gehrig's 49 in 1936. Chuck Knoblauch praised Tino's defensive skills when he said, "He basically catches anything I throw in his direction. As an infielder you appreciate that."**

Yankee fan Jeff Maier aided his heroes with this catch of a ball hit by Derek Jeter in the eighth inning of the first game of the 1996 ALCS against the Orioles. He has clearly reached into the field of play to make the catch, but the umpire ruled the play a home run. The hit tied the game, which the Yankees eventually won, as they did the remainder of the postseason schedule.

rare afternoon affair, Yankee fans queued up for hours like true Londoners to buy the few tickets available. Most of them would certainly admit that the wait was worthwhile, thanks to a twelve-year-old New Jersey lad named Jeffrey Maier, who had come to Yankee Stadium armed with a black Mizuno fielder's glove and grungy braces on his teeth. In the eighth inning, Jeffrey graduated to instant Yankee folk hero when he stuck out his glove in right field, thereby preventing Baltimore's Tony Tarasco from making a play on Jeter's fly ball. When Umpire Rich Garcia signalled home run on the drive, Orioles manager Davey Johnson heatedly objected, as did many television viewers. But the decision stuck, leaving it up to Bernie Williams to settle the matter with a game-winning home run in the bottom of the eleventh.

Those who chastised Maier for his "illegal" play on Jeter's fly ball must have forgotten what it was like to be young—and a fan. Jeff had done what any energetic lad would have done under such circumstances. Imagine turning away a Jeter ball hit right in front of his eyes—and glove!

The next day the Yankees lost, 5–3. But when they journeyed to Camden Yards, the Yankees surprised everyone by upending the Orioles in three straight games. Pettitte won the conclusive game with the help of a six-run third inning. Big Daddy belted a three-run homer in that big inning, his second four-bagger of the series, and Williams wound up being anointed the MVP. So the Yankees climbed back into the World Series for the first time since 1981, and Torre finally got there after over 4,000 games as both manager and player.

The Yankees' foe in the World Series was Atlanta, and the odds strongly favored the Braves. Atlanta had a pitching rotation—John Smoltz, Greg Maddux, Tom Glavine—that reminded people of the Koufax-Drysdale routine of the Los Angeles Dodgers, plus a nice mix of veterans and youthful athletes. When the

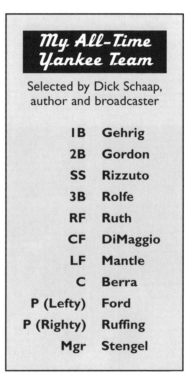

My All-Time Yankee Team

Selected by Dick Schaap, author and broadcaster

1B	Gehrig
2B	Gordon
SS	Rizzuto
3B	Rolfe
RF	Ruth
CF	DiMaggio
LF	Mantle
C	Berra
P (Lefty)	Ford
P (Righty)	Ruffing
Mgr	Stengel

Yankees were drubbed in the first two games at Yankee Stadium, 12–1, 4–0 (Maddux hurled the shutout), "it looked extremely rocky" for New York, as De Wolfe Hopper might have adjudged it. But this was a team that had proved itself capable of turning things around—and they did exactly that. In Atlanta's Fulton County Stadium, where the noise level (thanks to the infamous tribal chop chant) often rivaled Yankee Stadium turbulence, the Yankees stormed back for three consecutive victories. In the fourth game, the Yankees were behind 6–0 in the sixth inning, but rallied by degrees to overcome that margin. Leyritz's home run with two on tied the game in the eighth. In the tenth the Yankees won it with the help of an intentional walk to Williams. The final two games saw Pettitte outduelling Smoltz in a 1–0 contest, while Key and four relievers turned back the Braves in a 3–2 goose-pimpler finale, at Yankee Stadium.

The capacity crowd held its breath as Wetteland, in still another appearance, came on in the ninth inning. He yielded a run and had the tying and winning runs facing him on the bases, with two out. The Braves' Mark Lemke then hit a foul pop-up near the Atlanta dugout, which was wildly pursued by Charlie Hayes, the third baseman that the Yankees had acquired late in the year from the Phillies. Hayes couldn't make the catch, although at least one observer, announcer Tim McCarver, felt that the third out should have been awarded to the Yankees because of possible interference from a Braves player. This time, unlike the Jeff Maier episode, the Yankees didn't get the call from the umpires. In a moment, however, Lemke raised another pop-up, almost in the same place, and Hayes circled under it and made the play. At 10:56 P.M. the ball landed in Hayes's outstretched glove for the final out of the Yankees' twenty-third World Series victory.

With such a stunning comeback the Yankees

proved that like so many of their teams of the past they possessed a peculiar knack for four-game Series wipeouts. The 1927, 1928, 1932, 1938, 1939, and 1950 Yankees had victimized their opponents in four straight games. Now they had done it again, except this time they had accomplished it the hard way, after two bad defeats in their home quarters.

The Yankees' triumph produced a range of so-phistic explanations for what they had achieved: pure luck, Kismet, karma, law of averages, balls taking some funny bounces. But whatever the reason, it caused New York City to erupt—from the moment the players toured the Stadium on a victory lap, with Wade Boggs, fist in the air, atop a policeman's horse, until the tumultuous ticker tape pa-rade three days after the clinching game. David Cone was convinced that there was "an angel up there orchestrating the whole scenario," while Torre believed that "it was strange and weird, like it was all just supposed to happen."

What had preceded the Yan-kees' ascendancy, after so many years, couldn't have been devised with more twists and turns by a cun-ning novelist. In June, Rocco, Torre's brother, who had been a po-lice officer, died suddenly of a heart attack. Meanwhile, Joe's older brother, Frank, a one-time player with Milwaukee in the 1957 and 1958 World Series (against the Yan-kees) was awaiting a heart replace-ment at the Columbia Presbyterian Hospital, the same plot of land on which the Yankees (then the High-landers) played almost a century be-fore. Prior to the final Series game, Frank received his new heart—fit-tingly, from a Bronx resident—with the successful procedure performed by a doctor named Oz!

When the Yankees wrapped up the Series the next day, Frank, wearing his Yankee cap, watched the tense struggle on TV, scarcely looking like a fellow whose life had been ebbing away only hours before.

The ticker tape tribute, down Broadway's Canyon of Heroes in lower Manhattan (where Lucky Lindy, Generals Eisenhower and MacArthur, John Glenn, and others once rode in triumph), attracted more than a million adoring onlookers. They cheered, whistled, and applauded under a sea of Yankee headgear, as con-fetti rained down on them. The crowd was at times twenty and thirty deep, a gleeful assemblage of happy

"I'm a better hitter the bigger the situation," Jim Leyritz once told Joe Torre. "I rise to the occasion." On this occasion he has just belted a three-run homer in the fourth game of the 1996 World Series, a hit that tied the score in the eighth inning and propelled the Yankees to an extra-inning victory over the Braves. The Series turned on this blast. A loss would have sunk the Bombers to a 3–1 game disadvantage and probable elimination.

There were never any concerns voiced about Chuck Knoblauch's batting skills. In 1999, he hit .292 with a career high of 18 home runs. But during that season he began to experience difficulties in throwing the ball to first base accurately, an unaccountable lapse that continued into 2000. At one point he spoke of retiring and moving to the Cayman Islands. In 2001, he was moved to left field.

neighbors. On the steps of City Hall, Torre, poised as only an ex-broadcaster could be, asked: "How did everyone get into my living room?" Beginning their season in April's snowflakes, the Yankees concluded in a hailstorm of "New York cole slaw."

As the 1997 season began, Jim Kaat, the veteran pitcher who had become a Yankee announcer, wisely uttered a caveat to the true believers: "You honor the past, but don't lean on it." Torre appreciated Kaat's message as he got his club ready for another season. But he never bargained for the sturm und drang that enveloped his club.

To begin with, as the Yankees picked up their championship rings, talk bubbled around New York about the future of Yankee Stadium. Would the Yankees still be playing in the great theatre in the Bronx after 2002? Would the citizens of the west side rebel against a Manhattan venue that would cost over a billion dollars (most in taxpayer money)? Would the Yankees end up somewhere in New Jersey? How about the Hoboken Yankees? Would Steinbrenner settle for a refurbishing of the area around the Stadium, a solution that might make the area more appealing for both residents and visitors? Did anyone doubt that the majority of Yankee fans believed that baseball's counterpart of Paris's Eiffel Tower should stay right where it was?

Aside from the problem of the future home of Yankee Stadium, Torre had to confront other anxiety-making issues. The overhyped and overweight pitcher from Japan, twenty-eight-year-old Hideki Irabu, joined the club for a reported $15 million. Yes, he strongly resembled Babe Ruth—who could pitch better than Irabu—but he was never a model of consistency. Irabu worked for the first time at the Stadium on the night of July 10, with 50,000 on hand. But the novelty of the temperamental right-hander soon wore off. He ended the season with a 5–4 mark and a 7.09 ERA, in nine starts.

The stouthearted Cone had a difficult time with tendinitis, missing a month. Bernie Williams was out for 33 games and Tim Raines missed more games than that. Fielder stopped banging long-distance clouts and, without his horse under him, Wade Boggs felt insecure when he wasn't in the starting lineup. The mercurial pitcher David Wells, who really appeared to be as much of a Yankee fan as any of the club's most avid supporters, had a hard time keeping his mouth shut around the press, which eagerly gobbled up his bon mots.

The highlight of the season had to be the three fevered days in mid-June at Yankee Stadium when over 170,000 fans came out to see the Yankees battle their upstart Queens rivals, the Mets. This was the most people to crowd the old ballyard since the place had a face-lift in 1976. It also marked the introduction of interleague competition. These two clubs had never played each other in the regular season and the hoopla surrounding these games was raucous and persistent. In the first game, Dave Mlicki of the Mets tossed the first shutout of his career. The next night the Yankees evened it up, 6–3. The third game, on a cloudy afternoon, turned out to be the most dramatic. There was

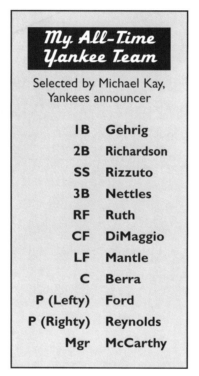

My All-Time Yankee Team

Selected by Michael Kay, Yankees announcer

1B	Gehrig
2B	Richardson
SS	Rizzuto
3B	Nettles
RF	Ruth
CF	DiMaggio
LF	Mantle
C	Berra
P (Lefty)	Ford
P (Righty)	Reynolds
Mgr	McCarthy

a "foul" home run, a crucial game-tying balk, and six no-hit innings by Cone, the one-time Met. The Yankees finally pulled it out in ten innings, 3–2, which had to please Mr. Steinbrenner mightily; he never cared to be second to anybody, especially the Mets.

A touch of tenderness took place on the night of August 30, when Don Mattingly was honored before 55,000 fans. His number 23 was retired that evening. Thus, Don joined others who had achieved Yankee immortality. The list was familiar: Gehrig (number 4), 1939, the Babe (number 3), 1948, DiMaggio (number 5), 1952, Mantle (number 7), 1969, Stengel (number 37), 1970, Dickey and Berra (number 8), 1972, Ford (number 16), 1974, Munson (number 15), 1979, Maris (number 9), 1984, Howard (number 32), 1984, Rizzuto (number 10), 1985, Martin (number 1), 1986, and Jackson (number 44), 1993. Others will follow in the years to come. One can only guess now who they will be.

Through all of the season-long traumas the Yankees survived sufficiently to win 96 games. But that was only enough to earn them the wild card niche. Their rival was Cleveland in the American League divisional battle. And for a while it looked as if the Yankees were going to surprise the naysayers. Back-to-back-to-back home runs by Raines and O'Neill wiped out a 5–0 Indians advantage in the first game, as the Yankees won, 8–6. Cleveland won the second game, 7–5, when they roughed up Pettitte and his successors on the mound. Wells put the Yankees ahead in the third game, with the help of O'Neill's bases-loaded homer. But Gooden and Pettitte failed to hold down the Indians in games four and five. In that crucial last game at Cleveland, the twenty-one-year-old fireballer, Jaret Wright, gave a pretty fair imitation of Bob Feller, the Indians' Hall of Fame phenom of the prewar era, as he sent the Yankees home for the year.

At last, October had turned cold for New York.

Another in a long line of players who have blossomed in pinstripes is Scott Brosius, who hit .203 for Oakland in 1997, then hit .300 with 19 homers and 91 runs batted in for the Yankees a year later. In 1999, he earned his first Gold Glove Award. He has been especially visible in World Series play, batting .471 in 1998 against the Padres.

Yankees shrewdly acquired Scott Brosius, who had just come off an injury-riddled, mediocre season with Oakland. The Yankees gave up their unpredictable southpaw, Kenny Rogers, and also threw in $5 million to get Brosius. Chuck Knoblauch came over from Minnesota to give Jeter a capable partner at second base. He was also a base-stealing threat, a department that had been lacking in the Yankee arsenal.

But the biggest fish of all to land in the Yankee camp was the Cuban emigré hurler, Orlando "El Duque" Hernandez, who had made a highly publicized escape from his native island. The Castro regime had ruled that Hernandez, one of Cuba's national sports heroes, should be banned from baseball for life because he had made contact with a sports agent. He had become "the Shoeless Joe Jackson of Cuba, living in the shack behind the house of his best friend," reported Tom Verducci of *Sports Illustrated*.

And one could hear that sad refrain of the old Brooklyn Dodgers, "Wait 'Til Next Year."

Next year was 1998. And Steinbrenner, who had promised after the loss to Cleveland in 1997 that the Yankees would win it all this time, turned into a prophet. In order to make good on his prediction, Steinbrenner did not unload buckets of cash, as he might have done in the past. What he did do, with the help of thirty-year-old Brian Cashman—who had become the second youngest general manager in history (Randy Smith of San Diego had been the first)—was to make key moves designed to strengthen the club in its weak links. Only one expensive free agent, Chili Davis, a designated hitter, was purchased. In order to make up for the loss of third baseman Boggs, the

In December 1997, El Duque made his departure from Cuba in a 20-foot boat that moved at 20 knots an hour. He was jammed in with seven others, including his girlfriend, Noris Bosch. The group's destination was Anguilla Cay in the Bahamas, a small island that often had been used as a staging area for Cubans trying to enter the United States. The group intended to meet a boat sent from Miami. But the rendezvous failed, causing El Duque and his friends to be stranded for three days, until they were picked up by a United States Coast Guard helicopter. The United States proceeded to grant asylum to El Duque, something they might not have done for a lesser mortal. Holding himself out as a free agent, El Duque was signed by the Yankees to a four-year contract for $6.6 million,

Orlando Hernandez joined the Yankees in June 1998 and won his first start 7–1 against Tampa Bay. He went on to win 12 games. With the Yankees trailing Cleveland two games to one in the 1998 ALCS, he pitched seven shutout innings, lifting the Yanks to a 4–0 win. He was known as "El Duque" in Cuba, a nickname happily adopted by Yankee fans.

possibly the most prudent investment that Steinbrenner had ever made.

In Cuba, Hernandez had owned the all-time winning percentage among pitchers, a fact that was persuasive for the Yankees. But he was still subjected by the Yankees to a brief minor league apprenticeship at Class A Tampa and Triple A Columbus before reporting to New York in June. However, it wasn't only El Duque's Cuban record that had impressed the Yankees, it was also his refreshing personality and childish smile. That went along with his dramatic high leg kick that could be seen even in the far-off bleachers. Despite his minimal English vocabulary, El Duque connected immediately with Yankee fans. It was his strong right arm that spoke out clearly for him.

Oddly, the 1998 season began in miserable fashion for the Yankees. They dropped their first three games, causing Steinbrenner to comment caustically that "we're even behind Tampa Bay." But from that low point the club became almost unbeatable. They romped away to 17–6 in April, 20–7 in May (on May 17 "Boomer" Wells, their unreconstructed clubhouse comic, delighted 49,000 fans at the Stadium with the second perfect game in Yankee history), 19–7 in June, 20–7 in July, 22–10 in August, and 16–11 in September.

By the end of the year this well-balanced club was hailed by many as the greatest team of all time. With their 114 victories, the Yankees were second only to the Chicago Cubs of 1906, who had won 116 games in the dead ball era. But the 1998 Yankees had eclipsed all American League teams, including the Cleveland team of 1954, which had triumphed 111 times.

The Yankees finished the year 66 games over .500

and 22 games ahead of Boston, the widest margin in franchise history. Perhaps their most astounding accomplishment was that these Yankees held a lead in 48 consecutive games, starting in June and ending in August. They also reached the century mark in wins on September 4, the earliest that any club had ever attained that target. The club also rolled up 62 victories in the comfortable confines of Yankee Stadium. Only the 1961 team, with 65 victories, had won more at home.

Even as they entered the always precarious postseason, these Yankees were being measured for Olympian greatness. They were linked with the Big Red Machine of Cincinnati, the Orioles of 1970, the Cubs of 1906, and, of course, with the almighty Murderers' Row Yankees of 1927, a team that was jampacked with Hall of Famers. (Some have insisted that some marginal players on the 1927 club made the Hall simply because they were identified with this juggernaut.) Was the 1998 team more accomplished than the 1939 Yankees, when the youthful Joe DiMaggio took over from the dying Lou Gehrig?

The Yankees proceeded to buttress their reputation—if there were still any doubters—by wiping out Texas in the Division series. Pitchers Wells, Pettitte, and Cone yielded only one run in the three games, as

After pitching a perfect game against the Minnesota Twins in May 1998, David Wells celebrated. He revered Yankee traditions, and chose uniform number 33, a double-digit version of Babe Ruth's number. Early in the 1997 season he wore a cap on national TV that once belonged to Ruth, a relic that he paid $35,000 for. "Kids change their minds a lot," he said, "but I've always had a thing for the Yankees."

late-season call-up Shane Spencer contributed two home runs. (Shane had also hit three grand slams in ten days in September, proving that this team had everything—and even more to come!)

Right before the Yankees were to play Cleveland for the league crown, it was discovered that Darryl Strawberry had still another struggle on his hands—this one against colon cancer. Following surgery, which presumably was successful, Strawberry's doctors said that Darryl might be expected to play in 1999. How many times would Strawberry be faced with major crises in his life? How many times would the dread disease invade the Yankee clubhouse?

In the series with Cleveland, the Indians went ahead, 2–1. But the Yankees bounced back with alacrity. They took two straight at Cleveland, then won a final 9–5 victory in New York. In this series four different Yankees—Brosius, Davis, O'Neill, and catcher Jorge Posada (now being groomed as the next number one Yankee backstop)—hit home runs, emphasizing still again that this was not a one-man or two-man Yankee operation.

When the World Series came along, with San Diego the opponent, the Yankees did what so many other all-conquering Yankee clubs had done in the past; they won four straight. In the third game, Brosius hit homers in back-to-back innings, as the ace reliever of the Padres, Trevor Hoffman, couldn't stop the New Yorkers. The next day Pettitte wrapped it up for the Yankees, with help, as usual, from the near-invincible Rivera.

"They've got one helluva club," acknowledged the San Diego hitting machine Tony Gwynn. "They did whatever they needed to win." When O'Neill and Williams, the Yankees' number three and four hitters, did hardly anything against the Padres, it was the bottom-of-the-order Brosius who stepped up and did most of the damage for New York. He was named the World Series MVP, with his six RBIs and .471 average.

Finishing out the year with seven consecutive postseason triumphs, the Yankees had shown that they could beat other clubs in so many different ways. "Like fingerprints and snowflakes," said *Sports Illustrated*, "no two of their wins

After a six-year minor league apprenticeship, Jorge Posada joined the Yankees in 1997 and split the catching duties that season with Joe Girardi. A year later he made the transition to full-time duty handsomely, batting .268, hitting 17 homers, and becoming the sixth Yankee to homer from both sides of the plate in a game against Texas in August. He added two homers in postseason play and hit .333 in the World Series.

were alike." With their sweep of San Diego, the Yankees boasted an overall record for the year of 125 victories and only 50 defeats. This may, in the long run, be a team mark almost as invulnerable as the individual 56-game mark set by DiMaggio in 1941. Could anyone believe that any ball club would ever experience a better season?

Had the Yankees, at last, returned to baseball supremacy? Thirty years before, Leonard Koppett wrote in the *New York Times* that he didn't believe that "a Yankee dynasty could ever come back . . . it is no longer possible for any baseball team to achieve such superiority—and it never will again."

But what occurred in the magic season of 1998—and what would occur in the immediate years to follow—contradicted the usually astute Koppett, as well as any number of other baseball savants.

During the winter of 1998 the Yankees re-signed free agent Bernie Williams to a seven-year contract. In his quiet, unassuming way Bernie had become a tower of strength in the Yankee alignment. There were two men on this team who were essential to the club's future: one was Williams, the other was Jeter. Williams always had wanted to remain in New York. Now his wish had been granted. In a few years the Yankees would have to deal with Jeter, in an era of swollen wages that made .250 hitters multimillionaires overnight.

In February 1999 the Yankees gave Torre a two-year extension through the 2001 season. This appeared to be an acknowledgment of how much his leadership meant to the club. "He's a common sense guy, quiet in a storm, a

Mariano Rivera's fastball regularly sizzled in the mid-90s, but what made it almost impossible to hit was the movement on the pitch. "When it's coming you think you're going to hit it," Baltimore's Jerry Hairston said, "and then it goes right through your bat." From 1997 to 2000 he averaged 40 saves per season, and boasted a combined ERA of 2.14. He was named the Most Valuable Player of the 1999 World Series.

On April 2, 2001, Roger Clemens moved up to seventh place on the career strikeout list, passing Walter Johnson. Joe Torre said, "The one word to use with Roger Clemens is the one word you used with Bob Gibson, and that is 'war.'" Clemens once described his expectations succinctly: "I expect to be dominant and exciting and aggressive."

pro's pro, who comes to the park every day accepting and embracing the idea that baseball, no matter how much you love it, can break your heart," wrote Dave Kindred in *The Sporting News*.

The next month, DiMaggio, "the greatest living ballplayer," died in Florida at the age of eighty-four. Was he truly the greatest player of his time, or all time? It can be argued that way. Certainly he was a living legend for a longer time than anyone else in memory—and he had practiced hard at such imagery. His famous hitting streak would probably endure for as long as baseball was played, but his reputation would in time come under intense postmortem scrutiny. "Every hero becomes a bore at last," Ralph Waldo Emerson said. He may have had some celebrated generals in mind, but Joe DiMaggio would not have escaped his notice.

Suddenly, in spring training, another one of those fateful thunderbolts struck the Yankees. A visit to the doctor revealed that Torre had prostate cancer, and surgery was prescribed. Torre underwent the procedure, but promised that he would be back. By late May he fulfilled his promise. His energy level seemed to have returned to its normal level. During Torre's absence, the indomitable Don Zimmer filled in for him. He obviously had absorbed a good deal of Joe's wisdom, for after almost two months, the club stood at 29–20, just barely behind the Red Sox.

In June, the future Hall of Famer (and only slightly scuffed up) Roger Clemens, who once possessed the most fearsome fastball in his league, served notice that he was still a force to be reckoned with. He gained his eighteenth straight victory (ultimately the streak ended at 20). On June 5, El Duque, whose style and brio had captivated New Yorkers, added still another fillip to the brew; he fielded a hard grounder hit by the Mets' Rey Ordonez and threw his glove, with the ball stuck in it, to first baseman Tino Martinez. The Cuban pitcher had figured more ways to get batters out than anyone else had contemplated.

The next month, Cone joined his pitching brothers Don Larsen and Wells on the list of Yankee pitchers who had carved perfect games. Cone's masterpiece arrived on Sunday, July 18, against Montreal, before 45,000 fans at the Stadium. Pitching in near 100 degrees, David was never hotter. And how ironic it was that the silver-haired Larsen was on hand to throw out the first ball on a day that had been dedicated to his old teammate Yogi Berra. Now the maestro of his own museum in Montclair, New Jersey, Berra neatly summed up Cone's accomplishment. "Those pinstripes make you do something," he said. Overcoming the trials that he had been through with his health, Cone was magnificent as he threw only 20 called balls and struck out 10. He also managed to outlast a half-hour pregame ceremony that included a $100,000 donation to Yogi's museum from the Yankee Foundation, and a third-inning rain delay of 33 minutes. A few days after Cone's chef d'oeuvre, the Yankees scored 21 runs against the Indians, the most they had scored in the Stadium since a game in July 1931.

At the end of August, the Yankees were at 81–50, putting them 7 1/2 games ahead of Boston. When they underwent a late-season malaise, with a 17–14 September, their margin over the Red Sox dwindled to

David Cone sank to his knees and was tackled by battery mate Joe Girardi after the third out was recorded in Cone's perfect game against Montreal on July 18, 1999. Inexplicably, Cone's next 42 starts produced a record of six wins and 19 losses. "I know a lot of people would say it's time to walk away," he said. "I know I got to go out there again. I got to keep trying. . . . The final chapter hasn't been written." In 2001 he pitched for archenemy Boston.

Before there was a Bob Sheppard, the Yankees employed a short, stout man named Jack Lenz to make public address announcements. Lenz served from 1915 through the mid-thirties, using a megaphone the size of an oversized pylon, since there was no amplified sound system in those days. He worked more than 2000 consecutive games, first at the Polo Grounds and then at Yankee Stadium.

Bob Sheppard at work in his tiny cubicle at Yankee Stadium. The 2001 season marked his fiftieth as the Yankees' public address announcer, a dynasty all his own.

But the only Yankee Stadium public address voice that most of us remember now belongs to Sheppard, a tall and elegant gentleman who has become a Yankees immortal in his own right. Amid the audio-visual clamor that currently pervades Yankee Stadium, Sheppard's voice soothes like a lullaby. His debut in 1951 coincided with Mickey Mantle's first season and Joe DiMaggio's last. He loved intoning "Mickey . . . Mantle." He said it was the perfect baseball name.

Sheppard was a professor of public speaking at St. John's University for many years. In addition to his baseball duties, he has been the public address voice for the New York football Giants since 1956. In 1998, the Baseball Writer's Association presented him with the William J. Slocum Award for "long and meritorious service." Two years later he stood near the pitcher's mound at Yankee Stadium prior to a game for the unveiling of a brass plaque presented in his honor. The plaque was later placed in Monument Park with the rest of the Yankees' deities.

"Most men go to work," he said. "But I go to a game. How many men would love to do that?"

---

four games. But that was still enough to give them their third flag in four years. Their 98 wins was hardly a rebuke to their talent, but it certainly wasn't as exhilarating as the 114 victories the previous season.

The main contributors to the Yankees cause had been, as expected, Jeter, with 219 hits to lead the league, and Williams, who hit .342 with 25 homers. Jeter just failed to win the batting title, as Nomar Garciaparra of Boston beat him .357 to .349. Williams also had 212 hits, making the Jeter-Williams combine the first pair of Yankees to make 200 or more hits since DiMaggio and Gehrig did it in 1937.

In the division series, the Yankees again thrashed Texas in three straight games, giving up one run to a team that was widely considered to have solid hitting. Then the Yankees banged the Red Sox around in five games in the League Championship Series, taking advantage of sloppy play on the part of the underachieving Red Sox. Williams's homer in the bottom of the tenth inning of the first game was the signal that the Yankees had not gotten tired of winning. But did anyone believe that the New Yorkers would obliterate Atlanta in four straight in the World Series? But it happened exactly that way. The icing on the cake was provided by Clemens, who hurled 7 $^{2}/_{3}$ shutout innings in the final game to give the Yankees their twelfth straight triumph in the World Series.

The Yankees had ended the century with a twenty-fifth world championship, and the third world crown in four years. Even the most pernicious of Yankee haters, most of them holdovers from the years when the club was equated with U.S. Steel, had to admit that Torre and his men were talented and relentless.

"We had to win in order to validate what we did last year," said Torre, who had become a master of understatement. He might have added that it was a season also marred by the intrusion of cancer, and the deaths of the fathers of O'Neill, Luis Sojo (the ever-valuable utility man), and Brosius. Steinbrenner echoed his manager's words when he reminded people that the Yankees were "a tough team that accurately depicted the town" in which they played.

So once again it was a sparkling autumn in New York—another fall to remember—with thousands assembling to hail the victors. They paraded all the way to City Hall, where Mayor Rudy Giuliani, the self-confessed ultimate Yankee fan, presided over the festivities. Those who cheered and shouted and laughed were men and women, the known and unknown, the young and old, who were all shades of white and black and brown. The times had irrevocably changed, for the Yankees now truly represented "this gorgeous mosaic of a city," as former Mayor David Dinkins had on occasion described it.

In the year 2000 there seemed to be jobs for everyone and money in almost everyone's pockets. Little attention was paid to those chronic pessimists who sought something to fear, even when they couldn't find much to fear. The country's second-term president, Bill Clinton, was in his twilight days in office, and two men, Vice president Al Gore and Texas Governor George W. Bush, fought all summer and fall to succeed him.

Against this background, the Yankees looked for an almost unthinkable third straight world championship, aware that no team had performed the feat since the Athletics of 1972–1974. The Yankees had a five-star manager, a five-star pitching staff, and a remarkably mature five-star shortstop. But some savants shook their heads at the team's reliance on veterans like the thirty-seven-year-old O'Neill, the thirty-three-year-old Brosius, and the thirty-three-year-old Martinez, now in his tenth year of big league baseball. Catcher Posada would no longer have the knowledgeable Girardi to "learn him" (as Dizzy Dean might have said it) the finer points of his position. And their second baseman, Knoblauch, who was an effective leadoff man, had become a defensive high risk at his position.

As the season moved along, these imperfections became more glaring. Adding to the team's miseries was the puzzling performance of Cone. In his first five seasons with the Yankees, David had been a reliable stopper, with a 60–26 record and a 3.34 ERA. But in his first 16 starts in 2000 Cone emerged with only a single victory. Nothing seemed to work for him. His frustration became etched in his taut face.

Faced by the upstart competition from Toronto and Boston (always in the race, thanks to pitcher Pedro Martinez), the Yankees sadly resembled Chicago's Hitless Wonders of 1906. By July they were only two games over .500, and the second guessers were having a field day writing the team off. Obviously, something had to be done about the stillness of the Yankee artillery. As usual, the front office took over, as it had so many times in the past. This time, it

My All-Time Yankee Team

Selected by John Sterling, Yankee announcer

1B	Gehrig
2B	Gordon
SS	Jeter
3B	Nettles
RF	Ruth
CF	DiMaggio
LF	Mantle
C	Berra
P (Lefty)	Ford
P (Righty)	Ruffing
P (Relief)	Rivera
Mgr	Torre

was by happenstance. General Manager Cashman made a phone call to Cleveland's assistant general manager, Mark Shapiro, asking for the address of Gary Tuck, a catching instructor with the 1999 Yankees, who was entitled to receive his World Series ring. In the course of the chat, Shapiro informed Cashman that outfielder David Justice might be available since the Indians were trying to cut down on their national debt. Cashman thought (to himself) that Justice, a longtime star with Atlanta, would be a perfect fit for a Yankee lineup that had suddenly gone flat. In May and June the Yankees had compiled a dismal mark of 23–28.

A trade was arranged on June 29, with the Yankees sending their young, uncertain outfielder, Ricky Ledee, to Cleveland. As it turned out, the deal worked immeasurably better for New York than if they'd gotten home run slugger Sammy Sosa from Chicago or Juan Gonzalez from Detroit. Justice became the team's catalyst, winning games with his homers, and assuring Yankee fans he had considerably more going for him than the fact that he was once the husband of actress Halle Berry. His southpaw swing was a delight to watch as he pumped out 20 home runs for the Yankees to add to the 21 he'd hit for Cleveland. When the year ended, he had 118 RBIs. The Yankees made other moves during this period, adding the big-muscled Glenallen Hill and equally big-muscled Jose

David Justice joined the Yankees from Cleveland on the last day of June 2000 and did not disappoint, batting .305 over 78 games, with 20 home runs and 60 runs batted in. He added three homers and 12 runs batted in during the postseason. At the end of the season he voiced the sentiments of many players who joined the Yankees late in their careers when he said, "I really feel blessed to wear the same uniform as all the greats."

Canseco. The mercurial Denny Neagle joined the pitching staff and Luis Sojo and Jose Vizcaino helped to stabilize the infield. But it was Justice who seemed to come out of nowhere to rally the club.

One day in July, when the team was performing like an aging heavyweight champ battling to retain his title in the final round of a punishing fight, the club rallied from a seven-run deficit against Baltimore. This exhilarating victory put them a half-game back of Toronto, just as they prepared to move into a series with the Mets. In a two-game set earlier in the season against their Queens rivals in the other league, the Yankees had won one of them. But another game was cancelled because of rain. This meant that a doubleheader would have to be played between the two teams on July 8, with one game to be played at each ball park. This unique arrangement had only a single precedent. That was in 1903, almost a century before, when the New York Giants played the Brooklyn Superbas.

The fans and the media enjoyed this arrangement. But the Mets' Mike Piazza didn't. The catcher, in the midst of a splendid season, came to bat against the Yankees' Clemens in the second inning of the nightcap. In June Mike had hit a bases-loaded home run off Clemens, and the latter was reputed to have a long memory. This time he fired a pitch that hit Mike in the helmet, sending him hurtling to the ground. The incident, which caused Piazza to suffer a concussion, served to reinforce Clemens's general reputation as a headhunter. "A surly intimidator," wrote Robert Lipsyte of the *New York Times*. Others, like Ralph Branca—Mets' manager Bobby Valentine's father-in-law and the pitcher who threw the ball to Bobby Thomson in 1951 that became known as "the home run heard 'round the world"—had little doubt that Clemens had tried to hit Piazza. Mike was inclined to agree with Branca.

The Piazza brouhaha overshadowed the Yankees' doubleheader victory. However, in some perverse way, the episode became the catalyst for a turnaround in Clemens' season. From that point he went 7–2, providing the kind of Cy Young Award (five times) pitching that the Yankees had expected from him after they obtained him in 1999. No matter what some said about him ("If he were a prizefighter, he'd have bitten more ears than Mike Tyson," wrote Mark Kriegel in the *Daily News*.) Clemens remained a valuable cog in the team's drive for another flag. Teaming up with Pettitte and El Duque, he gave the Yankees the kind of starting pitching, to go along with Rivera in the bullpen, that would keep them in the race.

Rousing themselves, as they had so often in the past, the New Yorkers put together an excellent stretch of baseball from the start of July until September 10. They compiled a record of 44–22 to take over the divisional lead and stay there. The Boston threat was obliterated with a three-game sweep over the Red Sox at Fenway Park—yes, the Curse of the Bambino was still alive and well. With 18 games left on the schedule, the Yankees were up by nine games, which looked unassailable. Just when it was assumed that the team would roll along easily into the postseason, all their wheels seemed to fall off. If what was afflicting them at this stage was complacency, this was countered by the inconsistency of the Red Sox. The morale of the club was also, without doubt, affected by the absence of their able pitching coach, Mel Stottlemyre, who left the club on September 11 to undergo treatment for blood plasma cancer. O'Neill wasn't helped, either, by a hip injury that bothered him for a month, and Cone couldn't shake off the injury jinx as he dislocated his shoulder in early September.

Whatever the concatenation of circumstances that caused it, the Yankees dropped 16 of their final 21 games, often by blowout margins. Of their last 18 games, they lost 15. They finished the year by losing their last seven games, an ignominious way of entering the playoffs. They had the "honor" of being the first team to advance into the postseason without winning at least five games of their final fifteen.

Was Torre worried about this curious turn of events? Certainly, he was concerned. But publicly he dismissed it by saying that the team was simply "trying too hard to close the deal . . . I think the real team shows up tomorrow."

The Yankees' first playoff foe was a surprising Oakland club, which was young and on the rise.

Thanks to their late-season collapse, the Yankees lost the chance to open at home against Oakland, a factor that was often important in a short series. One of the least appreciated managers in the American League, Art Howe, was prepared to lead his "men in green" against New York. His club had won 18 of its final 22 games and one sensed they had an emotional advantage over the Yankees. In the first game, Howe started Gil Heredia against Clemens. Roger threw bullets for a few innings, but in the end Oakland won, 5–3, as the Yankees extended their losing ways into the postseason. As Pettitte faced Kevin Appier in the second game, Yankee fans had the feeling that this was a "must" game. In the past, Steinbrenner had been more negative than positive about Pettitte. But this time the pitcher kept the Yankees alive, with 7²/₃ shutout innings. The 4–0 New York victory tied the series and left it up to El Duque. He certified his claim as a money pitcher by surviving a bumpy road and winning, 4–2. Seeing an opportunity to sew things up, Torre called on Clemens, with only three days rest. But Roger was simply not up to it under those conditions. He allowed a half-dozen runs in a game ultimately won by the Athletics, 11–1.

This brought the Yankees' future down to a fifth game, back on Oakland home turf, after a long overnight trip. The odds seemed to favor the younger Oakland team. But the sputtering Yankee bats suddenly came alive in a rousing six-run first inning. Not accustomed to such an outbreak of hitting, Pettitte almost piddled away the lead, as Oakland charged back with five runs accumulated over the next few innings. However, those bullies in the Yankee bull pen saved the day, sending the team into the American League Championship Series against Lou Piniella and his Seattle club. By this time Torre was as emotionally exhausted as anybody who had been following this enigmatic Yankee season. After

the final out in Oakland, he walked off the field with tears in his eyes. Tears of joy or tears of relief? No matter, the Yankees would now confront the Mariners.

Seattle had just won three straight games over the Chicago White Sox, a team reputed to be full of heavy hitters. Few people had ever heard of the Seattle hurlers, but they stilled the Chicago bats. Was there a likelihood that they would be able to do the same with the Yankee lineup? The answer was yes. Freddy Garcia, a right-hander, totally stymied the Yankees in the first game in a 2–0 win, and southpaw John Halama took a 1–0 lead into the eighth inning of the second game, reminding fans of the impotent Yankees of September. But these Yankees refused to die. They had been able to come back from the grave before. Now they did it again. They were still a team of intelligence and enterprise. They had even become endearing. And what happened next would further endear them to those who still believed in them.

Justice, for a half season the key hitter on this club, banged a double off the wall in left field to lead off the eighth inning, and a moment later Bernie Williams singled him home to break the scoreless skein that had been woven by Mariner hurlers. With that, the floodgates opened and six more runs paraded across the plate to give the Yankees a much-needed 7–1 triumph. The next day Pettitte was masterful and the Yankees had a relatively easy time in an 8–2 win. With the fourth game coming up, Torre had a well-rested Clemens in his rotation—and the Rocket performed brilliantly, with a touch of malice thrown in.

This time it wasn't Piazza that Clemens chose to pick on. Instead, he made Alex Rodriguez, Seattle's superlative shortstop, his target of choice. In the first inning Rodriguez twice went down in response to the Rocket's 95-miles-per-hour "purpose" pitches. And,

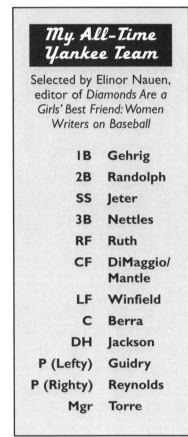

My All-Time Yankee Team

Selected by Elinor Nauen, editor of *Diamonds Are a Girls' Best Friend: Women Writers on Baseball*

1B	Gehrig
2B	Randolph
SS	Jeter
3B	Nettles
RF	Ruth
CF	DiMaggio/ Mantle
LF	Winfield
C	Berra
DH	Jackson
P (Lefty)	Guidry
P (Righty)	Reynolds
Mgr	Torre

like Piazza, Rodriguez had little doubt about the hurler's motivation. Clemens hardly needed to resort to such intimidation, for on this night he was on his way to a one-hit shutout and 15 strikeouts. He was Walter Johnson, Bob Gibson, and Bob Feller all rolled into one angry package. (In the off-season, Rodriguez, who had become the most delectable free agent in the business, left Seattle for the Texas Rangers for a massive bundle of money ($252 million) that must have helped to salve his feelings over the impasse with the Rocket.)

The Yankees tried to wind it up with Neagle on the mound in the fifth game. But he wasn't up to duplicating the Rocket's effort as the Mariners won, 6–2. (After the season, the Yankees saw Neagle leave for Colorado.) It was back to the Bronx for the sixth game, which was put into the hands of El Duque. Until the seventh inning, it looked as if this series was going to go down to the bitter end, as the Yankees fell behind, 4–3. Again, it was Justice who stepped up to do the job. His booming three-run home run into the right-field stands sent the capacity crowd into near hysteria. Building on Justice's clout, the Yankees amassed a 9–5 lead, which looked pretty safe considering that Torre was about to call on the inevitable Rivera to shut down the Mariners. But on this night, the skinny Panamanian, who was protecting a record of 33 1/3 post-season innings without yielding a run, proved he was human after all. Seattle got back two runs in the eighth off him (there was never any chance that Torre would replace Rivera) and then had the tying run come to the plate in the ninth inning, in the person of Edgar Martinez, one of the game's most productive designated hitters. When Martinez rolled out meekly to shortstop, the Yankees, after all the sturm und drang, were on their way to the World Series for the third straight time. Their rivals would be New York's own Mets, who had finished fast to win the wild card.

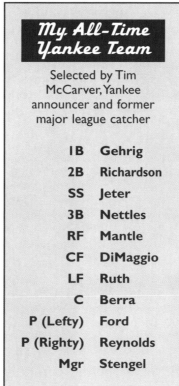

My All-Time Yankee Team

Selected by Tim McCarver, Yankee announcer and former major league catcher

1B	Gehrig
2B	Richardson
SS	Jeter
3B	Nettles
RF	Mantle
CF	DiMaggio
LF	Ruth
C	Berra
P (Lefty)	Ford
P (Righty)	Reynolds
Mgr	Stengel

This fourteenth Subway Series in New York history would serve to introduce the current generation to a provincial tradition going back to 1921, when John McGraw's Giants faced Babe Ruth's Yankees at the Polo Grounds. The last time there had been an intracity dispute was in 1956, when the Yankees, with the help of Larsen's perfect game, licked Jackie Robinson and the Brooklyn Dodgers in seven games. Dwight D. Eisenhower was running for a second term as president that year against the Democrats' Adlai E. Stevenson.

For the media and the fans—at least, the older fans—this intramural competition brought on a rush of fond memories. It represented, as Glenn Collins of the *New York Times* wrote, "a triumph of continuity and revival for a city in both history and baseball." Also, and this wasn't something to be sneered at, it gave all the interested and dementedly partisan fans an opportunity to blow off steam, to brag and bray. For one week the universe of New York would discover whether this Yankee dynasty was ready to be put to bed, or whether the Mets would return supremacy to Queens, under the voluble leadership of Mets pilot, Bobby Valentine. If history was the judge, the Yankees would be in the driver's seat, for in the previous Subway brawls they had emerged on top 10 times: four out of six against the no-longer-New-York Giants, and six out of seven over the disappeared Brooklyn Dodgers. Any way the duel would evolve it was a certainty that the city would be almost totally and maniacally involved, from its scrappy, Yankee-loving mayor, to bus drivers, doormen, secretaries, stock brokers, delicatessen store operators, cops, baby boomers, the elderly, and the young, whether they came from Manhattan, the Bronx, Brooklyn, Queens, or Staten Island. Even if the outside world, meaning the rest of blasé America, didn't feel it had much of a stake in the affair, New Yorkers most certainly did.

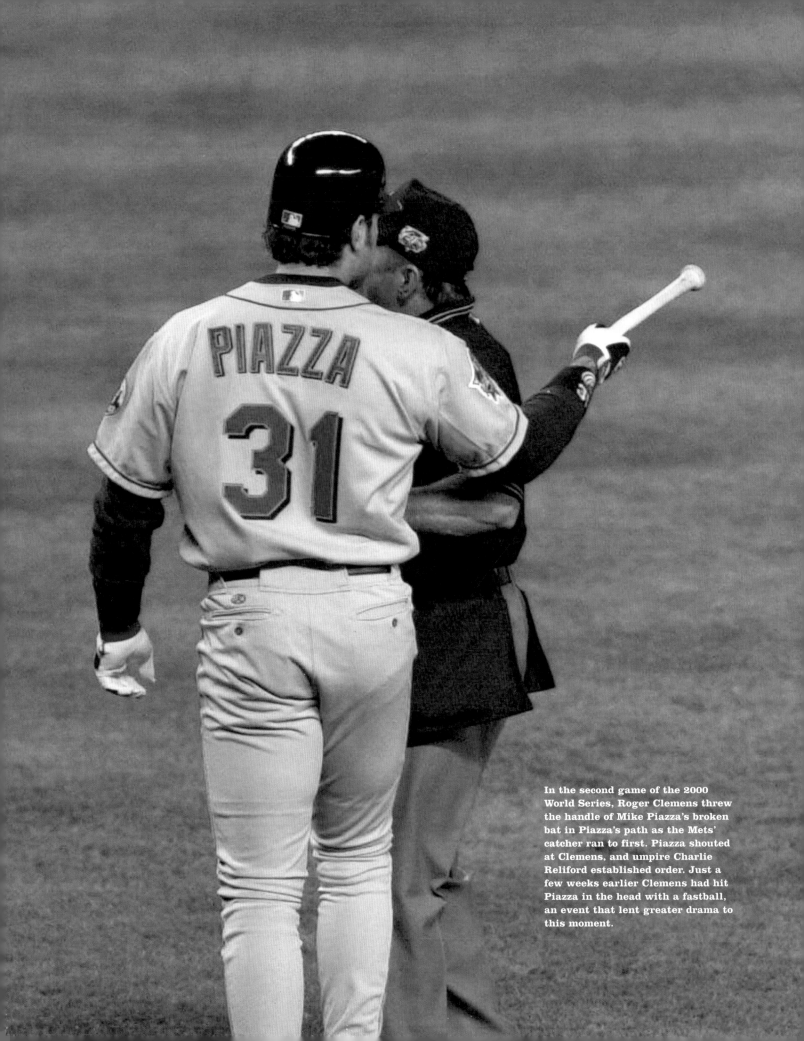

In the second game of the 2000
World Series, Roger Clemens threw
the handle of Mike Piazza's broken
bat in Piazza's path as the Mets'
catcher ran to first. Piazza shouted
at Clemens, and umpire Charlie
Reliford established order. Just a
few weeks earlier Clemens had hit
Piazza in the head with a fastball,
an event that lent greater drama to
this moment.

On a surprisingly warm (75 degrees) October night at a packed Yankee Stadium, the first Subway Series game in 44 years got under way, with the Mets' intense southpaw, Al Leiter, facing Pettitte. The script turned out to be as unpredictable as the presidential election between Al Gore and George W. Bush that would take place the next month. The Mets trailed, 2–0, until the top of the seventh, when they scored three runs to go ahead. But prior to that moment they had squandered enough opportunities to win most games. The chief squanderer was Timo Perez, a late-season fill-in, who had provided brio to the Mets' lineup. This time his brio let him down. In the sixth inning, Timo stood at first base watching the flight of Todd Zeile's long fly ball to left field. Thinking it was going over for a home run, he failed to run hard. When the ball bounced off the top of the padded wall, Perez set sail. But it was too late. A relay from Justice to Jeter, who made a dandy off-balance throw home, nailed Timo. Such hesitation on the bases was not the way to beat the Yankees.

Trailing the Mets, 3–2, in the last of the ninth, the Yankees had to face the big right-hander Armando Benitez, one of the brutally tough closers in baseball. And Benitez came within two outs of turning back the Yankees. After retiring Posada, Benitez faced O'Neill, who was as skilled a professional hitter as any in the lineup—when he was in shape. He tested Benitez through an excruciating 10-pitch contest, four of which he defensively fouled off to stay alive. Finally, O'Neill had his base on balls. As the pressure mounted, Polonia stroked a pinch hit single, moving O'Neill to second base. Vizcaino's single loaded the bases, giving Knoblauch his big chance. His response was a left-field fly deep enough to permit O'Neill to score the tying run. The game then proceeded into extra innings, with Jeff Nelson, Rivera, and Mike Stanton coming on through the twelfth inning to stifle the Mets. Meanwhile, as the clock moved toward one in the morning, the Yankees had equal difficulties with the Mets relievers. Finally, it turned out to be Jose Vizcaino's night after all.

In the bottom of the twelfth, with one out, Martinez singled off Turk Wendell and Posada doubled him to third. With first base open, Valentine ordered O'Neill to be intentionally walked. Sojo prolonged the suspense by popping out for the second out. But Vizcaino jumped on Wednell's first pitch for a game-winning single. The battle had gone on for four hours and fifty-one minutes—the longest game in World Series history (twice as long as another spellbinder, the movie *Casablanca*)—but wasn't that the way a Subway Series was supposed to be?

Rested for a week, Clemens took the mound for game two against lefty Mike Hampton. The waiting had increased the combative Clemens's anxiety and anticipation. If there was any baseball fan in New York not familiar with the Rocket's earlier mano-a-mano with Piazza that person had to be catatonic. In the first inning, Clemens fanned Timo Perez, then Edgardo Alfonzo, on fastballs and splitters that fairly smoked as they hurtled past these two batsmen. Now it was Piazza's turn to face his old antagonist. Clemens quickly got two strikes on Mike, then a ball. On the next pitch Mike managed to connect, but in doing so his bat splintered apart. The handle remained in Piazza's hand, while another cracked segment flew out to the left side of the infield. The biggest part of the bat—the barrel—bounced out towards Clemens, even as the ball headed for foul territory in the region of first base.

What occurred next was as bizarre as anything

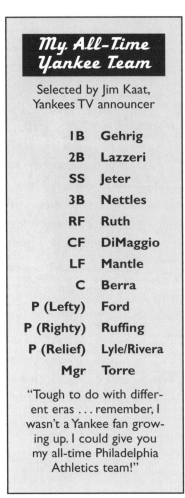

My All-Time Yankee Team

Selected by Jim Kaat, Yankees TV announcer

1B	Gehrig
2B	Lazzeri
SS	Jeter
3B	Nettles
RF	Ruth
CF	DiMaggio
LF	Mantle
C	Berra
P (Lefty)	Ford
P (Righty)	Ruffing
P (Relief)	Lyle/Rivera
Mgr	Torre

"Tough to do with different eras . . . remember, I wasn't a Yankee fan growing up. I could give you my all-time Philadelphia Athletics team!"

that has ever happened in a Series game. Clemens seized the jagged hunk of bat, as if he were fielding it, and threw it angrily in the direction of the first base line, where Piazza was running. Fortunately, the flying object didn't strike Piazza. But the baffled Mike looked out at the pitcher and yelled at him, "What's your problem? What's your problem?" Oddly, not a punch was thrown in a highly combustible situation.

Later Clemens insisted that he thought the bat fragment was the ball. "My emotions were extremely high," he explained. "I went in and really had to calm down." Whatever had taken place in Clemens's mind had not gone unremarked by observers and some Mets. The substitute Mets catcher, Todd Pratt, suggested that "competition can often bring out the best and worst in people." Obviously, he thought it hadn't worked wonders for Clemens. Tim McCarver, in the TV booth, proclaimed Clemens's action was "indefensible," and possibly for the first time Joe Torre found himself on the wrong end of a heated argument. In trying to defend Clemens, he, too, might have been doing the indefensible.

The fractious moment might have been unsettling for many fans, but the Yankees didn't blink at all. They rolled up a 6–0 lead behind their controversial pitcher, who actually flourished in the cool (56 degrees) night air. His quick temper remained under control after the first inning. In a last gasp in the ninth inning, after Clemens had given way to relievers, the Mets banged out five runs, including homers by Piazza and outfielder Jay Payton. But it was too late to influence the result of the game.

Going into the third game the Yankees appeared well on their way to another four-game sweep, which had become habit for them. It looked especially promising—with El Duque Hernandez on the mound, the odds were strongly in their favor for a third straight win. Hernandez's postseason mark of 8–0, even more spectacular than the earlier pitching feats of such Yankee icons as Lefty Gomez, Herb Pennock, and Whitey Ford, was good reason to suspect that Shea Stadium would be no more hospitable for the Mets than Yankee Stadium. But, as the Yankees sought their fifteenth straight World Series victory (a truly remark-

able achievement for any team in any professional sport), El Duque finally came up short. But not by much. He stayed even with the Mets' Rick Reed at 2–2 over six innings, and only faltered in the eighth inning, when the Mets, with the help of a clutch hit by Hawaii's Benny Agbayani, put across the go-ahead run. The flu-ridden El Duque had thrown 134 pitches and refused to come out after seven innings. "He deserved the right to get the decision in this one," said Torre, who felt that his hurler had as much heart as any pitcher he'd ever managed. In losing, Hernandez racked up 12 strikeouts, the most that any Yankee pitcher had ever registered in the 204 Series games the club had played.

The victory assured the Mets of playing two more games at their home headquarters, even if the noise level at Shea proved to be mixed. It was clear that among the 56,000 fans at the third game there were plenty of Yankee enthusiasts, who had emigrated to Shea. However, it didn't take long in the fourth game for the Yankees to give notice that they were not about to blow their advantage over the Mets. On the first pitch of the game, Jeter pumped a home run over the left-field wall off right-hander Bobby Jones. Not since Cincinnati's Pete Rose hit a first pitch against Oakland for a homer in 1972 had any batter performed such a feat. The Yankees went on to tack on single runs in the next two innings, with triples by O'Neill and Jeter playing a part in each run. A two-run homer by Piazza in the third inning brought the Mets back to 3–2. But after that it was left up to the merciless Yankee bull pen to protect the one-run margin.

In a move that obviously irked Neagle, the starting pitcher in this game, Torre removed him in the fifth inning with two out and not a Met on base. Neagle was about to face Piazza, but there came that man, Torre, hopping out of the dugout to inform him that he was through for the night. As his quirky choice to replace Neagle, Torre signaled for Cone, the forgotten man of the staff. Pitching for the first time at Shea in eight years, David made short work of the slugging catcher, getting him to pop up. That left the rest of the game up to the usual triumvirate—Nelson, Stanton, Rivera—as they split up the chores and sent the

On September 2, 2001, Mike Mussina, pitching in Fenway Park, extended a perfect game into the last of the ninth inning. He retired two batters, rang up two strikes against Boston's Carl Everett, then saw the dream burst when Everett singled to left. "Moose" took a deep breath and retired the last hitter to complete his 1–0 masterpiece.

So the fifth game arrived, with Mets fans clinging to the hope that the Yankees might still fail as they faced Leiter for the second time in the Series. It had been an exciting Series and a memorable one, even without the Clemens contretemps thrown into the mix. And most of New York was still losing sleep each night to watch it. Leiter had once pitched for the Yankees and wanted nothing more than to send the Series into a sixth game, back at Yankee Stadium. For eight innings he battled Pettitte, who was pitching another strong game. It was, as an old New York Giants catcher, Wes Westrum, once characterized such games, "a real cliffdweller." With the fans hanging on each pitch in the top of the ninth, Leiter struck out Martinez and O'Neill. Surely he could retire one more Yankee and leave it up to his team to try to win it in the bottom of the ninth.

But Posada worked out a walk after nine pitches, though Leiter threw a pitch that he thought was a third strike. The pitcher's broad shoulders seemed to sag—the type of body language that spoke more than words at that point. Second guessers in the stands, as well as at home, probably were convinced that Valentine should have removed Leiter in favor of a fresh arm. But after throwing 138 pitches, Leiter was determined to stick it out to the bitter end. Apparently Valentine felt that way, too, believing that Leiter had enough left on his four-seam fastball to get out of the inning. But Brosius came up and lined a single to left field, and Sojo, one of those unsung players on the Yankees ("He of the ancient craftsman's face," as Pete Hamill described him), banged a little teaser through the middle, inches past Leiter. Payton, in center field, raced in quickly on the hit as it squirted out to him, and his strong throw home on the slow-

Mets fans home unhappy in a 3–2 loss. It was exactly the type of ball game that the Yankees had patented under Torre. The final two innings were owned by Rivera, who threw 28 pitches, including 20 strikes. The Yankees had proven it was very hard to lose when a game could be turned over to the sangfroid Rivera. They had shown in their first three victories over the Mets that they could play "little ball," by running the bases well and taking advantage of blunders made by the opposition. They could hit when it counted and make the big play when it counted.

footed Posada was right on target. But as Piazza waited behind the plate to tag out Posada, the throw hit Posada's hip and caromed off into the Mets dugout. Not only did Posada score, but so did Brosius. At last, the depleted Leiter came out of the game, and John Franco came in to get the third out.

The enterprising Yankees had done it again, capitalizing on a tired but gutty pitcher and a throw that misfired by a whisker. In the last of the ninth inning Rivera was there again to close out the game and the

Series. He got pinch hitter Darryl Hamilton on strikes, walked Agbayani (who had been a thorn in the Yankees' side during these games), got Alfonzo to fly out to O'Neill for the second out, then, fittingly, Piazza came up one more time, at midnight. His big bat swung around on Rivera's pitch and for a split second the flying ball seemed to have enough trajectory to zoom over the wall in left center field. But Bernie Williams moved back a few steps, near the warning track, and smothered the ball in his glove.

The Subway Series of 2000 was over and the Yankees had won their fourth world championship in five years and their third in a row. Every game in this captivating Series was decided by two runs or less, the first time this had happened since 1915, when the Red Sox beat the Phillies. Jeter, the Most Valuable Player of the midsummer All-Star Game, was named as MVP of the World Series (with his .409 batting average), the only time any player had accomplished that in the same season.

In the twenty-five years since the coming of free agency, the Yankees had become the only team to triumph in three straight World Series. Torre, once dismissed as a loser in his previous assignments as manager, had posted a 16–3 mark in Series play, better than any other manager who has managed in more than a single Series.

The 1936–41 Yankees triumphed four times in five years, and Yankees General Manager Ed Barrow unequivocally stated that the 1939 team was the best Yankee team of them all. The 1947–53 club won six times in seven years, and these teams were literally cluttered with Hall of Famers. Often named as "the greatest team of all time," the Yankees of 1927 also won in 1928; they didn't win in 1926, with essentially the same talent on hand.

The debate about which is the great-

Alfonso Soriano, his path to shortstop stardom blocked by Derek Jeter, established a position for himself in 2001 when second baseman Chuck Knoblauch was moved to left field. He is another in a long and distinguished line of players born in the Dominican Republic, where he reportedly started playing baseball at the age of six.

Don Zimmer and Joe Torre, inseparable in the dugout, posing here before the start of the 2000 World Series. Torre once told a hotel chambermaid that he was the Yankees' manager, and she replied, "Oh yes, you're the one who sits next to that round guy." Only Connie Mack, Casey Stengel, and Joe McCarthy have won more world championships than Torre.

est baseball team ever is as old as the game itself and will continue as long as there are Hot Stove Leagues and hotheaded fans.

It's probably unfair to render a final, dogmatic judgment that makes one of these Yankees teams the greatest team of all. However, it may be said, with emphasis, that the Yankees of 1996–2000, a dynasty if ever there was one, were the greatest *postseason* teams ever assembled.

Torre himself would heartily agree with such an estimate. "Winning four World Series out of five years in this day and age, when you have to go through layer after layer of postseason play, means we can put our record, our dedication, our resolve up against any team that's played the game. We may not have the best players—but certainly we have had the best team."

In the Roaring Twenties, the boyish-looking Waite Hoyt, the future Hall of Fame right-hander, mused that, "it's great to be young and to be a Yankee." Seventy-five years later Derek Sanderson Jeter, in the prime of his life, is an affirmation of that simple sentiment.

Jeter may not be the best hitter in the game. He may not be the best infielder in the game. He may not be the best base runner in the game. And he may not have the sweetest smile in the game (although that is as arguable as some of the other points). But after only five full seasons with the Yankees, he is the indispensable man on the club. His employer, George Steinbrenner, has been wrong in judgment and action on more than a few occasions, and may even admit it in his more malleable moments. But he was absolutely prescient when, during Derek's rookie year, he proclaimed that there wasn't a better shortstop anywhere than Derek.

Born in June 1974, in Pequannock, New Jersey, Jeter has become the most popular Yankee in the last decade. He seems to cut across party lines, too, ranging, in his support, from squealing teenage girls to old-time Yankee fans who remember DiMaggio and Mantle. He has proven himself to be an athlete of grace, talent, and maturity, who does not permit his intense competitiveness to stand in the way of his good sportsmanship. When he says repeatedly that he would like to be a Yankee for the rest of his career, he can be believed—even in an era when players show limited loyalty to their clubs of the moment.

Probably more responsible for the success of his team than any other Yankee, Jeter refuses to accept such credit. He insists that "every player wants to win here . . . guys play better here because they want to be here." He could have added that one of the reasons they may want to play here is Jeter's own presence on the field day after day.

From the start of his career in the Bronx the big city has never intimidated Jeter. "The game is the same, it's baseball, whether you're here in New York or Kansas City," he says. "It's just that off the field you're going to face more scrutiny and more questions."

In 2000, Jeter's numbers were down for the year over the previous season. But he still finished with 201 hits, 15 homers and 73 runs batted in, despite two weeks on the sidelines in May, caused by a strain in his abdominal muscle. In 1999, he had knocked in 102 runs. But the dropoff in production never fazed him. "I just want to be consistent," he says. "And as long as I'm having fun, I don't worry about the statistics. I hope to have a lot of good years left."

It has been said of Jeter that in a time of great shortstops, he may not be the best of them. There is his pal, A-Rod Rodriguez, now of Texas, and Nomar Garciaparra of the Red Sox, who may be better hitters than Jeter. The Mets' Rey Ordonez is a fancier fielder. But Derek's emphasis has always been on scoring runs and winning. If that is the test, he is succeeding mightily. At his age he has already played in 19 World Series games. At the rate the Yankees are going, he may eventually surpass Berra and Mantle in this category.

"My job is to score runs. That's the bottom line," he says. "But a lot of people focus on RBIs. When you're hitting first or second in the lineup that isn't really something you strive for. As long as I'm getting on base that's what I worry about. Obviously, I'd like to hit more home runs, but that's not my job."

Jeter is aware that baseball is a game of failure. He knows that hitters fail more often than they succeed—by almost four to one. But in trying to battle such odds, Jeter—a very coachable man, according to the coaches on the team—has been willing to make adjustments in his batting stance. There was a time when he held his bat so high, and in such an unorthodox manner, that Ira Berkow of the *New York Times* suggested that he looked like he "was sprouting an antenna from his helmet." In a period in which pitchers were jamming him, Jeter backed away from the plate in order to cope with inside fastballs better.

Among his fellow Yankees he is regarded as the

In 2000, Derek Jeter became the first player in history to win both the All-Star Game and World Series MVP awards. Reggie Jackson said he was "a champion in the truest tradition of what it is to be a Yankee." He has coped with the demands imposed on New York celebrities maturely and good-naturedly. "He's more than just a talented kid," Joe Torre said. "He's a good kid who has his priorities straight."

team's perpetually sunshiny guy. He goes about his balletic work in the field—where he is a joy to watch—and his work at the plate with great concentration. He is not surprised at what he's able to accomplish. But there's no braggadocio about him, which is what endears him to other Yankees.

"He's our energy," David Cone once remarked about him—and David is a man thoroughly familiar with the psychological aspects of baseball. "There's a bounce to his step that everyone picks up. Players feed on that. And he doesn't take himself too seriously. He is the team's de facto captain," added Cone, now gone from the Yankees. (The Yankees have been without an official captain since Don Mattingly left in 1995.)

In time Jeter will be rated against other outstand-

ing Yankee shortstops. Some already put him ahead of Rizzuto and Crosetti. But it may be a bit of a reach, as of now, to regard him on a level with the Babe, Lou, or Mickey. That could come, of course, with the passage of years.

In a baseball world, and a sports world, of runaway egos, where athletes and owners are not accustomed to think much about their obligations to fans, Jeter is unique. He behaves with poise and like a gentleman, even if, on occasion, he may sound a bit scripted and overly careful. "You can't compare him to Joe DiMaggio," author Gay Talese has written, "for DiMaggio didn't have bad manners. He had *no* manners. Here's a hero who is actually polite and that's from good parenting."

For all Americans, 2001 was a distressingly noir year. It began with the aftermath of a bitter and controversial presidential election and was followed by the ghastly destruction of more than five thousand lives in the terrorist attacks on New York's World Trade Center and the Pentagon on September 11.

With such events as a backdrop, the Yankees played through to an unprecedented November 4 conclusion (the weather remained kind, despite the date), as they attempted to win their fourth consecutive world championship. In the end, their seemingly unconquerable relief pitcher, Mariano Rivera, was conquered by the Arizona Diamondbacks, when a bloop hit fell behind shortstop in the ninth inning of the seventh game of the World Series. So the Yankees had finally faltered, in the thirty-fourth seventh game played in Series history. But it was not before they had unreeled two stunning ninth-inning comebacks in games four and five at Yankee Stadium, moments that will surely be remembered as long as the Stadium stands, and much longer than the painful finish of the seventh game.

Derek Jeter: a Yankee for all seasons.

It is fair to say that many chronic haters of the Yankees actually learned to love the Yankees in postseason, in part to assuage the psychic wounds that had been dealt to the scarred people of New York. In those last hours of a preposterous World Series, when all the talk in New York was about anthrax and baseball, not necessarily in that order, the Yankees had emerged as sentimental favorites of millions.

The "Damnyankees" had metamorphosed into the "Damnice Yankees." Arizona could have delivered the ultimate love letter to the Yankees by rolling over meekly in the Series. But pitchers Curt Schilling and Randy Johnson, winners of all four games against New York, didn't choose that option. Their sizzling pitches ended the latest Yankee dynasty. Now it remains to be seen how the Yankees will be reformed and rejuvenated, yet again.

During the regular season the Yankees posted a 95–65 record, hardly brilliant, but sufficient to beat out the troubled Red Sox in their own division. The highlight of the Yankees season was the pitching of the thirty-nine-year-old bulldog Roger Clemens, the expatriate from Boston and Toronto. Roger became

the first pitcher in American League history to start the season at 18–1. His fellow right-hander Mike Mussina was Steinbrenner's major pickup in the off-season. He came over from Baltimore and won 17 games. On Sunday, September 2, Mussina was one pitch away from hurling the fourth perfect game in Yankees history. But he had to settle for a 1–0 masterpiece, after Carl Everett of Boston hit a single to left center to thwart the Stanford graduate's bid, at Fenway Park.

For the most part, the team performed with consistency during 2001, despite early injuries to Jeter, who didn't have his best year at bat, and the death of Bernie Williams's father on May 14, which, for a while, appeared to diminish Bernie's ardor in the field. Chuck Knoblauch, in left field, was simply not a power hitter and often played inelegantly in the outfield. His successor at second base, Alfonso Soriano, had a brilliant freshman campaign and promises to be a Yankees fixture for years. Paul O'Neill, the intense and much-appreciated outfielder, had an injury-plagued season and announced he would retire after the World Series. The team's best month was July, when they won 19 and lost nine, while their worst mark was in August, when they won 15 and lost 14.

Coming into the first tier of playoffs against Oakland, with its array of sluggers, the Yankees lost the first two games amid premature announcements that they had died. Facing elimination, the Yankees managed to hold on to a 1–0 lead in the third game at Yankee Stadium, when Jeter orchestrated a play that has already advanced into Yankees mythology. He backed up an errant throw from Shane Spencer in right field as he played the role of Third Man, or third cutoff man—and then tossed a soft quarterback handoff to catcher Posada to nail Oakland's runner, who, unwisely, failed to slide. TV announcer Tim McCarver marveled at Jeter's instincts. "Just what was he doing there?" McCarver asked. Derek's gambit put an end to Oakland's bid, as the Yankees charged back to win the divisional playoff.

Next in the American League Championship Series came Seattle's Mariners, with a record-tying 116 triumphs during the season. However, to the surprise of many, Manager Lou Piniella's hard-hitting team, led by Ichiro Suzuki, who had amassed 242 hits during the season, was shut down by Yankees pitching. Ichiro, little more than a quaint footnote, was treated to taunts of "Sayonara," as the Yankees marched into their thirty-eighth World Series against Arizona.

Whatever propelled the Yankees—magic, mystique, miracles, aura, divine intervention, plain luck—or whatever the curbstone philosophers suggest—it finally ended in the cauldron of the Arizona ballpark. But few would deny that the Yankees of 2001 were a team that refused to give up. They exhibited enterprise, character, teamwork, and toughness, and a measure of that overworked word, *class*. All this in a year when their bats at times were as still as the Hitless Wonders of an earlier era. "They've got guts," said Keith Hernandez, the former Mets first baseman. And millions who watched them on TV knew that was the unvarnished truth.

1921	NY Giants defeated the Yankees, 5–3
1922	NY Giants defeated the Yankees, 4–0, one tie
1923	The Yankees defeated the Giants, 4–2
1926	St. Louis Cardinals defeated the Yankees, 4–3
1927	The Yankees defeated the Pittsburgh Pirates, 4–0
1928	The Yankees defeated the Cardinals, 4–0
1932	The Yankees defeated the Chicago Cubs, 4–0
1936	The Yankees defeated the Giants, 4–2
1937	The Yankees defeated the Giants, 4–1
1938	The Yankees defeated the Cubs, 4–0
1939	The Yankees defeated the Cincinnati Reds, 4–0
1941	The Yankees defeated the Brooklyn Dodgers, 4–1
1942	The Cardinals defeated the Yankees, 4–1
1943	The Yankees defeated the Cardinals, 4–1
1947	The Yankees defeated the Dodgers, 4–3
1949	The Yankees defeated the Dodgers, 4–1
1950	The Yankees defeated the Phillies, 4–0
1951	The Yankees defeated the Giants, 4–2
1952	The Yankees defeated the Dodgers, 4–3
1953	The Yankees defeated the Dodgers, 4–2
1955	The Dodgers defeated the Yankees, 4–3
1956	The Yankees defeated the Dodgers, 4–3
1957	The Milwaukee Braves defeated the Yankees, 4–3
1958	The Yankees defeated the Braves, 4–3
1960	The Pirates defeated the Yankees, 4–3
1961	The Yankees defeated the Reds, 4–1
1962	The Yankees defeated the San Francisco Giants, 4–3
1963	The Los Angeles Dodgers defeated the Yankees, 4–0
1964	The Cardinals defeated the Yankees, 4–3
1976	The Reds defeated the Yankees, 4–0
1977	The Yankees defeated the Dodgers, 4–2
1978	The Yankees defeated the Dodgers, 4–2
1981	The Dodgers defeated the Yankees, 4–2
1996	The Yankees defeated the Atlanta Braves, 4–2
1998	The Yankees defeated the San Diego Padres, 4–0
1999	The Yankees defeated the Braves, 4–0
2000	The Yankees defeated the Mets, 4–1
2001	The Arizona Diamondbacks defeated the Yankees, 4–3

1903–1907	Clark C. Griffith
1908	Griffith and Norman Elberfeld
1909	George T. Stallings
1910	Stallings and Harold H. Chase
1911	Harold H. Chase
1912	Harry S. Wolverton
1913	Frank L. Chance
1914	Chance and Roger Peckinpaugh
1915–1917	William E. Donovan
1918–1929	Miller J. Huggins
1930	J. Robert Shawkey
1931–1945	Joseph V. McCarthy
1946	McCarthy, William M. Dickey, and John H. Neun
1947–1948	Stanley R. Harris
1949–1960	Charles D. Stengel
1961–1963	Ralph G. Houk
1964	Lawrence P. Berra
1965	John J. Keane
1966	Keane and Ralph G. Houk
1967–1973	Ralph G. Houk
1974	William C. Virdon
1975	Virdon and Alfred M. Martin
1976–1977	Alfred M. Martin
1978	Martin and Robert G. Lemon
1979	Robert G. Lemon and Alfred M. Martin
1980	Richard Howser
1981	Eugene R. Michael and Robert G. Lemon
1982	Lemon, Michael, and Clyde E. King
1983	Alfred M. Martin
1984	Lawrence P. Berra
1985	Berra and Alfred M. Martin
1986–1987	Louis V. Piniella
1988	Alfred M. Martin and Louis V. Piniella
1989	G. Dallas Green and Russell E. Dent
1990	Dent and Carl H. Merrill
1991	Carl H. Merrill
1992–1995	William M. Showalter
1996–	Joseph P. Torre

Originally Baltimore, 1901. Moved to New York, 1903.

Yr.	Pos.	W	L	Pct.	Yr.	Pos.	W	L	Pct.	Yr.	Pos.	W	L	Pct.
01	5	68	65	.511	35	2	89	60	.597	69	5	80	81	.497
02	8	50	88	.362	36	1	102	51	.667	70	2	93	69	.574
03	4	72	62	.537	37	1	102	52	.662	71	4	82	80	.506
04	2	92	59	.609	38	1	99	53	.651	72	4	79	76	.510
05	6	71	78	.477	39	1	106	45	.702	73	4	80	82	.494
06	2	90	61	.596	40	3	88	66	.571	74	2	89	73	.549
07	5	70	78	.473	41	1	101	53	.656	75	3	83	77	.519
08	8	51	103	.331	42	1	103	51	.669	76	1	97	62	.610
09	5	74	77	.490	43	1	98	56	.636	77	1	100	62	.617
10	2	88	63	.583	44	3	83	71	.539	78	1	100	63	.613
11	6	76	76	.500	45	4	81	71	.533	79	4	89	71	.556
12	8	50	102	.329	46	3	87	67	.565	80	1	103	59	.636
13	7	57	94	.377	47	1	97	67	.630	81	1	34	22	.607
14	6	70	84	.455	48	3	94	60	.610		6	25	26	.490
15	5	69	83	.454	49	1	97	57	.630	82	5	79	83	.488
16	4	80	74	.519	50	1	98	56	.636	83	3	91	71	.562
17	6	71	82	.464	51	1	98	56	.636	84	3	87	75	.537
18	4	60	63	.488	52	1	95	59	.617	85	2	97	64	.602
19	3	80	59	.576	53	1	99	52	.656	86	2	90	72	.556
20	3	95	59	.617	54	2	103	51	.669	87	4	89	73	.549
21	1	98	55	.641	55	1	96	58	.621	88	5	85	76	.528
22	1	94	60	.610	56	1	97	57	.630	89	5	74	87	.460
23	1	98	54	.645	57	1	98	56	.636	90	7	67	95	.414
24	2	89	63	.586	58	1	92	62	.597	91	5	71	91	.438
25	7	69	85	.448	59	3	79	75	.513	92	4	76	86	.469
26	1	91	63	.591	60	1	97	57	.630	93	2	88	74	.543
27	1	110	44	.714	61	1	109	53	.673	94	1	70	43	.619
28	1	101	53	.656	62	1	96	66	.593	95	2	79	65	.549
29	2	88	56	.571	63	1	104	57	.646	96	1	92	70	.568
30	3	86	68	.558	64	1	99	63	.611	97	2	96	66	.593
31	2	94	69	.614	65	6	77	85	.475	98	1	114	48	.704
32	1	107	47	.695	66	10	70	89	.440	99	1	98	64	.605
33	2	91	59	.607	67	9	72	90	.444	00	1	87	74	.540
34	2	94	60	.610	68	5	83	79	.512	01	1	95	65	.594

57, 68–70, 97, 103, *229*
death of, 230
Gehrig compared with, 57–59, 68
illnesses and injuries of, 73, 77, 95–96, 99, 103–4, *110*
Italian heritage of, 75–76
MVPs won by, 89
Old-Timers' Day appearances of, 76–77, *183*
popularity of, 59, 61, 69–70
retirement of, 104, *106*, 108, 110, *110*
salaries of, 62–63, 68–69, 72
scouting report on, 108
Stengel's relationship with, 95–97, 104
in World Series games, *59*, 61, 63–64, 66, 71, 75, 89–92, *90–91*, 104, 108–9, *110*
Yankee debut of, 59
DiMaggio, Tony, 77
DiMaggio, Vince, 77
DiMaggio, Zio Pepe, 77
Dinkins, David, 233
DiSalvatore, Bryan, 3
Ditmar, Art, 133, 141
Doby, Larry, 125
Donovan, Wild Bill, 15, 250
Downing, Al, 156
Doyle, Larry, 4
Dropo, Walt, *107*
Drysdale, Don, 157, 221
Dugan, Joe, 19, *34*, 37, *37*, 39, 92
Dunn, Jack, 23–25
Duren, Ryne, 134
Durocher, Leo, 28–29, 40, *53*, 70–71, 80, 82–83, 89–90, 108–9, *112*, 120, 151
Durst, Cedric, *34*, 41
Dyer, Eddie, 150
Dykes, Jimmy, *130*

Earnshaw, George, 39, 44–45
Eastern League, 30, 49, 170
Ebbets Field, 63
 lights installed at, 85
 MacPhail and, 83–84
 World Series at, 71, 90–91, 100, 111, 126, 131
Edwards, Bruce, 90
Ehmke, Howard, 28
Eisenhower, Dwight D., 109, 127, 131–33, 222, 237
Elberfeld, Norman, 5, 250
Ellis, Dock, 176
Emerson, Ralph Waldo, 230
Erskine, Carl, 118
Essick, Bill, *68*
Etten, Nick, 80, 85
Evans, Harold, 138
Everett, Carl, *242*
Evers, Johnny, 5

Falkner, David, 176, 192
Farley, James, *157*
Farrell, Frank, 3, 6–7
Felker, Clay, 108
Feller, Bob, 59, 72, 104, *107*, 119, 224, 237
Fenway Park, 97, *97*, *140*, *180*, 181, 235, *242*
 playoff games at, *184*, 186–87
Ferraro, Mike, 191

Ferrell, Wes, 64
Fielder, Cecil, 218–21, 224
Figueroa, Ed, 176
Fimrite, Ron, 65
Fisher, Jack, 148
Fisk, Carlton, 170
Fitzgerald, F. Scott, 28, 39
Fitzsimmons, Freddie, 70–71
"Five O'Clock Lightning" rallying cry, 34, *35*, 37
Fletcher, Art, *34*, 41
Flood, Curt, 159
Fohl, Lee, 21
Forbes Field, 36, 56, 142
Ford, Whitey, 25, 28–30, 101, 111, 118, *121*, *122*, 128, 135, *136*, *142*, 150–51, 156–57, *160*, 163, 210, 241
 on all-time Yankee teams, 7, 18, 22, 30, 39, 61, 83, 88, 113, 126, 131, 134, 143, 171, 182, 185, 188, 192, 203, 221, 224, 233, 237, 240
 in World Series games, 75, 126, 141, 150, 157, 159
Foster, George, 176
Fothergill, Fatty, 218
Fox, Nelson, *164*
Foxx, Jimmie, 39, 52, 128, 153
Franco, John, 243
Frazee, Harry, 13–14, 17, 19
Frazier, George, 193
Freeman, Andrew, 205
Frick, Ford, 149
Frisch, Frankie, 20–21
Fuchs, Emil, 55–56
Fulton County Stadium, 221
Furillo, Carl, 90, 99, 118

Gallico, Paul, 28, 33, 49
Gamble, Oscar, 176, 182, 192
Garagiola, Joe, 115
Garbark, Mike, 83
Garcia, Freddy, 236
Garcia, Mike, 104, 111, 119, 134
Garcia, Rich, 221
Garciaparra, Nomar, 232, 245
Gardiner, John Lion, 22
Garvey, Steve, 182–83
Gazella, Mike, *34*
Gehrig, Christina, 47–49
Gehrig, Eleanor, 63, 69, *81*
Gehrig, Lou, 12, 14, *19*, 28–33, *34*, *35*–49, *42*, *49*, *52–53*, 55–61, 63–66, *92*, 108, 113, 119, 128, 143–44, 152–53, *168*, 170–71, 201, 218, *218*, 227, 232, 247
 on all-time Yankee teams, 7, 22, 30, 39, 61, 66, 83, 88, 126, 131, 134, 143, 151, 163, 182, 185, 188, 192, 203, 221, 224, 233, 236–37, 240
 background of, 47–49
 consecutive game streak of, 32, 47, 63–64, 207, 212
 death of, 69, 171
 DiMaggio compared with, 57–59, 68
 film based on life of, 69, *81*
 four home run game of, *42*, 44–46
 Huggins's death and, 41
 illnesses and injuries of, 47, 64–65, *65*, 103–4
 monument for, 69, 190, *190*

MVPs won by, *33*, 60
popularity of, 52, 63, 69
RBI record of, 42
retirement of, 64–66, *65*, 120, 153
retiring number of, 224
Ruth compared with, 47
on Ruth's called home run, 46
salaries of, 28, 36–37, 47, 63
in World Series games, 30, 32, 36, 39, 46, *59*, 60–61, *62*, 64
Gehringer, Charlie, 55, 66, 72
Giamatti, A. Bartlett, 89
Gibson, Bob, 159–60, *230*, 237
Gilliam, Jim, 126–27, *127*
Gionfriddo, Al, 90–92, *90–91*
Girardi, Joe, 218, *228*, *231*, 233
Giuliani, Rudy, 233
Glavine, Tom, 221
Glory of Their Times, The (Ritter), 9, 182
Goetz, Larry, 71, *73*
Goldwyn, Samuel, 69
Golenbock, Peter, 90
Gomez, Lefty, 22, *40*, 42, 44, *53*, 59, 66–67, 156, 210, 241
 on all-time Yankee teams, 66, 151, 163
 in World Series games, 62, 66, 88
Gonzalez, Juan, 218, 234
Gooden, Dan, 215
Gooden, Dwight, 169, 215–16, *215*, 224
Gordon, Joe (ball player), 3, 5, *6*, *52*, 62, *68*, 71, 74, 80, 85–88
 on all-time Yankee teams, 22, 30, 66, 221, 233
Gordon, Joseph (team president), 3
Gore, Al, 233, 240
Gorman, Tom, *122*
Goslin, Goose, 55
Gossage, Goose, 126, *175*, 184, 187–88, 192–93
Gould, Joe, 62–63
Gould, Stephen Jay, 2
Gowdy, Hank, 12
Grabowski, Johnny, 33, *34*
Graham, Billy, 124
Graham, Charles, 77
Grant, Eddie, 12
Grant, Ulysses S., 19
Gray, Pete, 82–83
Great Depression, 41, 44, 52, 57
Green, Dallas, 203–4, 250
Greenberg, Hank, 55–56, 60, 66, 69, 72, 75, 83, 153
Greenwade, Tom, 104, *137*
Griffey, Ken, Jr., 214
Griffith, Clark, 3–5, *5*, 89, 250
Griffith Stadium, 118
Grimes, Oscar, 83
Grimm, Charlie, 46
Groat, Dick, 142
Groh, Heinie, 21
Grove, Lefty, 39, 42, 44
Guerrero, Pedro, 193
Guetterman, Lee, 205
Guidry, Ron, 177, *178*, 182, 185, 201, 204, 210
 on all-time Yankee teams, 188, 236
Gullett, Don, 177
Gwynn, Tony, 210, 228